Feminist Futures
Contemporary Women's
Speculative Fiction

Studies in Speculative Fiction, No. 1

Robert Scholes, Series Editor

Alumni/Alumnae Professor of English and
Chairman, Department of English
Brown University

Other Titles in This Series

Feminist Futures
Contemporary Women's Speculative Fiction

by
Natalie M. Rosinsky

UMI RESEARCH PRESS

Ann Arbor, Michigan

BCW

Produced and distributed by
UMI Research Press
an imprint of
University Microfilms International
A Xerox Information Resources Company
Ann Arbor, Michigan 48106

Library of Congress Cataloging in Publication Data

Rosinsky, Natalie M. (Natalie Myra)
  Feminist futures—contemporary women's
speculative fiction.

  (Studies in speculative fiction ; no. 1)
  Revision of thesis—Unviersity of Wisconsin, Madison,
1982.
  Bibliography: p.
  Includes index.
  1. American fiction—20th century—History and
criticism. 2. Future in literature. 3. Feminism in
literature. 4. American fiction—Women authors—
History and criticism. 5. Science fiction, American—
Women authors—History and criticism. 6. Utopias in
literature. 7. Sex role in literature. I. Title. II. Series.
PS374.F86R6 1984 813'.0876'099287   84-2762
ISBN 0-8357-1578-7

Contents

Acknowledgments

I wish to thank Professor Annis V. Pratt of the University of Wisconsin-Madison, whose guidance made the initial version of this study a much better written work. I also wish to thank Dr. Raymond M. Olderman, who first gave me the confidence and inspiration to pursue formally this subject close to my heart. Finally, I wish to acknowledge most lovingly my debt to my husband, Donald F. Larsson. Without his good humor, patience, and intelligence, I could never have accomplished what I have.

Introduction

A Feminist Continuum: Androgyny to Gynocentrism

There was a time when you were not a slave, remember that. . . . You say there are no words to describe this time, you say it does not exist. But remember. Make an effort to remember. Or, failing that, invent.[1]

Monique Wittig's injunction in *Les Guérillères,* her speculative novel of an all-female society in conflict with patriarchy, is a fitting introduction to this study. In the following chapters, I examine comparable speculative fictions written by contemporary American women (and one British woman writing about the American scene) and illustrate the ways in which contemporary feminisms have significantly influenced the development of this genre.[2] "Remembering" or "inventing" non-sexist possibilities for people and societies is a major ideological force underlying much of the "social science fiction" increasingly written during the last two decades.[3] A shared commitment to feminist inquiry leads the writers I discuss to focus on similar themes and motifs; however, their treatments of these themes often differ dramatically. For, as recent theorists demonstrate, feminism is not one cohesive viewpoint but rather an ideological framework which contains a range of views.[4] These diverging beliefs may be articulated politically (for example, socialist vs. capitalist feminism) as well as in more general philosophical terms. It is in this latter, more fundamental sense that I analyze the feminist ideologies that shape the content and form of much recent speculative fiction.

As the following chapters demonstrate, opposing concepts of human potential provide one of the philosophical frameworks for recent feminist debate. Some feminists believe that human potential is not predetermined by physiological gender but is instead "androgynous"; proponents of this "androgynous vision" claim that nurture, rather than nature, is the dominant influence on women's and men's mental as well as physical development. Thus, the traditional divisions of labor into circumscribed "feminine" and broader "masculine" spheres are artificial constructs which reflect social prejudice rather than actual human capabilities. To feminist proponents of androgyny, women's and men's abilities are potentially equal. (Feminist androgyny differs from the classical or traditional Western concept of androgyny, whose advocates often literalize its symbolic representation in a hermaphroditic or sexually epicine figure to support their own physiologically deterministic outlook. The suggestion that traditionally masculine and feminine traits (e)merge as a direct result of physical sexual ambiguity is fundamentally essentialist.[5] Furthermore, as I discuss later in this work, many proponents of traditional Western androgyny continue to hierarchize "masculine" and "feminine" traits from an androcentric perspective.[6])

In contrast to this re/vision of androgyny, other feminists maintain that there are indeed innate psychological or spiritual differences between the sexes.[7] Their emphasis on "essential" mental differences between women and men is potentially the mirror image of the androcentric essentialism that has fueled patriarchal stereotypes of women as naturally limited, inferior beings. Instead of perceiving women as inferior, though, proponents of "gynocentric essentialism" view our supposedly distinct traits as superior ones—abilities which furthermore do not preclude women's fulfilling traditionally male roles. Whether or not this belief in women's encompassing, innate superiority leads to sexual discrimination against men depends on the degree to which it is upheld. The relationships among these ideologies may be expressed visually:

gynocentric essentialism ⌐‾‾‾‾‾‾‾⌐ feminist androgyny

androcentric essentialism ⌊_____⌋ androcentric androgyny

NON-FEMINIST
IDEOLOGIES

As this schema suggests, these views are the poles for a wide range of possible feminist beliefs. While none of the works I examine is solely an ideological tract for either feminist viewpoint, each may be productively analyzed along the continuum of beliefs that exist between these poles.

In chapter 1, I examine contemporary feminist authors' speculative re/visions of the theme of classical metamorphosis. This chapter discusses Lois Gould's *A Sea Change*, Rhoda Lerman's *Call Me Ishtar*, Angela Carter's *The Passion of New Eve*, and June Arnold's *Applesauce;* it also briefly traces the connections among these works, the contemporaneous body and performance art movements, and their ideological predecessor, Virginia Woolf's *Orlando*. Chapter 2 analyzes feminist re/visions of the heroic quest and utopian model of a traveller educated through experience in a strange land. Its focus is Dorothy Bryant's *The Kin of Ata Are Waiting for You* and Mary Staton's *From the Legend of Biel*. This chapter also discusses the ways in which these novels are more ideologically complex and formally innovative than a somewhat earlier work of feminist speculative fiction, Ursula K. Le Guin's influential *The Left*

Hand of Darkness. Chapter 3 examines the ways in which different feminist ideologies affect theme and form in three authors' depictions of a future "battle between the sexes." This chapter focuses upon Joanna Russ's *The Female Man*, Sally Miller Gearhart's *The Wanderground: Stories of the Hill Women*, and Marge Piercy's *Woman on the Edge of Time*. Drawing upon these analyses, chapter 4 is a theoretical overview of the evolving, symbiotic relationship of feminist politics and poetics in contemporary speculative fiction. In this concluding chapter, I discuss the impact of diverse feminist ideologies on theme and form in such fiction; I also examine SF's potential as both a genre and a social movement (or "subculture") to inculcate and foster fundamental feminist praxis. Such praxis is effected through the unconventional reader/narrative relationship that, to varying degrees, each of these works creates. For, as the following chapters reveal, the empowerment of the individual (reader) through her de/construction of textual meaning is an underlying ideological and aesthetic bond among these often disparate fictions.

1

Metamorphosis: The Shaping of Female Identity

"Androgyny was only attractive because it was too hard to be a woman."[1]

When Lucy Lippard, feminist art critic, expressed this sentiment in 1976, she was documenting an issue central to the contemporary women's movement and the fictions it has produced. In our struggle to understand and ultimately altar patriarchal norms, to explore actual and possible sex roles and gender identity, feminists have in the last fifteen years reestablished ideological perspectives with widely divergent concepts of personal identity. Some theorists—such as June Singer, Carolyn Heilbrun, and Julia Kristeva— advocate an androgynous vision of human nature, maintaining that sex roles and characteristics conventionally associated with gender identity are learned, rather than innate traits.[2] The prominent French psychoanalyst Kristeva claims that "Woman can never be defined . . . cannot, should not since the term is a social and not a natural construct. . . . The belief that 'one is a woman' is almost as absurd and obscurantist as the belief that one is a man."[3] This viewpoint is in sharp contrast to the other ideological framework current in feminist circles, that of innate psychological differences between the sexes. This essentialist position, with its gynocentric emphasis on women's spirituality, physiology, and history, has led to a reclaiming and renaming of "woman" by such theorists as Hélène Cixous, Mary Daly, and Susan Griffin[4] and has both fostered, and been fostered by, a resurgence of interest in matriarchal cultures and religions.[5] (At its most inflexible, gynocentric essentialism may be perceived as sexism which discriminates against biological males, rather than females. Its corollary, androcentric essentialism, is the ideology underlying patriarchy's historical discrimination against women.)

And so in Lippard's comment we may perceive the dilemma that, seeing social changes due to feminism and realizing that *seeing* changes us, many people have had to resolve during the last two decades. Having asked "Who are we" and then, "Who *can* we be," we receive two seemingly dichotomous answers. Some individuals, like Lippard, ultimately reject one viewpoint for the other;[6] some respond with less certainty or with the belief that there is valuable terrain between these polar opposites. I will examine some of the ways in which contemporary women novelists have articulated this dilemma. And, because their work provides illuminating parallels and insights into the texts I consider, I will also discuss the responses of some contemporary visual artists.

Lois Gould's *A Sea Change* (1976),[7] Rhoda Lerman's *Call Me Ishtar* (1973),[8] Angela Carter's *The Passion of New Eve* (1977),[9] and June Arnold's *Applesauce* (1966)[10] all employ classical metamorphosis as a multi-valenced metaphor for the search for female identity. Gould's and Arnold's protagonists are women who become men, while Carter's title character—like Woolf's Orlando—is a man who unwittingly becomes a woman. Lerman's Ishtar, a suburban Syracuse housewife, is transformed into the ancient Babylonian deity for whom she is named. Through this focus on the corporeality of their protagonists and its subsequent, fabulous transformation, these authors fully confront feminism's controversy about human nature and potential. Is female or male physiology a significant enough factor to alter—or originally predetermine—an individual's character, personality, and abilities? While essentialists (whether gynocentric or androcentric) would answer this question affirmatively, feminist proponents of the androgynous vision would strongly demur.

Orlando (1928) and such early twentieth century works as Charlotte Perkins Gilman's "If I Were a Man"[11] also address this question, but they are not the only overtly political predecessors of these novels.[12] Nor are their predecessors solely literary ones. Within the context of the new feminisms of the late 1960s and early 1970s, these novels are allied with a politically motivated, contemporaneous trend in the visual arts—"body art."

Because women have traditionally been validated or invalidated, identified as "womanly" or not, by the extent to which their bodies conformed to social norms,[13] it is not surprising that female conceptual artists, once overtly influenced by feminism, turned to "body art" to question and search out their identities. These quests often reflected the ideological currents of contemporaneous feminisms. Lippard has written of the reemergence of self as subject matter in the late 1960s and early 1970s, of the "costumes, disguises and fantasies" used by women artists to "detail the self-transformation that now seemed possible," to identify "the self not outwardly apparent...that challenged the roles they had been playing."[14] Within these avant-garde self-identifications and challenges to roles, one may discern elements of gynocentric essentialism or of feminist androgyny as well as consciousness-raising inquiry. Eleanor Antin's photographic essay of her weight loss over several months, titled *Carving: A Traditional Sculpture* (1974), is one example of this reexamination of the significance of flesh to selfhood;[15] other examples include Martha Wilson's photographic essay *Posturing: Drag* (1917), in which the artist androgynously records herself first as a man, then as that man dressed as a woman, and Adrian Piper's street appearances. Piper has thought-provokingly costumed and presented herself on the streets of New York City as both the apparently male "Mythic Being" of her imagination and as an inappropriately soiled or disfigured woman—inappropriate just because women are to be clean, unblemished, and conventionally attired in order to be defined as "women" by our society.[16] Such performance art, violating the conventionally implicit demarcation between life and art, observer and observed, active "male" and passive "female," especially forces audiences to identify and question our own internalizations of rigid social norms. These questions may then lead to efforts to transcend such patterned response.

Noting such rigid social prescriptions for "true womanhood," theologian and critic Carol Christ has suggested that fantasy may be as significant a form of discourse for women seeking to shape a "sacred story" of transcendence, questing for self and spiritual awareness, as more conventionally realistic, serious modes.[17] This observation, supported by numerous critiques of recent feminist fantasy and speculative fiction and substantiated by the growth of this genre,[18] is particularly relevant to an understanding of the ideological import of the four fantasies I discuss. These authors are not merely writing light, diversionary, or "escapist" fiction but are analyzing and responding to vital contemporary issues.

But emphasis on the body and fantastic metamorphosis are not the only links between feminist women's visual and literary creations. In a recent issue of *Screen*, a journal of cinema studies, Judith Barry and Sandy Flitterman analyze trends in women's visual artmaking during the last two decades, noting in their survey the diverging feminist ideologies I have mentioned. Opposed to the androgynous impulse, as represented by the works of collagists such as Mary Kelly and videomakers such as Martha Rossler, who "deconstruct" social roles rather than re-present them as innate aspects of female/male psychology, are artistic works that are a "glorification of an essential female power."[19] Barry and Flitterman cite Gina Pane's performances, which involve minor, "sacrificial" self-mutilation and the ritualized drawing of her own blood, and Hannah Wilde's presentation of her own body as subject, modified by vaginally shaped pieces of chewing gum, in the latter category. And, as these authors note about separatist artists, galleries, and community groups involved in establishing an alternative female culture, even "the very notion of positive (lesbian) images of women relies on the already [socially] constituted meaning of 'woman.'"[20]

Barry and Flitterman do not, however, analyze works like Judy Chicago's *The Dinner Party* that seem to defy such categorization. While Chicago's vaginal imagery and use of such traditionally "womanly" crafts as needlepoint attest to the femaleness of her celebrated "guests," the very naming and juxtaposition of these historical or mythological figures, famed for their unconventional, "unwomanly" acts, comments upon the contemporaneous roles and identities as women that they rejected. Thus *The Dinner Party* includes the Virgin Queen Elizabeth as well as the Great Goddess, superficially "feminine" Emily Dickinson as well as flamboyantly androgynous George Sand.[21] This ability to resist easy classification characterizes both the recent novels I examine and their spiritual forebear, Virginia Woolf's *Orlando*.

The import of Orlando's miraculous transformation remains a source of critical debate, with writers like Elaine Showalter claiming that it represents Woolf's "flight into androgyny [which] helped her evade her painful femaleness"[22] and others, such as Carolyn Heilbrun, maintaining that it is "representative of the range of human possibility."[23] The ideological bases for these differing interpretations are, of course, found in the dichotomous views of human nature I have already outlined. (Showalter's assessment of Woolf's stance echoes Lucy Lippard's opening self-assessment.) And, certainly, the novel's complexities can support both views. Woolf insists that her protagonist remains the same after her metamorphosis, save for a slight dimming of memory,[24] that she *learns* to be a woman by the confining, if deferential treatment she receives as a female—discovering, for example, the pleasure of having succulent portions of meat offered to her even as she realizes she cannot readily escape from a sinking ship in her cumbersome skirts (O, pp. 154-55). Woolf, however, also suggests that the new Orlando responds instinctively as a biologically determined "woman." Unwed in Victoria's England, Orlando is plagued by a ringfinger that twitches uncomfortably until an authentic gold band soothes it (pp. 240-43). And, as Claudine Hermann has noted, Orlando seems to perceive space and nature differently as a woman than she did even as a nature loving outdoorsman[25]—a further weighting toward covert, undifferentiated essentialism in this androgynous fantasy. Ellen Morgan's observation that Orlando *must* change sex, either literally (when she becomes a woman) or, later, psychically (when she seeks the freedom of London's streets in male disguise), in order to comprehend the sexual "other" further suggests an essentialist view of human nature linked to gender in this novel.[26]

Woolf's *Orlando,* then, open to multiple critical interpretations,[27] is a key to understanding its literary offspring: Gould's *A Sea Change,* Lerman's *Call Me Ishtar,* Carter's *The Passion of New Eve,* and Arnold's *Applesauce.* Rather than conveniently providing an apologue for either pole of the ideological dichotomy (feminist [or androcentric] androgyny on the one hand, gynocentric [or androcentric] essentialism on the other) that I have described, these novels range along a continuum between these extremes. *A Sea Change* most clearly embodies the essentialist viewpoint while *Call Me Ishtar* and *The Passion of New Eve* subsume elements of both views. *Applesauce,* retaining a degree of ideological ambiguity, is nonetheless closest to the feminist theoretical construct of androgyny. In this diversity and complexity, these novels parallel the "body art" and conceptual performances that in the last decades have gained cultural currency.

Gould's *A Sea Change* is the tale of Jessie Waterman's metamorphosis into the Black Gunman who had raped her during a burglary. This novel seems closest to the essentialist end of the continuum in its positing of absolute values and characteristics for both men and women.[28] All Gould's male characters are insensitive or brutal to one degree or another; to prepare herself for the metamorphosis she recognizes she is about to undergo, Jessie "studies" violence, urging a Coastguardsman to rape her so she may observe and learn from his pleasure in her own brutalization. She also treats Kate, her friend and new lover, with calculated brutality to perfect the role Jessie will soon—according to Gould—be suited to and expected to play.

Gould's consistent use of water imagery similarly suggests an acceptance of fixed female attributes. The protagonist, whose last name is Waterman, experiences "oceanic currents pulling at her from within" (SC, p. 25) as Hurricane Minerva assaults her Long Island home, and the energy of this storm is often described as female in its intensity. The stereotypical association of woman with nature and man with culture[29] is unquestioningly upheld through Gould's depiction of men who ineffectually guard coastlines, and of male scientists' efforts to disarm this storm by penetrating and seeding it. Jessie observes in these attempts "gang rape as a tool of basic research" and muses that "the first man who ever flew into a hurricane had said, 'Let's go and penetrate the center—just for the fun of it'" (SC, pp. 74-75). While these observations are indicative of the character's growing preoccupation with rape and sexual politics, Gould does not present an alternative viewpoint. Thus, with personal identity intrinsically linked to physiology in these ways, Jessie's metamorphosis can result only in role reversal—one more womanizing, rather than womanly, man is added to Long Island's population.

A Sea Change, in this sense, embodies Barry and Flitterman's observation that "an aesthetics of simple inversion," based on essentialist definitions of self, results in "bondage rather than bonding between women."[30] Indeed, the novel concludes with Kate's seeking out Jessie/B.G. to once again be one of a cruel man's playthings, his "woman." Kate is originally described as a "drowning victim" (SC, p. 35) because she relies so heavily on others, particularly men, for her sense of self. Her continued association with Jessie/B.G. appears to doom her to continued alienation from the potential, "natural" powers of womanhood as represented by the forces of Hurricane Minerva.

And yet, this novel is not totally essentialist in outlook. Like all the texts I discuss, it is fragmented, elliptical—indicating that the search for self is complicated and uneasy. Flashbacks to the burglary/rape are interspersed throughout the novel; some are recounted from Jessie's perspective while others are voiced in her complicated reconstruction of the original B.G.'s thoughts and motives. Each episode reveals more, and some, with Rashomon-like complexity, contradict one another. Moreover, the transformed Jessie/B.G. does not totally forget the insights that her society had forced upon her, the view of limited options and infantilization of women that has led her to tell her youngest daughter, "[W]e will tell secrets about what we want to be *unless* [my emphasis] we grow up" (SC, p. 22). She uses her metamorphosis to escape—and take her daughter and step-daughter away—from her husband, a man who has "*defined* her as his problem" (SC, p. 44), who has seen her as a work of art rather than a person. Unfortunately, her new self-definition may prove abusive to the other women in her new life.

It is interesting and perhaps revealing that this problematic work centers on a beautiful woman's, a fashion model's, metamorphosis. Her physical perfection, and thus, by conventional definition, her perfection as a woman, is transmogrified into the "perfect" machismo of B.G. This transformation is therefore a rigid, circumscribed one in accord with traditional gender roles, unlike the self-explorations undertaken by some of the "body artists" whose works I have described. Kate can perceive Jessie's disquiet, visualizing her as a damaged "lovely Victorian glass painting . . . glass held together securely by the heavy gold frame . . . a delicate cobweb of crazing across the face. . . ." (SC, pp. 45-46), but neither she nor Jessie can productively identify the sources of this damage. The validation of perfection, of symmetrically polar male and female opposites, embodied in the "countless photographs of Jessie all over the house . . . wearing enigmatic smiles, quizzical frowns, seductive winks" (SC, pp. 46-47) has been too complete. Jessie's daughters, less socialized, may perceive more. Their famous women doll collection, consisting of women heroes who suffered mutilation or deformity of some kind, which thus identified them as other than "women," perversely suggests not just the impact of social convention but possible ways to circumvent it. The oldest girl begins to exercise control over her own self—that is, the female body by which society defines and confines her—by rebelliously gaining ten pounds each weekend her domineering father visits "his" women. Although now recognized by some feminist theorists as a self-assertive tactic,[31] this strategy—anticipated, paralleled and at times parodied by women's conceptual art—has limited efficacy and implicit hazards. And so, Gould recognizes, however covertly, that B.G. will have more options than Jessie or her daughters, but Gould herself limits these options to the stereotypical male ones. B.G. will take advantage of and brutalize "his" women in stereotypically male fashion.

A Sea Change is not totally irredeemable, a schematic reversal of character, for yet another reason. Like *Call Me Ishtar* and *The Passion of New Eve,* it plays with and questions facticity. What we *know* is true may just not be so. Gould opens the novel with undocumented "facts" about sex change in certain sea creatures, and, while this information superficially lends authority to her fantasy, it also has the potential to undermine it. We need to verify her statements about "sea wives," juxtaposed suspiciously both in the title and the preface with Ariel's misleading lament for a live king, just because they *are* presented as fact, and to document their accuracy. In the 1970s and '80s we have learned how unreliable scientific truths can be. Thus, Gould's predominantly essentialist treatment of human personality revealed through fabulous metamorphosis includes some structural as well as thematic narrative elements that subvert its dogmatic stance.

Call Me Ishtar, a wonderfully comic tale of the reincarnation of the goddess Ishtar as a Syracuse housewife, questions facticity to similarly ambivalent ends.[32] The modern Ishtar's relationship with her overbearing Jewish husband seems to be a paradigm of the displacement of the mother religions by monotheistic patriarchy and thus seems to place Lerman's work within the gynocentric, essentialist worldview, but Ishtar's "womanliness" is not a static identity. Ishtar, representing womankind, is a multifaceted goddess—destroyer as well as creator, mother as well as lover. The purported job applications which open the novel attest to both the diversity of female ability and the ludicrousness of our society's attempts to formally label it by gender. Babylonian Ishtar's "Social/Community Activities" have included the "[l]aying of cornerstones, setting of foundations, sacred prostitution (organizer) etc., etc. . . . ," while her "Major Responsibilities" have been "Fashioning stars, worlds, suns, people (everything, etc.) Prime moving. . . . Birth, love, death, disease, seasons, etc." (I, pp. vii-viii). Our forms of discourse are unsuited to recognizing or perpetuating great truths, whether cosmological or epistomological; as Lerman's merged protagonist punningly laments, it is difficult to be "both cunning and lingual" (I, p. 71) in our society— particularly for women. Thus the "unemployed" deity attaches a business communiqué addressed "To Whom It May Concern" (I, p. 166) to her employment applications, but by the end of the novel abandons such conventional discourse. She abruptly translates a parodically baroque form letter, warning against harmful encroaching technology, into "Don't fuck with Mother Nature" (I, p. 168). This cliché is no less factual—perhaps more so, given Ishtar's reincarnation—than the elaborate verbal structure it replaces.

Lerman's metamorphosis of dissatisfied, suburban Ishtar into a feathery-crotched goddess (and how *that* transformation shocks both husband and stereotypical male gynecologist in this novel!) enables the author in another significant way to question facticity and to indicate the complex strands with which our comprehension and identities are woven. Myth and history are continually revised from the goddess's more knowledgeable perspective, and we learn that the "polyester" fiber of patriarchal technology has indeed obscured memories of the "luminous threads . . . of the legendary white mare of Ireland" (I, p. 2). Women's positive traits and gyn/ecological interpretations of myth, folklore, and matriarchal religions have been lost to us. In five different typefaces—which themselves indicate the complexity of "truth" and the concomitant paucity of conventional discourse—Lerman redefines significant elements in woman's cultural identity. Ishtar, the maligned "witch," was trying to *help* Snow White, who stupidly, vainly refused to heed the incantation necessary to properly use the poisoned apple; the ugly step-sisters mutilated their feet not to displace Cinderella from her golden slipper but to spare her the loathsome embraces of the Foot Fetishist; Hansel and Gretel were ungrateful, greedy children who betrayed a witch—Ishtar again—who benevolently was attempting to rescue them from their parents' cannibalism.[33] Sons have continually sought to possess the mysterious generativity of their mothers, symbolized by womblike "caskets," "[p]hilosophic eggs," "boxes," and—in this parodic novel—"cookie jars," but have then blamed imprudent or failed attempts on women—Pandoras (I, pp. 114-15).[34] In contrast to Genesis II's validation of male supremacy,[35] Ishtar drily recounts the evolution of man as an unloved, treacherous genetic sport—"Moses Mutant" (I, pp. 18-19).[36]

And so Lerman's novel traverses the terrain between ideological poles. Its "re-visions" of myth and history, as well as its deployment, however humorous, of the Great Mother herself as a central figure, are closely allied to the gynocentric vision, but its questioning of facticity, of essential truths, is removed from such clearly defined absolutes. Indeed, the very first line of the first chapter of Ishtar's search for self and fulfillment mocks such absolutes, so often rooted in physiology rather than personal psychology: "I am civilized. I am discontent. I have a hungry cunt. Truly" (I, p. 1). By capsulizing her predicament in these Freudian terms and then explicating the specific social causes of her "malaise," Syracuse's Ishtar parodically unmans Freud's essentialist views of women's destinies as biologically determined.[37] Singly and, most certainly, once embodied with the knowledge of her foremothers, Lerman's protagonist is representative of hard-won, individual selfhood; like another fictional questor who can name or "call" himself only after acquiring arduous knowledge—Melville's Ishmael—Ishtar is shaped by experience, not mere physiologically-engendered essence.

Thus, anticipating Kristeva's view of gender identity as social construct, Lerman's protagonist comes to realize that her narrow-minded husband needs her, however aberrant her behavior or appearance, because "without her . . . he is not a man" (I, p. 62). Physiology alone will not suffice, nor does it necessarily endow an individual with the stereotypical or potential traits of either gender. Many secondary women characters in this novel are alienated from the anarchic "female" qualities Ishtar comes to represent; conversely, conventional male sex roles disquiet some male characters, such as the rock singer Mack whom Ishtar, searching for a son who will share rather than steal her powers, adopts as a protegé. Furthermore, in Lerman's world-view mere metamorphosis is not enough to alter personal identity. Ishtar confronts a transexual, a male who like Jessie in *A Sea Change* was once female, and recognizes only confusion and emptiness inside him. Ironically, his artificially created penis has earned him the sobriquet of "Twentymiles, the best hung rock star in the Northeast..." (I, p. 108). Ishtar attempts to educate the other members of the rock band she manages—specifically Mack and Claire—to the gynocentric tradition almost destroyed by patriarchy not solely to convert them into adoring worshippers but to make them psychically whole and happy in ways that Twentymiles is not. As she realizes, patriarchy's degradation of certain spiritual and emotional values has adversely affected the psychological development of its followers.

Lerman's parodic account of Ishtar's mis/adventures as this character attempts to transform the dominant twentieth century world view has serious and extensive conceptual antecedents. For example, intelligent reverence for nature and respect for female sexuality are typical of the many matriarchal religions (including worship of Ishtar's diverse manifestations) which flourished before the hegemony of pre-Judeo-Christian patriarchies.[38] Today, these values are not merely absent from valorized patriarchal thought and civilization but actually posited as the "opposite" of (technological) progress and civilization. Perhaps because of their original association with religious and social structures that validated female autonomy and power,[39] these potentially revolutionary concepts have within patriarchal society become associated with women and our "naturally" inferior roles. This degradation of nature and sexuality is a further aspect of the stereotyped dichotomy between "male" culture and "female" nature. Lerman parodies this dichotomy early in the novel through Ishtar and her husband Robert's responses as they drive across Niagara Falls. They surreptitiously engage in sex play, but their motives are different. Ishtar is excited by the Falls' spectacle of untamed, natural power while Robert's excitement stems from the vision of all that energy harnessed for his cloth factory's expanding production.

Robert is representative of individuals who fear to step beyond conventional gender roles—in particular, men who fear to associate themselves with the purportedly inferior attributes of inferior women—and have thus come to ignore aspects of their own personalities and lived experience. Carl Jung termed such self-fragmentation in the individual male the absence of the "anima" (traditionally female or "feminine" qualities), in the individual woman the absence of the "animus" (traditionally male or "masculine" attributes).[40] Yet Jung's analysis is androcentric in its focus on the male quest for psychic wholeness. Rather than being grounded in feminist analysis of religious and cultural history, it indeed accepts and fosters conventional sexual stereotypes in the positing of the "healthy" female psyche as passive.[41] (Robert insists that

Ishtar see a psychiatrist when her activities unconventionally increase and diversify.) But the paradigm proferred by Jungian theory—that of human potential fragmented into so-called masculine and feminine spheres—is, as feminists have come to understand, one that has validity and relevance. It not only describes the impact of sexual stereotypes and roleplaying on individuals but also describes the truncated versions of human history and the distorted versions of human myth propogated by dominant patriarchies. In this sense, Lerman's use of women's myth and history as significant elements in the quest for personal identity is akin to Jungian theories of psychic potential.

Rejecting the inevitable psychological transformation that Gould through her characterization of Jessie/B.G. posits as a component of sexual metamorphosis, Lerman's novel is less ideologically intransigent than *A Sea Change*. The complex, often imperfect formation of cultural as well as personal identity is a major theme in *Call Me Ishtar*. Lerman parodies the gynocentric, essentialist view of human nature through Lerman's personal foibles and her plan to restore psychic balance to humanity through herbally-transformed Hostess cupcakes (a delightful play upon both her identity as the Great Hostess and the womblike form in which so-called female knowledge and power have been thought to be contained); however, Lerman does recognize this view as a valid metaphor for the unexplored or "lost" elements of human potential. Unlike Angela Carter who rejects the reemergence of matriarchal myth and history as "consolatory nonsense,"[42] Lerman validates, in her text, the personal and cultural efficacy of such consolatory, consolidating knowledge. And, by stripping patriarchal myth and history of their "sensible" facticity, Lerman makes "nonsense" a laudatory rather than a pejorative term.

Call Me Ishtar concludes ambiguously, after the Syracuse housewife/goddess has faked her own suburban death, and we are left to determine which ending is most appropriate to this bawdy fantasy just as we have been shown that we have the option to significantly transform our identities, to determine which "ending" is most appropriate for our own lives. Lerman writes of the absconding Ishtar and a new-found companion that "They kissed for a long time.

> And disappeared into the sunset.
> And disappeared into the morning.
> And disappeared into the night.
> And didn't disappear at all.
> Check one. (I, p. 247)

By placing the narrative ultimately in our hands, Lerman undermines narratorial authority and reinforces her undermining of social, historical, and psychological "authority" throughout the text. This final emphasis on *psychological* mutability (her own as an author eager to cede authority; Ishtar's as a character able to metamorphose psychically and socially, as well as psychically; and ours as readers able to accept and then authoritatively modify textual ambiguity) is yet another indication of *Call Me Ishtar*'s ideological complexity. This complexity arises from Lerman's treatment of androgyny and gynocentrism. While she describes the androgynous potential of men as well as women to develop psychically, she paradoxically frames this development within a simultaneously laughable but necessary gynocentric context.

Angela Carter's novel, which details the unwilling transformation of Evelyn, a licentious, irresponsible young Englishman into the "New Eve" of its title, also concludes ambiguously, but this novel is unquestionably further along the ideological spectrum between essentialism and androgyny than Lerman's work. *The Passion of New Eve* savagely satirizes the gynocentric vision that *Call Me Ishtar* merely parodies; its protagonist overtly voices conclusions that Lerman's reader must infer from the combination of plot lines, complex narration, and characters' casual, seemingly elliptical asides. Carter's donnée *is* the question of personal as opposed to gender identity; Lerman's work, with frequently interspersed parodic episodes of upper middle class suburban life—its marriages, bar mitzvahs, counselling sessions, and funerals—and the interweaving of the romantic subplot of Mack and Claire's relationship, is more diffuse in focus. And yet, both novels not only employ physical metamorphosis as a metaphor for the search for individual identity but also situate that search in a specific historical milieu and employ some similar narrative devices to indicate its complexity.

Evelyn, heir to and professor of cultural values and prejudices, leaves London at the end of the first chapter for a university teaching position in New York. It is in America, the source since World War II both of world-wide cultural norms and the most recent wave of feminism, that he will "dis-cover" selfhood. By situating her protagonist in the New World and depicting his personal growth during an automobile trip from East to West Coast, Carter is able to idenfity satirically the multiple layers of naturalized gender identity. America, supposedly idyllic home of the "New Adam,"[43] is shown in this near-future setting to be in civil and social chaos. Blacks and militant feminists conduct guerilla warfare in the cities, while conservative Christian zealots battle a San Francisco-based coalition of liberals, feminists, and Chicanos for control of the "Free State of California" (NE, p. 166). America's initial aspirations, represented by the tradition of the "New Adam" or "Eve,"[44] contrast with its social actualities; both aspirations and actualities are removed from the cultural values that English Evelyn has been indoctrinated with through the media—romanticized Hollywood images of femininity and masculinity.[45]

The Passion of New Eve opens in London, but it is set specifically in a revival movie theater where Evelyn watches yet another old Hollywood film starring Tristessa de St. Ange, the glamorous celluloid heroine, "the very type of romantic dissolution," (NE, p. 7) who has shaped his perceptions of all women. It is these perceptions, and the corresponding vision of masculinity, that will be altered during Evelyn's grimly parodic recapitulation of so many semiautobiographical "road" odysseys by 1950s male American writers.[46] Carter thus does comment on the absurdities of American life, but her satire—evident in the picaresque form of the novel as well as in its content—is more pointed than Lerman's and more integral to the philosophical questions the novel overtly addresses. As he recounts this last evening in a London cinema, the older, altered Evelyn who appears to be our narrator notes that "A critique of these symbols is a critique of our lives" (NE, p. 6). As a result, we begin our reading of this text with a statedly critical outlook.

Carter presents essentialist views of self as the subject most deserving of such critical scrutiny. Initially, these views are detailed through Evelyn's perception of woman as other, a "fiction of the erotic dream" (NE, p. 30) propagated by American media, and the attendant ease with which he can in New York abandon the Black street waif Leila, left sterile after aborting his child. And, certainly, the poet Zero whom Evelyn later encounters in the desert further satirically embodies such patriarchal solipsism. Zero, a self-proclaimed producer of verbal culture, believes that biological man is a superior, culture producing being, while biological woman is an inferior, "naturally" animalistic creature. He carries this self-serving belief to its logical conclusion by forbidding any of his seven common-law wives to speak except in gibberish. He also feeds them garbage (which they must consume "naturally" without cutlery) and forces them to cohabit with his pigs, the most valued members of his communal household. He has convinced these women that his semen is an elixer vital to their well-being and is obsessed with discovering the secret desert home of retired Tristessa de St. Ange, that ultimate "woman," who he is convinced has bewitched him into sterility. He is certain Tristessa has such malign power because she was reputedly uninterested offscreen in heterosexual liaisons and thus possibly a lesbian. Such irrational beliefs and actions are prototypically sexist, stemming from a sense of superior selfhood. Carter pointedly furnishes this character with a bust of Nietzsche in his dishevelled study and with a predilection for Wagner. But this traditional sexism is not the sole, or even the main, focus of Carter's satire. Its feminist correlative, excessive and misanthropic gynocentric essentialism, is at least equally rebuked, depicted in deliberate counterpoint to the pathetic self-delusions of abject inferiority held by Zero's wives. Their internalized values reflect only too well those of patriarchal culture and religion, the aptly-named "Church of Zero" (NE, p. 99).

Seeking "that most elusive of all chimeras, [him]self" (NE, p. 38), Evelyn journeys cross-country to the desert, where he is captured by a well-organized, technologically-advanced unit of feminist separatists—Goddess worshippers who are determined to restore society to its "natural," specifically female order, to "[r]eintegrate the primal form" (NE, p. 64) first by raping Evelyn and then by surgically castrating him and transforming him into a woman. "To be a *man*," their leader proclaims, "is not a given condition but a continuous effort..." (NE, p. 63), an unnatural state. She will remedy this disorder. Before Evelyn is assaulted, he witnesses a religious ceremony in which ancient goddesses from diverse cultures are invoked, and is privy to the modern *reductio ad absurdum*—according to Carter—of such traditions and their litanies: "I am the Great Parracide, I am the Castratrix of the Phallocentric Universe, I am Mama, Mama, Mama!" (NE, p. 67). When the castrated Evelyn awakens, he learns that he is to be impregnated by his own semen, preserved for this purpose following his ritualized rape, and thus ultimately to embody for these misanthropic essentialists their parthenogenetic ideal.[47]

In this satiric description of Beulah's "Women," Carter lampoons what is only one segment of a significant movement in contemporary feminism. Drawing upon rediscovered knowledge of matriarchal history and myth, gynocentric essentialists emphasize woman, rather than man, as the human norm and maintain (like proponents of patriarchal, androcentric essentialism) that there are indeed innate psychological and psychic differences between the sexes. Within the gynocentric vision, however, these differences *favor* the physiologically female. Some enthusiastic advocates of gynocentric essentialism, focusing on women's historical loss of power and rediscovered, sexually-segregated matriarchies, advocate the contemporary establishment of separatist communities. It is this fringe element of gynocentric essentialism that is depicted, satirically, in *The Passion of New Eve*'s Beulah.

Thus, as the "unnatural, slippery, ersatz, treacherous, false-looking" corridors of these women's subterranean retreat remind us, "myth is a made thing, not a found thing" (NE, pp. 55-56). Despite their plastic surgeon leader's re-creation of herself as "her own mythological artefact" (NE, p. 60)—complete with two tiers of nipples, the ultimate Earth Mother—and her unqualifiedly successful metamorphosis over several months of Evelyn into the "New Eve," her new female must *learn* to be a woman. The process of "psychosurgery" that Eve is forced to undergo subsequent to her metamorphosis implicitly contradicts the principles upon which—both figuratively and literally— "Mother" has operated:

> Reproductions of... every single Virgin and Child... ever... painted... projected in real-life colors and blown up to larger than life-size, accompanied by a sound track composed of the gurgling of babies and the murmuring of contented mothers.... another, more inscrutable videotape composed of a variety of non-phallic imagery such as sea-anemones opening and closing; caves, with streams issuing from them; roses, opening to admit a bee; the sea, the moon.... the Liturgy of the Holy Mother... arranged for women's voices in a Monteverdi-like setting, repeated over and over again....   (NE, p. 72)

These images and sounds bombard Eve in Carter's satiric juxtaposition of all the cultural norms (both patriarchal and matriarchal) that today may construct "woman." Mother and her followers, we are shown, have a fallaciously limited, distorted definition of female identity. That they recognize the need for such psychological indoctrination and indeed accompany it with chilling revelations of social gynocide is itself tacit admission of nurture's, as well as nature's, influence on female identity. Furthermore, they fail to perceive their own internalized patriarchal values. The New Eve is designed as "a lyrical abstraction of femininity...a *Playboy* centerfold" (NE, pp. 74-75); her physical perfection, like that of Jessie Waterman is *A Sea Change,* is that of the conventional, media-hyped sex object. Ironically, despite their goal to separate their community physically from patriarchy and mankind, these women have not given equal consideration to the patriarchal norms they themselves must separate from their own gynocentric vision. This ideological confusion is further demonstrated through their treatment of Evelyn/Eve. In their abduction, rape, and attempted impregnation of her, the Women (as Eve/Evelyn names them) invert their own loving, life-giving myth of Demeter and Persephone;[48] it is Mother who now sequesters her new daughter in unwelcome subterranean darkness.

Although this technological womb is called Beulah by its inhabitants, it is not—for Eve—the Biblical promised land, Bunyan's peaceful country, or even the truly "married" state of opposites suggested by Isaiah.[49] This misnomer is instead one of Carter's ironic comments on the possibilities of self-deception during the quest for personal identity, and it applies as much to the gathered Women whose ideological excesses she depicts as it does to Eve/Evelyn, who must live as a woman in order truly to become one. Escaping Beulah and artificial insemination, she realizes that, though she "possess[es] a woman's shape...[she] remain[s]...in the state of innocence that precedes the fall" (NE, p. 83). Continuing such religious metaphors, Carter proceeds to demonstrate that Eve's "passion" is neither the curiosity which has been recorded as her Biblical forbear's downfall nor the lust that outraged mankind has since attributed to that first woman; instead, it is the passion of Christ: the agony and suffering of martyrdom. While the Women treat Evelyn as the male sacrifice necessary to "fertilize" an Eliot-like wasteland, the desert "landscape that matches the landscape of [his] heart" (NE, p. 31) also alludes to Christ's torment in the desert. Eve's anguish recreates this experience of accepting painful humanity. After this character's flight from Beulah, the major portion of the novel depicts the pain of her learning to be "woman" in our society, however cosmeticized that experience may be.

Eve's further initiation into the mutilated selfhood imposed upon women and men by an androcentric, misogynistic dominant society occurs through her interactions with Zero and the almost-legendary Tristessa de St. Ange, whom the poet ultimately locates. Zero's brutalization of his wives, including Eve, once again held against her will, begins the genuine transformation; physically female, she ceases "passing for a woman, like many women born" and "become[s] almost the thing [she] was" (NE, p. 101) after continual physical and psychological abuse. Summarizing the impact of repeated rapes, Eve notes that "[h]e turned me into a woman. More. His preemptory prick turned me into a savage woman" (NE, pp. 107-8). But violent rage in reaction to violence is not the sole component of womanhood, as Eve—and the reader—discover. Through Tristessa, we critically encounter the effects of other socially-fostered female stereotypes.[50]

To his and Eve's incredulous surprise, Zero—seeking to possess Tristessa's "self" and purported powers through rape—discovers that the aged, emaciated movie star is a transvestite, a person without "function in this world except as an idea of himself; no ontological status, only an iconographic one" (NE, p. 129). Tristessa has exemplified and perpetuated the false, impossible ideals of feminine passivity, ethereality, and glamour for millions of fans, including the narrator and himself; Eve surmises that "[h]e had made himself the shrine of his own desires, had made of himself the only woman he could have loved" (NE, p. 129).[51] It is at this point that the surgically transformed Eve begins to realize fully the impact of sex roles and stereotypes upon ordinary women and men. Violated by Zero, Tristessa is revealed as only a "poor, bound female man," (NE, p. 128) living sterilely in a "wedding cake" house, "her own mausoleum" (NE, p. 112) filled with Hollywood wax figures and illusions, and surviving on liquid protein to maintain his svelte figure—a far cry from the rebellious body art of contemporary feminists. To humiliate both the "false" woman (Tristessa) and the "true" woman (Eve), Zero forces them to participate in a mock wedding and then to copulate. His brainwashed wives participate gleefully in this savagery. Reestablishing through this burlesque of heterosexual coupling their own vindictive certainty in conventional, physiologically-based gender identities, these prejudiced characters further reaffirm for Eve and the reader (now dazed by yet another "metamorphosis") the inchoate nature of such identities and sex roles. Allied, the couple later escape, destroying in the process Tristessa's bizarre desert retreat, Zero, and his viciously degenerate wives.

Tristessa's philosophy, revealed to Eve during their flight, further confirms the lessons Eve has learned so painfully. Beginning to grasp now that maleness and femaleness are "masks" for the self (NE, p. 132), Eve listens to the transvestite recount the stages of his world-wide deception:

> At first . . . I used to conceal my genitals in my anus. I would fix them in position with Scotch tape, so that my mound was as smooth as a young girl's. But when the years passed and my disguise became my nature, I no longer troubled myself with these subterfuges. Once the essence was achieved, the appearance could take care of itself.   (NE, p. 141)

Woman's "essence," female self-identity, is, as Tristessa perceives in this none-too-fictional Hollywood culture, the assumption of properly limited, gender-defined roles. Tristessa, existing as a glamorous woman, the mysterious "other" of his own, Evelyn's and Zero's fantasies, thus becomes a true woman through feminine actions. S/he is able to secure this "essence" despite being physiologically male.[52] Tristessa's voluntarily assumed position in society, that of an aptly-named sufferer, confounds in this sense the extremes of both androcentric and gynocentric essentialist definitions of self. Finding a measure of peace with Tristessa, Eve at this point accepts uncertainty and ambiguity as positions closer to any true understanding of sexual dynamics or individual identity than absolutist creeds: "But what the nature of masculine and the nature of feminine might be, whether they involve male and female... that I do not know. Though I have been both man and woman, still I do not know the answer to these questions" (NE, pp. 149-50). With this statement, signalling a psychological transformation in Eve commensurate with her physical metamorphosis, Carter moves her protagonist still further along the ideological spectrum of feminisms from gynocentric essentialism (practiced with such fervent irrationality by the Women of Beulah) towards androgyny.

And yet, this is not the final stance that Carter, either through her protagonist or through the narrative, firmly takes. After Tristessa is slain by Christian child zealots—their nipples pierced by medallions praising, alternately, God and America (NE, p. 157)—because they are horrified by the couple's lovemaking and determined to rescue Eve from Tristessa's "male" animal passions, Eve enters a new stage in her psychosexual odyssey. Gingerly selecting words, she reflects that

> [e]ver since the interrupted continuum I refer to as myself had left Manhattan six—or was it seven or even eight months ago?—it had lived in systems which operated within a self-perpetuating reality; a series of enormous solipsisms, a tribute to the existential freedom of the land of free enterprise. But now I felt myself on the edge of a system of reality that might be perpetrated by factors entirely external to itself....   (p. 167)

This system of reality, sketched in the remaining twenty-five pages of the novel, acknowledges chthonic deities and to some degree validates the Goddess worship of Beulah.

The conclusion of *The Passion of New Eve* is extremely ambiguous, both reiterating and calling into question the issues Carter has raised throughout the text. Carter's playful treatments of facticity and narrativity further obscure her final ideological position. Fleeing the fourteen year old leader of the child zealots, whose maturing body is beginning to distort the reproduction of "The Last Supper" tattooed on his chest much as his crusade distorts the original tenets of Christianity (a further comment on body-mind anomalies), Eve encounters Leila. The supposedly invalided Harlem street waif is now leader of the Women's army, fighting to secure the "Independent Republic of

California" from seceding "Free State of California" zealots and John Birchers (NE, p. 166). Leila reveals that she is really the daughter of "Mother," surgeon-leader of Beulah, who "[w]hen she found that she could not make time stand still... suffered a kind of ... nervous breakdown," and "has retired to a cave by the sea for the duration of the hostilities" (NE, p. 174). While this fictional transfer of power from an isolationist, essentialist leader to a political activist may be interpreted as Carter's consistent repudiation of myth as "consolatory nonsense,"[53] other possible interpretations must also be considered.

Eve herself voices amazement at the transformation of "the houri of Manhattan" (NE, p. 172) into a detached, methodical military leader, and notes an uncanny resemblance between the present Leila and Sophia, the "wise" blonde, upper class Woman who had dispassionately nursed her in Beulah. While the change in Leila's demeanor may be explained as a manifestation of androgynous potential, this physical similarity (yet another metamorphosis!) is rationally unexplainable. The oneiric logic with which such understood "fact" is revealed as mysterious or misunderstood "fiction" in this novel—the Women's Army is camped, most appropriately, in the Benito Cereno shopping center and "relaxarama" (NE, p. 171)[54]—alternatively suggests that Mother and her followers may indeed have tapped an overlooked source of power, that of the Goddess.

The fantastic in this novel thus becomes, not the series of metamorphoses, transformations and coincidences that structure its plot, but the ordinary, "normal" man or woman—Evelyn/Eve—who has failed previously to perceive such powers or human potential. Tzvetan Todorov and Jean Paul Sartre analyze other works of fantasy in which such inversion of ordinary and extraordinary events occurs;[55] it is possible that *The Passion of New Eve,* however critical of gynocentric essentialism's excesses, similarly suggests in its baroque critique of patriarchal norms that we rethink the philosophical bases, the accepted concepts of reality and the "ordinary," that underlie these norms. Such metaphysical redefinitions, intimated early in the text through frequent references to alchemy (NE, pp. 13-16, 14), ally Carter with other contemporary writers of feminist speculative fictions concerned not only with the effects of patriarchal superstructures and ideology but also with the impact of the "new physics" of flux and uncertainty on our lives and self-concepts.[56] Eve's penultimate vision illustrates these concerns. Safely hidden from the civil war by Leila in Mother's naturally womb-like sea cave, Eve experiences "[t]ime... running back on itself" (NE, p. 183) and sees the "archaeopteryx.... bird and lizard both at once.... a mysterious, seminal, *intermediate* being whose nature [she] grasped in the desert" (my emphasis). This vision both in setting and imagery seems to repudiate patriarchal reality, to validate the mysteries of earth and goddess worship at the same time that its focus on an "intermediate" creature seems to validate the androgynous vision.

Alternatively, Eve may merely be deceiving us and herself, an unreliable narrator whose vacillations between conflicting ideologies are but one indication of psychological instability. Her accounts of Tristessa de St. Ange's Hollywood career may be construed as a further sign of such unreliability. She credits the transvestite with having starred—always opposite Tyrone Power— in *Wuthering Heights,* in *Little Women,* as Madeleine Usher, George Sand in the biography of Chopin, and as Faust's Marguerite. While these false film credits, distorting actual film history, may be perceived as yet another comment on both Hollywood's homogenization of femininity and on the dubious worth of "facticity" as we conventionally understand it, such obvious historical "errors" may also represent an unbalanced mind.[57] Evelyn/Eve's obsession, manifested early in the novel, with "the dark room, the mirror, the woman" (NE, p. 39), with things and situations alchemical, may be signs of early irrationality as readily as they may be the stirrings of a quest for Jungian wholeness—a "man's" search for his "female" anima. The new Eve's transformative experiences in the sea cave may just be hallucination. Carter toys with all these possibilities in her last chapter.

Barely half a page in length, this last, twelfth chapter places the whole preceding narrative literally in limbo. Beginning with the sentence, "We start from our conclusions" (NE, p. 191), the chapter displaces the narrative from any conventionally logical framework. Shifts from present to past tenses and the intimation that Eve, pregnant with Tristessa's child, has set herself adrift on the Pacific Ocean in a rowboat effect this displacement. Whose voice have we heard in this text? How can the author of this purported memoir be Eve, if its final sentence, "Ocean, ocean, mother of mysteries, bear me to the place of birth" (NE, p. 191), suggests simultaneously suicide and mystical rebirth rather than the termination of a written reflection? Who—if anyone—has intervened to present this tale to us, and what, if anything, has been added or deleted in the transmission? Like the reader of Eliot's poetry, alluded to in the first line's paraphrase of the *Four Quartets'* "In the end is my beginning"[58] as well as in earlier wasteland imagery, we are flooded by the possibilities of alternate systems of belief, cast adrift (as is Eve?) from patriarchal conventions of time, space, and history. Further clear reference to the *Four Quartets'* questioning and reordering of reality is made in the next sentence's use of the four elements that are that work's dominant metaphors: "I arrived on that continent by *air* and I left it by *water; earth* and *fire* I leave behind me" (NE, p. 191, my emphasis). Only the nature of the new order remains unclear. The novel's experience, as it is remembered, "confounds itself in a fugue" (NE, p. 191). But which themes are being counterpointed, and which portions of experience have been forgotten, misunderstood, or misremembered is uncertain.

Questions raised by the final pages of *The Passion of New Eve* strongly suggest that it is we, the readers, who must "start" from whatever conclusions the text has provided.[59] We know that Carter penultimately depicts her protagonist trading an alchemical necklace for an old woman's boat; the woman is described "with hair like a nest of petrified snakes, old enough to have been either man or woman" (NE, p. 191), but the significance of this simultaneously Medusan and androgynous figure remains moot.[60] Perhaps Carter is indicating the need to move past *both* rigidly-maintained essentialist and androgynous ideologies to arrive at a more profound understanding of our natures.[61] We are told that the dying old woman has her "dream" (NE, p. 178), sitting as she does in splendid decay on the beach singing "Everything is peaches down in Georgia" (NE, p. 177), and that Leila and Eve wonder if she might not be better off in this dream than in the coming post-apocalyptic world. The nature of the dream and outcome of the apocalypse, though, both remain unspecified. The penultimate observation of Carter's work is, in this sense, highly significant to this novel of multiple sexual metamorphoses. Someone—perhaps Eve, perhaps Carter herself—concludes that "the vengeance of the sex is love" (NE, p. 191); however, we are not told *which* sex is so afflicted. We may choose, or decide—at the conclusion of this novel—that the distinction is irrelevant.

The Passion of New Eve thus rests tentatively between the poles of the ideological spectrum of contemporary feminist ideologies. While Carter, drawing parallels between Zero's and young Evelyn's misogyny and the misanthropy of the Women, satirizes fringe elements within the feminist essentialist movement, her novel seems to support the authenticity of some of this view's historical, religious antecedents. Her protagonist comes to believe that gender identity is merely a social construct, but the text as a whole is more ambivalent about this possibility.

June Arnold's *Applesauce,* depicting "the primary struggle of a woman to be a woman" (A, Foreward) in contemporary society, questions the nature of self- and gender-identity in less pyrotechnic but no less probing ways than Carter's novel. Arnold's allusions are few but pointed. Those to Kafka's "Metamorposis" and "In the Penal Colony" (A, pp. 5 and 9, respectively) ironically draw our attention both to the possibility of untoward physical metamorphosis and to the social pressures to have self and self-knowledge "accurately" reflected by one's body. References to Swift's Gulliver place in new perspective women's "travels" in similarly foreign or hostile patriarchal lands.[62] Finally, allusions to Theophrastan characters, Peter Pan's Wendy, Rumpelstilskin, the old woman in the shoe, and Echo (A, pp. 230, 145, 215-18, and 240, respectively) create specific reminders of the conflicting, mythologized, one-dimensional stereotypes that women are supposed to embody. (Respectively, they refer to the sexless nursemaid, confined housekeeper-mother, and pining lover.) Praised by Ellen Morgan as a "feminist novel of androgynous fantasy,"[63] *Applesauce* is extremely close to that end of the ideological spectrum, but it is not merely an apologue for androgyny. Instead, after displaying the destructive absurdities fostered by our dominant culture's androcentrically essentialist stereotypes and sex roles, Arnold's work details as well some of the pitfalls of the androgynous vision. Complex, possibly unreliable narration; redefinition of accepted "fact" as opposed to fantastic "fiction"; and examination of the artificial, constricting limits of conventional discourse figure in *Applesauce* as they do in the other three contemporary novels discussed above.

Liza Durach/Gus Ferrari, Arnold's protagonist, whose third person viewpoint (with two brief first person exceptions) is ours throughout the text, initially seems to experience a sexual metamorphosis more akin to that of Woolf's Orlando than any of the others previously discussed. No hurricane, goddess, or plastic surgeon intervenes; Liza simply becomes Gus as the male Orlando simply awakens in female form. But, while Woolf seemingly implies that the distinction between male and female identity is as clear as the one between sleep and wakeful consciousness, Arnold rejects such easily-recognizable demarcations. Because relationships between gender and sexual identity are more nebulous in the world-view she creates, we are not shown or told of that moment of Liza/Gus's transition. Instead, we are presented metaphorically with the possibility of every person's androgynous potential, of gender identity's being totally a social construct. Noting the sexual ambiguity of people's features, so "often placed . . . by circumstantial evidence—names, dress, etc. Or . . . prejudiced in advance by . . . choice of pronoun" (A, p. 25), Liza/Gus demonstrates this observation for a visiting friend:

> "I am Gus Ferrari," he said to the mirror. A square forehead, imprecise eyebrows, set and solid flesh looked back at him in agreement. "I am Liza Durach." The mouth became fluid, the cheeks soft, the eyes almond-shaped in complicity.   (A, p. 25)

To this intimation that sexual "metamorphosis" is illusory only in the same sense that gender identity is a social illusion, the friend laughingly, conventionally responds that Liza/Gus is insane.

Narrational unreliability, stemming from Liza/Gus's possible insanity, must be acknowledged by Arnold's reader. The physical metamorphosis that Liza/Gus recounts, the androgynous physical presence that s/he observes in the mirror, is not perceived by each of the other characters in *Applesauce* and may indeed by a hallucinatory manifestation of this character's rage and thwarted goals. Bobby, the youngest Durach/Ferrari child, says "You're Mommy. Aren't you?" (A, p. 7), while Liza's old college roommate Jo cannot prevent herself from uttering the first syllable of her former friend's name— "Li-Gus"—even as she attempts to humor her by acceding to the presence of Gus Ferrari (A, p. 89). But further examination of *Applesauce* lessens the significance of this possible twice-removed aberration from conventional, "factual" reality.

Liza/Gus's plan to build a room within the room to which s/he has retreated for several years, to "enclose all of [her] so safely [she] won't bother to bring journeying bits of [her]self back to [her] body" (A, p. 59) may be perceived as a further sign of mental instability. And yet this ultimately life-negating behavior may also be viewed as a most rational response to the irrationalities of a sex-biased society. By attempting to literally build what Elaine Showalter has described (in relation to Virginia Woolf's works) as "female space, a space that is both sanctuary and prison,"[64] Arnold's protagonist is seeking the absence of conflict, "chaos without anxiety," the "rest according to the laws of physics" (A, p. 60) popularly-accepted in the mid-1960s.[65] Addressing the skeptical reader, Liza/Gus emerges from relative third person anonymity to clarify the sense and sensibility of this act:

> I have explained the room to you a hundred times, if you had listened. It is a concept which makes clarity and perfect sense; how could you not understand? It is simply a matter of *choosing what you can't avoid in any case.* I have been out in the world, and my brain is as good as yours, my heart perhaps less so but adequate, adequate—at least to begin with. I have tried to get through in as many ways as I can think up. What happens I don't know.   (A, p. 169, my emphasis)

Liza/Gus continues this rationalizing rumination:

> There's a two-year-old child on the beach out the window, racing for the surf. The waves knock him down once; he gets up, retreats, and sits on the sand to think it over. Another figure brings him something—a pail and shovel? Yes, a pail and shovel because the beach is made of sand. His mother's education was cutting out and pasting into scrapbooks colored advertisements from magazines (because *her* mother knew how to handle children: give them something to do). So this child does not keep on racing for the surf and being knocked down by the waves, retreating, racing for the surf, being knocked down, retreating, racing.... He will play in the sand instead, which is better.   (A, p. 169)

The room, its floor boards slanted, its distorted proportions painstakingly worked out, is Liza/Gus's methodical, pail and shovel retreat from the pounding surf of everyday existence. In place of the conventional sand castle, a suburban ranch home, s/he substitutes this paradigmatic equivalent. Arnold depicts the brutal effects of sex role socialization on women and men in such vivid detail that Liza/Gus's maddened responses become clearly comprehensible, if not desirable. The reader recognizes the authentic female experiences Arnold narrates through her personae,[66] and this psychological acuity counterweighs our distrust of a narrator whose probable unreliability is so clearly the result of systematic, constant pressures.

The "mother figure" (A, p. 169) in this character's rationale for her/his behavior is particularly relevant to the novel's overall structure. *Applesauce* is divided into three sections of approximately equal length, each of which is named for one of the three "dead" wives of Gus Ferrari: Eloise, Rebecca, and Lila. While these characters each typify one of the conflicting, stereotyped roles permitted women in our society—sexual playmate, intellectual, and mother, respectively—and each confronts different elements of sexism both within and outside her "marriage" to Gus,[67] they all absurdly appear to have the same dreadfully conventional mother, "Mrs. _____" (A, p. 36). First introduced as Mrs. Durach, this mother's relationship with her daughter is rigidly circumscribed by social norms and is further "evidence" in the psychological profile the reader constructs of Liza/Gus during the course of the novel. We begin to perceive through Mrs. _____'s presense in each section that Liza has, in attempting to fulfill maternal and social injunctions, fragmented herself before—into Eloise, Rebecca, and Lila. These personae are all different aspects of the conventional womanhood that she has tried to embody before her final, desperate retreat and "metamorphosis"—as Gus Ferrari—to her room within a room.

Mrs. _____ serves then as both metaphor and plot device in *Applesauce*. She figuratively represents the patriarchal social constraints that make Eloise feel "closeted and confined into the standard girl-mold" (A, p. 78) by her dresses, that tell intellectual Rebecca that she is not "really a woman" unless she "[a]dvertises that softness" (A, p. 109) that comes after giving birth and cries when upset, and that give Lila a hunger and emptiness that no number of children can satisfy. She is also an awful enough childhood influence to contribute significantly to the potential mental instability of young Liza Durach. Mrs. _____'s eyes shine only when her daughter is happy for the "right" reasons: when "her daughter [is feeling] this happiness from proper sources": in relation to her husband and children (A, p. 196). She resists this daughter's attempts to maintain selfhood through unconventional acts by saying they are "not natural.... You need only follow your natural instincts, darling. Don't be afraid to let what is inside come out" (A, pp. 167-68). Such androcentrically essentialist comments—prescribing and validating a specific, conventionally "inferior" set of emotions as "natural" for women solely on the basis of our physical gender—are bitterly ironic because of the fears that Eloise, Rebecca, Lila, and ultimately Gus share. Each of these personae is terrified by the vulnerability of conventional women in patriarchal society. This terror often manifests itself after unsatisfactory sexual intercourse in feelings of self-dissolution—"like my insides are outsides" (A, p. 44). Letting "what is inside come out" is the last thing any of these characters would choose to do. Lila notes of her mother's complete acculturation to dehumanizing social norms that "[s]he would never need to build a room. She would grow cataracts if necessary and print her world on their inner side" (A, p. 164, my emphasis). It is Mrs. _____, fulfilling the role of a socially responsible wife and mother by attempting to indoctrinate her daughter with patriarchal values (and alienating her in the process), who—along with her weak-willed second husband and self-destructive son—functions as the structural linchpin of Arnold's novel.[68]

Mrs. _____ is a rational explanation for Liza/Gus's possible irrationality; other logical explanations are found in the adult experiences that further circumscribe and confine this character until, "his body show[ing] only a ten per cent connection with his emotional life" (A, p. 80), s/he decides that self-confinement (in a room if not another body) will provide some measure of protection. Thus, the psychological reality of this character's felt need for Liza Durach's metamorphosis into Gus Ferrari outshadows the questions of its literal occurrence or narratorial unreliability. And, in this work of mingled psychological and social realities, the possibility of such a literal transformation becomes no more fantastic than the destructive social norms Arnold details. As in Carter's *The Passion of New Eve,* the fantastic or "fictional" may be perceived not as the extraordinary event (the possibility of Liza's actual transmogrification into Gus, or of the actual existence and deaths of Eloise, Rebecca, and Lila) but as the misperceived, misrepresented, supposedly benign everyday "facts" of patriarchal society. Liza/Gus's unreliability in this sense affirms Arnold's ideological opposition to essentialist sexism and its conventional delimitation of reality; ambivalent narration does not obscure this author's final position in the text as it does in Carter's novel. Arnold's detailing of the impact of implacably essentialist definitions of self upon men as well as women and of the paucity of conventional discourse to describe such destructive experiences and possible productive alternatives, further confirms these redefinitions of fantasy/facticity.

Liza Durach, as Eloise, is first drawn to the man she marries, whose identity she in some sense ultimately assumes, because "she saw, or thought she saw, or hoped she saw, that inside [him] there was still space—for her" (A, p. 32). She desires to possess—through association or mysterious/maddened incorporation—the freedom that such a person, with an "exterior sufficiently unambiguous that on any streetcorner he would be taken for a man" (A, p. 32), seems to possess in an androcentric culture. But Liza/Eloise is mistaken; even though she talismanically calls this character Gus because the name "has us in it" (A, p. 33), he too is constrained (though to a lesser degree) by rigid sex roles and stereotypes. Arnold's Gus is psychologically maimed because he is expected to be a "real" man like the "real men" (A, p. 121) with whom women have nothing in common, like the men who objectify women, telling them "You're much too pretty to talk, baby. Just look pretty" (A, p. 140), and who insist that women smile even when they are sad. Gus "refuse[s] to look at the surface of things, and that is almost as bad as never looking beyond the surface" (A, p. 230). The Dick and Jane storybooks that lock Liza-Eloise-Rebecca-Lila into circumscribed, inferior roles also inhibit Gus. And, to close this circle, upon completing *Applesauce,* the reader realizes that Gus's domineering mother, introduced briefly in the novel's first pages, is none other than Mrs. _____. The child in the narrator's breaking surf, pail-and-shovel metaphor for parental socialization is, we recall with new awareness, male.

While it may be argued that Gus is an artificial composite of stereotypically male foibles, that this character is just the distorted fictive construct of another, unreliable fictional creation (Liza), Arnold's depiction of Mrs. _____'s suicidal son Dick, also alluded to in each section of the novel, further confirms the text's emphasis of this corresponding dimension of damaging sexual prejudice. Dick is the victim who fails to survive Mrs. _____'s views about what "a natural life," a "normal" life for a biological man or woman should be (A, p. 208). His childhood confusion about the sex roles he is expected to fulfill parodies rigidly essentialist views of selfhood. Misinterpreting his parents' caustic remark about his "effeminate" pleasure in drawing, "that a boy would be a sissy if he drew pictures unless he was six feet two and squared off to a horse" (A, p. 211), the nine year old Dick destroys his sketches because he believes that he has been told that "he'll draw in public *when* he's a horse" (A, p. 210). This literalization of metaphor burlesques Mrs. _____'s sexual biases as it merely extends logically the absurd linkage of social role to physical form upon which the original remark is based. Dick retains the essence of Mr. and Mrs. _____'s illogic. At eleven, according to Mrs. _____, he "paint[s] his body like a woman's . . . he paint[s] himself *into* the body of a woman" (A, p. 212, my emphasis). At thirteen, he similarly attempts to transform the bodies of two of his friends. Superficially akin to contemporary feminist body art, this playacting, which horrifies Liza and Dick's parents with its intimations of homosexuality or transvestitism, can be interpreted darkly; to some extent, it is the presaging obverse of Liza's unhappy self-fragmentation. Thirty year old Dick later volunteers for the army, telling his sister that he plans to die.

Why do Liza/Gus and Dick fail to find more productive alternatives for their lives? Arnold's phantasmagoric rendition of their childhoods and adult experience, detailing the obstacles to be overcome, provides some answers; her allusions to feminist controversy and theory provide others. While the tribulations of *Applesauce*'s protagonists are a vehement argument against the worth of rigid gender roles or identities, Arnold also voices through her persona Rebecca apprehensions about the alternative of androgyny. Like some theorists who debate this viewpoint's value to feminists, suggesting that it may further elevate stereotypically "male" values at the expense of conventionally "female" ones, Rebecca notes that "[m]en" have "worshipped trees because that's what they wanted to be, male-female together.[69] The Tiresias complex" (A, p. 135). The emphasis here is on the primacy of "maleness." Androgyny as a theoretical construct contains the dangers for women of co-optation; just as the "tree . . . identified with the mother in primitive religious worship" became the Biblical tree of patriarchal knowledge and law (A, p. 135), androgyny may prove our undoing. To complete this analogy of potential loss, Liza/Gus's old family retainer reminds her that the growth of new young trees near well-established ones often portends the death of the older ones (A, p. 135). Arnold then alludes to Daphne who, seeking "to escape Apollo" (A, p. 135), turned into a tree: we do not know if this metamorphosis was a satisfactory refuge, as this tree (like Liza/Gus's room within a room) is both sanctuary and prison. Tellingly, though, Arnold does reveal elsewhere that Lila "dies" after falling from an apple tree.

The author voices reservations about *all* theoretical constructs early in the novel through this omnipresent apple imagery. A young Liza/Gus literalizes a grandmother's affectionate comment that [s/he] is "the apple of [her] eye" (A, p. 18) much as Dick literalizes his parent's remark about a horse; as with Dick, there is significant validity to the childish interpretation. Because women are stereotyped, classified by sex regardless of individual differences, they are intellectualized as a generic class, like apples. It is the soft "core" that must be protected from such ratiocination and its social corollaries, hidden in a different body or at least in a room within a room, to avoid its being mashed into "applesauce."[70] As undifferentiated specimens, apples (women), are merely pawn-like rhetorical devices, held "casually" between powerful personages and their audiences, useful as punctuation, "perfect to gesture with—a half-eaten apple held by a lean intellectual" (A, p. 19). Once bitten into, the apple (woman) may be carelessly discarded, with a "flash of hate" at its continued, awkward presence; "[i]t is always an existential conflict, to one who was once a boy, between the apple and the ball" (A, p. 20). It is this subsidiary role—of accessory or plaything—that Liza/Eloise/Rebecca/Lila experience in *Applesauce*. Liza/Gus maintains that s/he "would rather be peeled than be the object of such promiscuousness" (A, p. 18), and this wish is nearly figuratively granted before the novel's conclusion. The paucity of conventional discourse to communicate this character's plight, let alone function as a tool to alter it, is another social obstacle confronting her protagonists that Arnold examines.

In addition to gender pronouns that artificially determine people's identities,[71] to nouns—like apple—that classify rather than specify, Arnold's protagonist rails against patriarchal language that denies ambiguity, maintains hierarchies, and categorizes itself according to gender.[72] Rebecca translates "Quien Sabe?" into "of course" (A, p. 134) because this translation is the required conventional response—terse, unambiguous, reassuring—to a question about her mothering abilities. Her true sentiments can only be voiced in a foreign tongue. Later, she dismays a luncheon table full of academics with her inappropriate metaphors for literary analysis: "disjointing the carcass" of a text; "baiting and setting the trap" for meaning; knowing a poem so thoroughly that it "belongs to you as if you'd whelped it yourself" (A, pp. 131-32). The physicality of these first phrases is inappropriate because, as a woman, Rebecca is not entitled to use hunting metaphors taken from the traditional male sphere;

the last phrase is inappropriate, paradoxically, because it emphasizes her biological femaleness, her ability to "whelp." Rebecca, caught in the double bind of female scholars which this verbal conundrum typifies, cannot fit into the literary circles of the Rice Institute Arnold portrays. Arnold has this character/persona of Liza/Gus commit suicide—in an interesting parallel to the conclusion of Kate Chopin's *The Awakening*—by swimming out to sea. Unlike Chopin's turn-of-the-century protagonist, however, Rebecca worries about being raped before she plunges into the ocean and does not sink peacefully into oblivion. Sharks, drawn by menstrual blood, savagely attack her. When the probability of Rebecca's being one aspect of self-fragmented Liza Durach is considered, the metaphorical implications of this self-destruction precipitated by female physiology are clear.

Arnold also intimates the problems that written discourse holds for women as we attempt to redefine ourselves. In addition to coping with language which does not adequately reflect the emphases of actual female experience (verbal Rebecca realizes that a self-help book "entitled *How to Make People Like You*" is actually "a manual giving directions for constructing a people making machine: how to make people like *you*" [(A, p. 138]), Arnold—through narratorial comments and the text of *Applesauce* itself—confronts the limitations of semiotic conventions. There is no punctuation mark that adequately reflects the unsatisfactory sexual routines of Gus and Rebecca, "half question, half statement. . . . Unless: ./?? Or, perhaps, $\div$. But no typesetter," Rebecca observes, "can get that; I can hardly type it"(A, p. 123). Similarly, Arnold presents Mrs. Durach and Liza's argument over childbearing and sexuality in split page format—an innovation that reflects the simultaneity of the disagreement and its possible lack of resolution and leaves the reader uncertain as to the most informative order in which to read this page (A, pp. 165-66). Disrupting the patriarchal tradition of discursive linearity, this technique presents the reader in miniature with the problems of living without clear definitions, or within what were previously foreign ones, that Arnold's protagonist undergoes.[73] We must choose at this point how to construct or deconstruct the text. Contemporary feminist collagists deliberately present their audiences with similarly difficult interpretive choices in order to sensitize us to the artificial, man-made and often man-oriented texture of contemporary life and art. Arnold herself, through Rebecca, warns the reader of the "duplicity" of critics (A, p. 113), of the pitfalls possible in always-subjective literary interpretation, that we must avoid in reading this or any other text.

And so, even *Applesauce*, with its clear condemnations of patriarchal norms and—by extension—feminist theory that is comparably essentialist in scope, concludes ambiguously. Ellen Morgan notes the positive reintegration of personalities (bodies?) that concludes the novel, Gus Ferrari/Liza Durach realizing fully the social constraints on men as well as women, beginning to perceive the destructiveness of the room within a room as a way of life. Morgan notes that *Applesauce* concludes with Liza/Gus's victorious, self-affirming proclamation that "I AM LIZA" (A, p. 240).[74] However, this is only the novel's penultimate line. It literally concludes with a final, italicized sentence, which we must interpret for ourselves:

> *I am Liza, am Liza, Liza, Liza, za, za, a, a, a, a, . . . , said Echo.*

Is this a resounding, reaffirming chorus, celebrating Liza Durach's rebirth, or is this sentence a reminder of the frailty of individual resolve against mythologized sexual stereotypes? It is unclear at this point if Liza Durach will survive as herself or again pine away, like Echo, for obsessive love of a male-oriented vision. While Arnold confounds in *Applesauce* the basically essentialist views of a writer like Gould (whose Jessie Waterman, in an interesting coincidental inversion, draws upon mysterious "female" powers to rescue her child from a hurricane even as Lila permits hers to drown), she does not offer an *absolute* alternative vision. Androgyny contains potential dangers for women, just as—in Arnold's view—any theoretical construct does.

Mirroring contemporary feminist performance and body art, Lois Gould's *A Sea Change*, Rhoda Lerman's *Call Me Ishtar*, Angela Carter's *The Passion of New Eve*, and June Arnold's *Applesauce* broach issues and questions central to the women's movement of the last two decades. Through their characters' shifting identities and fantastic sexual metamorphoses, these novels, the literary offspring of Virginia Woolf's *Orlando*, range the continuum of feminist ideologies—gynocentric essentialism to androgyny—that are currently being debated, explored, and experimented with in contemporary society. *A Sea Change*, with its intimation of Jessie Waterman's supernatural ability to transform herself and harness the "female" forces of Hurricane Minerva, is closest to the gynocentrically essentialist end of this continuum. *Call Me Ishtar* and *The Passion of New Eve* are ambivalently at its center. *Applesauce*, despite metaphoric reservations, suggests that the androgynous vision has most merit.

These authors' common use as well of complex, at times unreliable narration; of plot devices and metaphoric systems that invert "fact" and "fiction"; and of discourse that questions the efficacy of conventional, partriarchal linear writing further shapes the impact of their works. Each novel concludes with some degree of ambiguity; instead of "receiving" the truth or law from an omnipotent author, the reader is led to accept responsibility and *authority* for the final construction of the text's meaning. This authority is comparable to the control that feminists currently seek to wrest from patriarchal convention and replace in freer women's and men's hands.[75] In this sense, these works of fantastic fiction, which may superficially seem like light or "escape" entertainment, are significant models for the replotting or mapping of our own lives.[76]

2

Questors and Heroines: New Myths, New Models

Let us step off the edge. . . . We must go beyond what we sense (I am assuming that we already are beyond what we *know*), and test our perceptions of reality. We must admit the entire cosmos as the ground on which such a search takes place. We must recognize the dissolution of the illusion of linear form. Yet we must go beyond, in effect, at the same time that we embrace the past and act openly in the present.[1]

At once invitation and command, exhortation and request, Robin Morgan's proposal for the future direction of feminist theory summarizes the complex relationships among reader, text, and ideology that some feminist writers of speculative fiction continue to initiate. At the same time that their protagonists "step off the edge" of known experience by participating in interplanetary, interdimensional, or transtemporal travel, such writers as Dorothy Bryant, Mary Staton, and (to a lesser degree) Ursula K. Le Guin propose through their narratives' complexity that the reader abandon the safety of a "readerly" text's conventional discourse.[2] Instead, such works as Bryant's *The Kin of Ata Are Waiting for You* (1971),[3] Staton's *From the Legend of Biel* (1975),[4] and Le Guin's somewhat earlier *The Left Hand of Darkness* (1969)[5] dissolve "the illusion of [textual] linear form." The structures of these works thus "test [the reader's] perceptions of reality" much as feminism challenges patriarchal realities. Furthermore, by placing authority for textual meaning within the *reader's* grasp, these authors (like the ones discussed in chapter 1) create models for the kinds of individual and grass roots activisim feminist theory encourages.

The plots and themes of these novels also reflect their authors' feminist vision. The mythological and literary tradition of physical metamorphosis is but one drawn upon by contemporary speculative fiction writers in their efforts to redefine the parameters of individual identity. Such authors also employ the classical quest motif[6] and the utopian model of an unwary stranger thrust into a distant, strange land[7] to convey their interest in current feminist ideologies. The questing or journeying protagonists of *The Kin of Ata* and *From the Legend of Biel,* the specific focus of this chapter, are forced by alien or unforeseen circumstance to examine strong preconceptions. They must confront, in particular, their own stereotyped beliefs about sex roles, gender identity, and human or social potential. In this confrontation they are much like the space-travelling protagonist of *The Left Hand of Darkness*. Light years and millenia, constituting the "fantastic" proportions of these novels' plots, thus become unifying metaphors for the strenuous psychological journeys their characters and the attentive reader undertake. For these complex novels experientially ally the audience, through the actual processes of reading and then constructing textual meanings, with their questing or journeying protagonists.

Inciting readers to speak and act, to construct meaning *beyond* as well as within the text, is, however, a point upon which these three novels diverge. While *The Kin of Ata* and *The Legend of Biel* both to varying degrees explicitly address the reader, overtly requesting personal involvement with the issues they raise, Le Guin omits such a plea from *The Left Hand of Darkness* itself.[8] This omission parallels her relatively more ambivalent stance towards feminist activism.[9] For despite their similarities of technique, plot and theme, these novels (like the ones discussed in chapter 1) display the scope and varied intensity of current feminist ideologies. "Stepping off the edge" has very different implications for each of these authors.

In effect, Bryant's and Staton's novels may be read as more politicized versions of Le Guin's watershed treatment of gender identity, sex roles, and sexual stereotypes. To appreciate Bryant's and Staton's ideological and textual daring, I therefore believe it is helpful to preface analysis of their works with a brief discussion of their literary forebear, *The Left Hand of Darkness*.[10] Le Guin's novel is an account of Earth envoy Genly Ai's difficult sojourn on Gethen/Winter, a planet of humanoid hermaphrodites who are sexually quiescent save for a few days each month when they may involuntarily assume the sexual functions of either gender. This book has received significant and varied critical attention.[11] Le Guin's depiction of Ai's dangerous misapprehensions in a world devoid of sex roles, sex-stereotypes, or gender identity has been linked to implicitly advocated Taoism or Jungianism as well as to a less philosophically-defined "journey of self-discovery."[12] This character only gradually comprehends that his diplomatic and life-threatening problems stem from his own divisive patriarchal heritage in which "women" are "more alien to [him] than [non-humans] are" (LH, p. 223). Ai survives on Gethen only because he learns to overcome his fears, to accept and reciprocate the friendship of Estraven, the alien other, "woman as well as ... man" (LH, p. 234).[13] Symbolically, this acceptance of Estraven's female component is equivalent to Ai's acceptance of his own female characteristics or "anima." The old Gethenian lay from which Le Guin purportedly derives the novel's title applies as much to Ai's psychological structures as it does to Gethenian physiology and attendant folklore:

Light is the left hand of darkness
and darkness the right hand of light.
Two are one, life and death, lying
together like lovers in kemmer,
like hands joined together,
like the end and the way.   (LH, p. 222)

This folk song echoes Jungian and Taoist thought in its suggestion that unified opposites (light and darkness; life and death; male and female lovers; the end and the way) are a necessary, integral component of human(oid) existence.

Le Guin's demanding use of complex narration has also been cited in support of varied critical interpretations. The novel develops through "official documents" purportedly written by several representatives of the Hainish empire, tape-recorded legends and myths from different Gethenian groups, diary fragments, and multiple first person narratives. It also consistently employs light/dark imagery that reflects its theme of unified opposites.[14] Active reader involvement is crucial to construct meaning in this variegated text. Bryant and Staton engage active reader involvement with their texts through similarly complex narration; however, it is the controversy about feminist ideology and literary practice in *The Left Hand of Darkness* that provides the context critical to understanding the significance of *The Kin of Ata* and *From the Legend of Biel.*

As the novel's mixed critical and popular reception indicates, Le Guin's deployment of feminist ideology and literary practice is ultimately too conservative for some readers.[15] This conservatism is most evident in the novel's relationships to traditionally androcentric Jungianism, the developing concept of feminist androgyny, and the emerging possibility of consciously feminist discourse. *The Left Hand of Darkness* is a feminist work in its consciousness-raising inquiries, but (as I shall demonstrate) it retains a significant number of androcentric or androcentrically essentialist elements. Le Guin's attempt to "go beyond" convention is not supported by equal efforts to "embrace the past *and* act openly in the present." In contrast, *The Kin of Ata* and *From the Legend of Biel,* both employing complex narration comparable to that of *The Left Hand,* overtly address the issues that this novel, its reception, and its problematic success as feminist polemic merely raise. Bryant's *Ata* merges traditional Jungian theory more successfully into its feminist polemic than Le Guin does, but *Ata* too remains ideologically ambivalent, poised between essentialist and androgynous views of personal identity. Staton's *From the Legend of Biel* is closer to the androgynous pole of the continuum of ideological feminisms in its overall treatment of Jungian theory, feminist androgyny, and innovative feminist discourse.

Le Guin has been faulted for this novel's consistent, male-oriented use of the generic "he" to describe the biologically androgynous inhabitants of Gethen and for her depiction of these characters solely within the traditionally male spheres of politics and physical adventure.[16] In response, she has written that this novel's "real subject ... is not feminism or sex or gender or anything of the sort ... it is a book about betrayal and fidelity."[17] Furthermore, she has "refuse[d] to mangle English by inventing a pronoun for 'he/she'."[18] This refusal is antithetical not only to much current feminist revision of linguistic theory[19] and to the experimental practices of such writers as June Arnold but (as we shall see) to the subsequently developing genre of overtly feminist speculative fictions. Le Guin clarifies her position as woman and writer vis-à-vis the women's movement of the 1960s and 1970s in her 1976 introduction to the reissue of an earlier novel, *Planet of Exile* (1966):

> I am often very angry as a woman. But my feminist anger is only an element in, a part of, the rage and fear that possess me when I face what we are all doing to each other, to the earth.... I cannot accept the premise [that the root of all injustice, exploitation, and blind aggression is sexual injustice]; therefore, I cannot act upon it.... I would write dishonestly and badly.... A political activist can take her answers from the current ideology of her movement, but an artist has got to dig those answers out of herself, and keep on digging until she knows she has got as close as she can possibly get to the truth.[20]

Le Guin's placement of feminism at the periphery of her ethical concerns and her positing of such political activism or ideology as elements extraneous to artistic endeavor or "truth" are misleading statements.[21] They simultaneously misrepresent *The Left Hand of Darkness* and the body of feminist speculative fictions that has developed since the novel's original 1969 publication. Despite her protestations, Le Guin does not transcend feminist ideology or its conflicts in this fiction. She herself has repudiated as immature its plot's implicitly essentialist "thought-experiment"—the depiction of an alien population whose androgyny results from physical hermaphroditism and sexual quiescence alternating with periods of estrus. Nonetheless, this heuristic device for "asking questions about the meaning of sexuality and the meaning of gender, in [her] own life and in our society"[22] results in a fiction that validates its own essentialist premises. This work does not move far beyond the overliteralized tradition of classical, androcentric androgyny to a gender-free or feminist vision. Just as the Gethenians' purported psychological androgyny is rooted in their ambivalent physicality, Gethenian society reflects some of the values conventionally associated with female physiology. (Le Guin's assumption that female physiology "dominates" during the long Gethenian periods of sexual quiescence is yet another stereotypical association of women with sexual indifference or passivity.) Commenting on the novel, Le Guin notes that the predominant "female principle" on Gethen has led historically to an absence of war and of social or ecological exploitation.[23] This author thus focuses upon and fictionally embroiders some positive traits traditionally associated with women's "essential" nature. Both gynocentric and androcentric essentialists also focus upon these traits—but to very different ideological ends.

The Left Hand of Darkness is in this sense a repository of concepts currently under feminist scrutiny and debate. Furthermore, Le Guin's reconsidered alternative to this novel's "thought-experiment" is similarly biased by essentialist concepts. Androgyny "appear[ing] conventionally and overtly, as a couple. Both in one; or two making a whole. . . . Yin does not appear without yang, nor yang without yin"[24] is, as many feminists would note, a heterosexist definition.[25] The issue of conventional heterosexuality as opposed to gynocentric separatism is, as we have seen most vividly in *The Passion of New Eve*'s satire, a continuingly controversial one.

Furthermore, relatively few polemically feminist speculative fictions assert "sexual injustice" as the root of all earthly/extraterrestrial evils;[26] instead, they examine the interlocking root systems supporting the social and cultural structures of fictional as well as actual societies that such sexism may foster. *The Kin of Ata* and *From the Legend of Biel* are in this sense illustrative of contemporary speculative fiction as feminist polemic. Their explorations of sexism's and patriarchal thought's impact on language, legend, and dream and upon personal relationships and social structures extend Le Guin's inquiries. These explorations give heightened meaning to her opening statement in *The Left Hand of Darkness* "that Truth is a matter of the imagination" (LH, p. 7). Both authors present "re/visions"[27] of conventional norms, often posited as biological or sociological givens, that have functioned in the past as such patriarchal "Truth." That these novels also embody multiple and at times seemingly conflicting feminist ideologies is evidence not only of the complexity of current feminist inquiry but of feminist fiction's ability to be more than ideological tract.

The problematic relationships of Jungian theory to feminism and women's fiction form one of the ideological debates central to all three novels. This debate can again be placed on the continuum of beliefs ranging from essentialist to androgynous definitions of selfhood. Some critics note the androcentric essentialism of Jung (and his followers) in detailing and validating as healthy only the male quest, in positing biological man as the embodiment of rationality who must search for his emotional component, his "anima," embodied in biological woman.[28] Others—like Annis Pratt, Carol Pearson, and Katherine Pope—have begun to explore the value of archetypal theory in understanding the female quest for selfhood represented in women's previously misread or unread fiction, matriarchal history, and myth. Their revisionist analyses suggest that, once identified by the modern reader, women's archetypes can be perceived as symbols both of women's past self-integrity and of our continuing search for that androgynous wholeness of selfhood usurped by historical patriarchy.[29] This feminist controversy, in which Jungianism is perceived as androcentric or negatively essentialist on the one hand but gynocentric or productively androgynous on the other, sheds even more light on Bryant and Staton's novels. We see that they are ideologically complex extensions of Le Guin's novel on yet another level. Though to greatly differing degrees, both extend Le Guin's seemingly traditional concept of Jungian theory to include the quest of a female hero.[30] Each then places this female quest, in fictional form as well as content, within the "politicized" arena Le Guin sees as peripheral to her artistic aims in general and *The Left Hand of Darkness* in particular. Multilayered, complex works emerge, with Staton's *From the Legend of Biel* achieving a more successful dialectic between feminist ideologies and a more clearly woman-oriented version of Jungianism than *The Kin of Ata.* As with the novels discussed in chapter 1, however, neither of these novels is without ideological ambiguity.

Like Le Guin, Bryant creates a central male character initially alienated from women both in his own society and within himself. A successful writer of raunchy popular fiction that depicts "indestructible [male] hero[es] and equal parts of sex and violence" (Ata, p. 25), this character has lived a life focused exclusively on the physiologically male "orgasmic plane, clutching and trying to hang on, falling and trying to get back" (Ata, p. 25). This "law of gravity of the soul" (Ata, p. 25), posited on cyclical mood (and phallic) inflation and deflation, obscures all other realities for him. The novel opens with his early morning argument with a woman, whose outraged screams of self-assertion—"I exist. . . . I'm a person" (Ata, p. 1)—are countered by his bored insistence that she is no more to him, no "realler" than a character in one of his books. Stoned and sleepless from his attempts to avoid chronic nightmares, he unintentionally strangles her; however, this nameless protagonist can only note, "It didn't feel like murder. It was all unreal, like a scene from one of my books. . . . [It] took me a few minutes to remember her name" (Ata, pp. 2-3). After three or four pages of such exposition, the novel proper begins with the narrator's failed attempt to flee the scene of this crime resulting in a car crash.

The ethically, emotionally, and psychically distorted "reality" of this Maileresque protagonist is then contrasted to the improbable "reality" of Ata, the agrarian, communal village to which he apparently awakens. The accident has badly broken one of his legs and left him feverish and bruised. This mysterious change in locale and the community itself initially seem unbelievable (both to him and the reader), perhaps the hallucinatory results of concussion; however, these improbabilities diminish through juxtaposition with the horrific emptiness depicted in the novel's opening pages. This emptiness is captured in such narratorial admissions as "the nightmares were, perhaps, the only real thing in my life" (Ata, p. 26). Once again, as in *Applesauce* and *The Passion of New Eve,* we are led to perceive the fantastic not in the extraordinary events of a speculative fiction but in the intolerably circumscribed, sexist "reality" reproduced through traditional fictional mimesis. Such reversal of conventional oppositions and, indeed, the negation of such rigid demarcations are integral to the themes of personal and social growth in this novel. Despite her repudiation of many other conventional dichotomies (such as masculine vs. feminine, communication vs. silence, dream vs. reality, wealth vs. poverty, or history vs. myth), though, Bryant does retain one such traditional division in this otherwise tradition-breaking text. She accepts and promulgates physiological gender as an inevitable human polarization. This paradoxical acceptance of innate duality is evident in Bryant's integration into the novel of traditional Jungianism, with its emphases on biological man needing biological woman, yang confronting yin, animus seeking anima, and light meeting dark.

When *Ata*'s unnamed narrator awakens, he finds himself in a domelike, hand-made tent, being tended by people whose simple, uniform garb and behavior, devoid of "superficial conventions of clothing, grooming and manner" and "free of sexual roles" (Ata, p. 19) make him unsure of their gender. He speculates that their "primitive" lifestyle, androgynous appearance, and unconventional silence are merely the trappings of a publicity-shy, counter-culture commune. But this facile assumption is rapidly undermined as his injured leg is miraculously healed by his eleven hutmates' apparent "prayer circle." He is also disconcerted to realize that their infrequent utterances are in no known language and that each person he encounters is mysteriously, constantly accompanied by a different totem creature or "familiar." Once mobile, he limps away from the village of twelve huts to a nearby mountain only to confirm his growing disorientation: Ata is located on an island, not the continental United States of his car crash, and magically seems to disappear from view at the approach of a highflying plane.

Bryant, operating within the utopian tradition, thus presents her readers with the exotic foreign education of a representative of our dominant culture to illustrate ways in which we might productively change our society and ourselves. That her narrator achieves his transfer to Ata mentally is further indication that such change must be personal, involving redefinition of self, as well as political and cultural.[31] Whether this transfer occurs though actual teleportation, the result of his intense subconscious desire for change as the Atans suggest, or through hallucination, another possibility suggested by the novel's ambiguous conclusion, is ultimately irrelevant. Bryant's protagonist is in either case psychically as well as socially compelled to seek less fragmented selfhood—unlike Le Guin's Genly Ali, who is only accidentally forced to confront his androcentrism and his sexist fear of woman as alien other through a chance assignment to Gethen/Winter. Along with her narrator's proportionately greater gynophobia, this psychic quest places feminism and its multiple ideologies within Bryant's text more overtly and polemically that Ali's randomly motivated "journey of self-discovery" does in Le Guin's novel. Only in this comparative sense is Le Guin's assessment of the peripheral relationship of feminism to *The Left Hand of Darkness* a valid one.

One of the methods of self-redefinition Bryant develops in *Ata* is the possibility of individuals' achieving their androgynous potential. The absence of sex roles in Ata, evident in people nurturing each other and working together regardless of gender, is reinforced by the forms and function of their rarely-used language. Bryant rebuts Le Guin's assertion that novelistic intervention into the standard, sex-biased English generic "he" would "mangle" English by distracting rather than engaging reader attention. Bryant creates a gender-neutral pronoun for people, roughly translated by her narrator into "Kin," which also serves as both singular and plural. Avoiding artificial division by gender, "Kin" simultaneously provides through this numerical flexibility a further sense of community.[32] Names, too, are not sex-specific in Ata but rather chosen intuitively by individuals as they reach mature self-awareness.[33] The patriarchally-acculturated narrator stereotypically thinks one aged, gentle Kin named Doe to be female until death reveals the nurturing character to have been male. Bryant's protagonist originally considers the infrequently spoken language of Ata an impoverished one, with a "small and general vocabulary" (Ata, p. 47), lacking even tense distinctions in its descriptions "only of now, the present moment" (Ata, p. 50). But this reaction occurs before his gradual assimilation of Ata's philosophy, of the personal and social implications of a culture in which two words—"nagdeo" and "donagdeo" (Ata, p. 118)— encompass all that is positive or negative but are "never applied to persons, only to acts. Persons [are] just Kin, neutral, neuter, unmodified" (Ata, p. 118). Ata is a community in which "[l]aughter [is] better than words; silence better than both" (Ata, p. 202) because its members have consciously decided to work together toward specific goals. This decisive activism is a contrast to the unthinking propagation of conventional norms through language as well as deed which he has previsiously experienced. The narrator only slowly realizes this distinction.

Heir to legends of bold men questing for gold and silver, he concludes that the Kin's special evening gathering place, the "la-ka," from which his convalescence had excluded him, must be the repository of their material wealth. His materialist upbringing convinces him that only a mutually hidden treasure could unite people of such diverse ages and appearances in an otherwise marginal existence. Once mobile, he surreptitiously observes the Kin at dusk and thinks he sees "some shining objects passed from hand to hand in the darkness" (Ata, p. 43), "rubies" being exchanged, and a "child's mouth open wide with joy . . . between her teeth . . . a pearl as big as an egg" (Ata, pp. 48-49). Bryant's protagonist has misunderstood the children's chant that opens the evening's rituals—"We seek/All/seek/Where? Where?" (Ata, p. 49) by translating it and the actual treasure of Ata into the modes of patriarchal heroism, the individual quest for conquest and material wealth, with which he is familiar. Mistakenly conflating high technology with culture, a relic of social Darwinism that one critic has termed the "mystification of technology" by contemporary society,[34] the narrator believes that unprocessed precious metals or gems are the only treasures such "primitive" people could have. Bryant's text indicates that, for her, this misapprehension is comparable to her narrator's gynophobia—that materialism and sexism are equatable in their distortions (both literal and figurative) of human perception. For rubies and pearls do not exist in Ata; they, like words, are only the roughest equivalent for treasured spiritual experience. The narrator only imagines that precious objects are being passed from hand to hand or are visible in a child's mouth because he cannot conceive of non-material wealth. The Atans are actually sharing their spiritual joy, calm, and affection. Kin recognize, as the narrator does not, the ineffable, untranslatable quality of such experience, and in Ata, the word for "word" also means falsehood or "lie" (Ata, p. 118).

Bryant's Ata is a community in which dreaming is the only reality. Its Kin tell one another their dreams each morning; follow the directions for daily life implicit in these visions; and believe that their society, the original human one, perpetuates the very survival of the "fallen" world from which the narrator has come through such visionary efforts to uphold constantly "the law of light ... stronger than the law of gravity" (Ata, p. 54). Through this further reference to "gravity," previously linked to the narrator's phallocentric outlook (Ata, p. 25), Bryant once more associates sexism with distorting materialism. Her protagonist conversely views Atan philosophy itself as "delusion and hallucination" (Ata, p. 66), but he is readily accepted into this community just because his arrival has been presaged in dream. When they cannot dream, cannot clearly interpret these night visions, or are tempted to stray from their imperatives, Kin retreat to shallow burrows beneath the earth, hol-kas, to regain their psychic equilibrium. This retreat, "go[ing] naked back into [their] mother [earth]" (Ata, p. 70) is a ritual integral to Atan culture. It is also an experience that the narrator himself finally undergoes several times to eradicate his chronic nightmares which have begun to reoccur. Bryant's emphasis on the healing powers of mother earth is, however, one of the points at which her depiction of a non-sexist community becomes ideologically complex.

The concept of "mother earth" suggests to some contemporary feminists the gynocentric essentialism that has sprung from renewed interest in matriarchal history and myth. Angela Carter satirizes the excesses of this viewpoint through her creation of the artificial labyrinths of underground Beulah, the paradoxically technological base of man-hating Women; however, in its non-parodic forms, this resurgence of interest in women's spirituality, in our ecological balance with nature, and in alternative woman-centered life-styles has had significant consequences. It has led to religious and social regroupings of some committed feminists which adumbrate some of the social structures, if not the particular mystical vision, of Bryant's fictional Ata.[35] As Carol Christ concludes in relation to other works of feminist speculation, "the surfacing of [traditionally] female values in alienated urban cultures may also be a return to some . . . of the values of traditional or less urbanized cultures."[36] Ata's emphasis on a spiritual plane more significant than daily existence and on individual communion with this spiritual plane is redolent of such "traditional" culture. Its deliberately small (about one hundred and fifty) population which shuns technological advance, produces food only for immediate consumption, and generally avoids physical contact with larger social networks is similarly typical of less urbanized cultures.

While such fictional (or actual) social reorganization may be viewed as radical political change, it may also be perceived as an abdication of responsibility to participate in and effect significant social reform. This has been the charge leveled at participants in the women's spirituality movement by some other committed feminists.[37] And, indeed, the relationship of Bryant's text to feminist ideologies and goals may be questioned in similar ways. *Ata* highlights patriarchal gynophobia, depicts a community without sex roles or stereotypes, and indicates the possibility of productively altering language to preclude sex-bias; however, it also embodies some significant patriarchal stereotypes of acceptably feminine—that is, truly "female"—behavior. The ethereal, religious female or "angel in the house," the demure lady, and woman's domestic sphere separate from the larger, outside world of commerce are all echoed in Bryant's work.[38] Her fictional community emphasizes the spiritual, the positive absence of language, political non-involvement, and physical passivity (the Kin peacefully forgive the narrator's murder of one man and rape of a woman during the first days following his convalescence). The Kin's means of achieving spiritual transcendence may thus be seen as reassertion, ironically, of women's stereotypically limited or "immanent" social roles and ambitions.[39] To determine whether Bryant's novel falls into stereotyping in its depiction of the individual quest for nonsexist selfhood or whether it indeed succeeds in transforming such stereotypes for its own ideological purposes, the reader must examine *Ata*'s relationships to Jungian theory. This novel's depiction of its second major character, the female Kin Augustine, is particularly relevant.

While Bryant has written that one of the first purchasers of this novel was a Jungian analyst who bought one hundred copies to distribute to patients,[40] the kind of archetypal theory embedded in her text remains problematic. Bryant parallels *The Left Hand of Darkness* in her creation of a central male character who seeks and achieves greater self-awareness and integrity through contact with a woman. *The Kin of Ata* thus seems to uphold traditional Jungianism's essentialist focus on biological man. Black Augustine, constantly accompanied by a butterfly to signal her rapport with "mother earth," forgives the narrator's rape of her and becomes "woman to [him]" (Ata, p. 107) because she dreams he cannot live without her. This self-abnegating role of handmaiden to a man's emerging psychic wholeness, paralleling Augustine's ancillary position as secondary character rather than first person narrator, is also consistent with traditional Jungianism's subordinate placement of anima in relation to questing animus. The narrator's nightmares cease and he begins to accept fully the alternatives Ata offers only when he symbolically accepts the significance of woman to his social and psychic well-being. Dreaming that he is dancing in front of the fire in the la-ka and that his fragmented selves are dying painfully, he confronts both his own past and potential future:

> After eons there were two of me left, facing each other across the fire pit. One of me was a woman, a hundred women, all the women, hurt, enraged and furious, that I had ever known. One of me was a man, myself, every rotten, opportunistic, cruel, avaricious and vain self I had ever been.
> We faced each other and danced obscenely, cruelly, furiously, ever alert, watching. For every move of the dance was a threat, an aggression demanding simultaneous reaction and defense.   (Ata, p. 129)

The narrator makes a final, blind effort to avert the "death" of his familiar, albeit limited and destructive, self before acknowledging the strength of his anima and his need for it:

> It seemed to go on for years. I was tired. I had to destroy her. I tried every way I could think of, but she anticipated my every move. Then she grabbed the initiative and I was defensive until I could get it back. But I was so tired. Finally I stopped doing anything but defensive, complementary moves. I let her dictate the dance.   (Ata, p. 129)

As he follows this female dream image, letting "her dictate the dance," it becomes "not threatening at all, but neutral" (Ata, p. 129). Then, "Her movements become great sweeps of grace, of joy, that [I] follow[ed] in perfect simultaneity as she turn[ed] darker, darker, black" (Ata, p. 129). It is at this point that the narrator awakens in pregnant Augustine's arms, to be told that she—"darker, darker, black"—was indeed there with him during this experience and that this "dance of the numbers" and "com[ing] out of the pit as one" (Ata, p. 131) is an exhausting but not unheard of component of Atan life. The chapter concludes with her reassurance that "I will always, always be with you when you call" (Ata, p. 131).

Allied with nature, with mysterious and fecund passivity in her quiet forgiveness, acceptance, and protection of the narrator and her birthing of his child, Augustine seems to uphold the traditional Jungian division of emotion and intellect between biological woman and man. She is Eros to the narrator's initially distorted, self-interested Logos; literal as well as symbolic darkness juxtaposed with his corporeal and symbolic "light." (For Jung as well as Freud, woman is associated with darkness, the moon or dimmer light, as opposed to the brilliance or sunlike quality of biological man's "reason.")[41] But Bryant then to some extent alters this schematic, sex-stereotyped assignation of attributes by depicting Augustine's own spiritual depth and growth. Always a "strong dreamer" (Ata, p. 138), Augustine begins to have visions directing the course of Ata's daily life and to heal the sick through a laying on of hands. During one evening festival, the "Life Tree" at the center of the la-ka bursts into light at her mere approach. A sign of spiritual strength within this community, this event also signals a symbolic assumption, in Jungian terms, of traditional male power by a woman. It reaffirms the equality of Ata's "law of light" for both sexes. Seven or eight years pass, and the narrator wishes to formalize his continuing relationship with Augustine. As he hopefully points out couples who have remained together for decades, though, Augustine's admonitions that none in Ata "possesses" (Ata, pp. 174-75) another in traditional marriage become increasingly sadder. Her growing psychic strength enables her to foretell the impossibility of such a lengthy future for them. Finally, as she has suspected, Augustine joins those Kin who have been "chosen" (Ata, p. 184), because of their spiritual strength, to sacrifice themselves for the world's salvation.

This sacrifice parallels both Talmudic lore of ten just men [sic] whose compassionate suffering for the world's injustice balances all its unrepentant evil and the diverse mythic or religious traditions which involve the potential yearly sacrifice of a spiritual leader.[42] The Kin of Ata similarly know that each spring one of them may be called upon by his or her dream visions to leave Ata for the outside world. There, "the suffering of living in [the narrator's—and our] world" (Ata, p. 187), for one accustomed to Ata, will provide the further necessary spiritual counterweight for an unregenerate, but potentially redeemable, human race. When the narrator speaks of his past life to Kin, they recognize many great philosophers' names as those of the formerly chosen. These reknowned figures, however, are exceptions. Like most Atans who are called, Augustine voluntarily leads a life of obscurity. She performs charitable works and joins social reform groups in inconspicuous ways. The narrator, having observed her new life each night in his dreams, also sees her death, the result of these activities: "[F]rightened men in a senseless riot ... set dogs upon her, but the dogs [refuse] to touch her" (Ata, p. 199). She is then shot by these men less in rapport with other human beings than dogs.

In this positing of the psychic journey of a strong, albeit secondary woman character, the depiction of Augustine's gradual transformation from undistinguishable Kin to one of the "chosen" who accepts the burdens of spiritual leadership, Bryant veers from traditional Jungianism's definition of the healthy female psyche as passive.[43] But this woman-centered version of the archetypal journey is once more relegated to the background in the novel's conclusion. There, it is once again the male narrator whose psychic integration is central to Bryant's vision, and it is his "voice" through which she explicitly addresses her audience. Following Augustine's death, the narrator continues to learn and grow in Ata until, years later, he too is "chosen." Leaving in the way of all chosen Kin, by walking into the flames of a ritual fire, the narrator is "reborn."[44] He awakens to find himself in a hospital being treated for injuries sustained in a severe car crash. While decades have passed in his experience of Ata, only weeks have transpired in non-Atan time since his original, unrepentant woman-slaughter. Rather than deny his guilt for this crime, the narrator confesses; he cannot return to his former indifference to the significance of women's lives. Sentenced to death, he begins the journal that the reader now belatedly realizes Bryant's novel to be.

Describing the epiphany the narrator experiences the moment after his confession, Bryant employs imagery that emphasizes the success of his psychic integration, the merger of animus with anima:

> And then there was light. Indescribably warm, glowing light. Light was everywhere. It shone on everything, through and into everything; it came out of everything, out of everyone. It was like a fire that does not consume, but not like a fire, like . . . like nothing else, nothing else was like it. But all things were full of it. The faces around the table, the table itself, the walls, the windows, everything was alive, everything lived in and through the light.
>
> And I too. I too. From the center of my being the light broke in waves, in orgasmic waves, outward to the extremities of my body, every cell of my body melting together in the waves of light that flowed outward from my center, and over me from the very air around me, from everything. I breathed it into me and it poured out of me, sweeping through me like a million orgasms. I was full and whole. I was part of the light and all the other things that shone in and with the light. All were one. And whole.   (Ata, p. 218)

He has not only perceived and, perhaps, brought Ata's ultimately gender-free "law of light" to conventional "reality" but has experienced this supreme, creative force in a way that transcends gender. Just as he has twice been "reborn" in a "fire that does not consume" (first in the la-ka's fire when he is "chosen" and then in this fiery light of spiritual awareness and rapport), the traditional "male orgasmic plane" on which he had lived prior to Ata is here metaphorically transformed twice. First, it becomes a physiologically female experience, and then it becomes an ultimately gender-free experience. "Orgasmic waves . . . a million orgasms . . . from the center of . . . being" describes female sexuality—center, multiple, and then diffusing—rather than phallic tumescence and detumescence.[45] The narrator's next statement, that "I was part of the light and of all the other things that shone in and with the light. All were one. And whole" refers simultaneously to the "rational" light of traditional Jungianism and to Ata's commensurately more encompassing, gender-free "law of light." Bryant's male narrator has progressed from an experience of femaleness to one of freedom-from-gender or androgyny. The narrator concludes his recollection of these moments with his vision of something "fluttering down from the chandelier above. . . . It circled my head once, then lit on my shoulder, a small black moth" (Ata, p. 218). This physical reminder of Augustine, in life always followed by a summer butterfly or a winter moth, is further symbolic indication of the narrator's psychic wholeness, his continued spiritual rapport with his anima as well as his more "rational" animus. The novel/journal concludes with his (and Bryant's) "call to action" to the reader, offset in three widely-spaced paragraphs:

> You have only to want It [the reality behind the
> dream], to believe in It, and tonight, when you close your
> eyes, you can begin your journey.

> The kin of Ata are waiting for you.

> Nagdeo.   (Ata, p. 220)

How persuasive, however, is this call to action, particularly for the feminist or female reader?[46] To what extent is Bryant's vision of an androgynous community, enabling each individual to achieve psychic integration, vitiated by elements of traditional Jungian or archetypal theory? Those who criticize the androgynous vision for its potential to subordinate women's traditional abilities or qualities to men's might also perceive profound cooptation in Bryant's text. While its male narrator experiences both feelings of female sexuality and psychic wholeness, Augustine's role in this text is a secondary, increasingly symbolic one until this character is figuratively reduced to an insubstantial black moth! While the fictional "reality" (so like our own actuality at its worst) which frames *Ata* is deadly to self-integrated men as well as women (witness the narrator's implied execution), Bryant's narrative stance thus remains problematic. Even as she posits communal alternatives to patriarchal, materialistic norms, her novel implicitly embodies sex-biased concepts. One might even view the dualism of Ata's and the narrator's original "reality" as a continuation of the separate sexual spheres: Ata provides a source of sacrifices, "feminine" in their willingness if not their gender, to maintain the traditionally male sphere outside the home. The implicit recapitulation of conventional sexual politics in such sacrifice is further heightened if one rejects the Kin's comforting definition of death as going "Home" (Ata, p. 22). Religious belief may once more be the placebo embraced by the oppressed to "cure" their ills. These ideological ambiguities implicit in *The Kin of Ata* may not themselves be resolvable; however, Bryant does comment in this work on ideological ambiguity, faith and reason, and the processes of inscribing or decoding meaning. These aspects of Atan lore are interesting and possibly illuminating in relation to the text itself, our perceptions of it, and its relationships both to *The Left Hand of Darkness* and the novels discussed in chapter 1.

The temporal disjuncture that suggests the narrator's possible unreliability, the discrepancy between his years "in" Ata and the weeks that have elapsed for his hospitalized body, simultaneously suggests one of Ata's profound truths. As he only gradually comes to understand, "the daily language of Ata lack[s] tense" for a particular reason. "There were times for doing things: times for planting, for dreaming, for eating, for telling dreams. There were times, but no time" (Ata, p. 137). When he confronts Augustine with this observation, she acknowledges this temporal fluidity (and the corresponding temporal simultaneity subsequently suggested by the narrator's experience) with equanimity. She is undisturbed by the possibilities of paradox:

> "Time doesn't exist here," I told Augustine.
> "There is only now," she agreed.
> "It's because nothing changes."
> "Change comes, but very slow and very sudden," she said.
> "You contradict yourself."
> "Yes," she said.   (Ata, p. 173)

This paradoxical simultaneity and the corresponding belief that timelessness is as significant a concept as measurable time have been identified by Sydney Janet Kaplan as components of the "feminine consciousness" deliberately articulated by some earlier twentieth century women novelists;[47] they are also concepts that have "come of age" in the 1970s through the new physics' substantiation of endless, universal flux and constant potential instability. Bryant's fictional community integrates these "feminine" or "new physics" concepts into a shared, supportive world-view. This communality is a contrast to the similar but isolated perceptions of individual characters described in Chapter 1 (or in the earlier novels Kaplan discusses); in these works, such insights are often a reflection of self-fragmentation or social alienation. Before Bryant's fragmented narrator acknowledges his anima and becomes fully Kin, he too has difficulty with these concepts. His attempts at categorizing his understanding of Ata's lore keep "overlapping or breaking down into new divisions" (Ata, p. 177). These "failures" relate directly to the relative positions of written discourse, legend, and truth in Ata.

Bryant polemically extends Le Guin's observation that "Truth is a matter of the imagination." While Le Guin is content to develop this observation with the reader's imaginative construction of *some* "truth" from the alien legends, purportedly official documents, and diaries that Genly Ai preserves, Bryant directly addresses our own cultural myths. Moreover, she flatly states through assorted Kin that these myths and any conclusions the reader has derived from them are inevitably distorted. For written discourse diminishes meaning in Ata rather than preserving it. Just as the transcribed Christian parable of the loaves and the fishes "is a corrupt version of the dream" of each person literally feeding another throughout life (Ata, p. 104), past efforts at preserving Ata's many myths and creation legends have "frozen" them (Ata, p. 201). Kin tell the narrator of this distortion:

"But then disputes arose as to which were the best versions of the dreams, and as to whether the mark gave the correct meaning. Many more marks were invented, and many worked on carving alternate stories. Kin split over which story was correct. Which should be carved and preserved? There was no time to carve all the stories; choices would have to be made.

"But even more serious was the effect that writing had upon the words of the story. It froze them. People began to mistake the word for the unknown behind it. Instead of expressing the unknown, the carved word became a thing between the people and the unknown which it should symbolize.

"All was donagdeo. The people ceased to dream high dreams. And so, one by one they stopped the writing and the reading. They went back to the old way of telling the dreams in spoken words that rose like smoke and disappeared into the air to intermingle there, where there was room for an infinite number of dreams, which could change and grow and become closer to the reality"   (A, pp. 201-02)

This concept of fluid realities not commensurate with conventional written discourse has been touched upon in Rhoda Lerman's multiple typefaces and reworkings of traditional myth, Angela Carter's shifting narrative stance, and June Arnold's typographical innovations and related musings in *Applesauce*. In this passage, however, Bryant reiterates it with new force as a cultural axiom. As Augustine tells the narrator early in their relationship, "Words get between us and the dance and the meaning behind the dance . . . one must dance the dance and go through it to the meaning" (Ata, p. 128).

The epiphany this protagonist experiences at the novel's conclusion thus incorporates a further awareness of the untranslatable nature of spiritual experience, of the impossibility of capturing such understanding of universal law in one metaphoric truth:

In that instant I understood all the stories and dreams and songs and dances of Ata, stories of jewels and of sun, of fire and of ocean. I understood the many versions of each story and the contradictions and paradoxes, and I knew that they were all, in their own way, true. For I had glimpsed the reality behind them.   (Ata, p. 218)

And so, in the final page of this text he rephrases Augustine's earlier advice to him. He ruefully notes that he has "had to leave out many things, and even those that [he has] told may be misunderstood, told, as they are, in the faulty medium of words, and frozen on paper" (Ata, p. 220). He urges the reader of "this hasty and incomplete account" to heed not the words but that "something that at some level of our being, [we] already know. Something [we] know as an echo, as a glimpse in a dream or as a fragile hope [we] are ashamed to voice" (Ata, p. 220). Whether this "echo" of androgynous potential is loud enough to drown this text's significant ideological ambiguities remains moot; *Ata* does provide self-integration for male questors, but its treatment of female questors is problematic. Extending the merger of Jungian quest and androgynous vision that Le Guin posits in *The Left Hand of Darkness*, Bryant's *The Kin of Ata Are*

Waiting for You may not extend far enough for some readers. It still implicitly poses many conventional answers to unconventional questions.

My analysis of Mary Staton's *From the Legend of Biel* highlights Bryant's problematic success in addressing issues central to both texts and their ideological predecessor, *The Left Hand of Darkness*. (There is no evidence that Le Guin is a *direct* influence on either author; however, she is their well-known chronological predecessor within a decade of exponentially increasing interest in feminism and feminist speculative fiction.) If *The Kin of Ata* is in this sense a "liberal" response to Le Guin's traditional Jungianism and relatively more conservative approach to androgyny, language, and their relationships within a work of fiction, Staton's novel is a "radical" response. It, too, draws upon the classical quest motif and utopian tradition of a stranger educated by exotic travel but focuses primarily on a female protagonist, alien humanoid Biel, as well as a secondary male character, Earth astronaut Howard Scott. More than three-quarters of the text is devoted to Biel's journey of self-discovery. In addition to this fundamental departure from the male emphasis of traditional Jungianism (evident in Bryant's novel as well as Le Guin's), Staton's work also differs structurally from *The Kin of Ata*. *Biel* even-handedly depicts tertiary characters, male alien Nyz-Ragaan and female alien Logana, who fail to integrate different elements of their personalities successfully, and portrays a significant, evolving relationship between two women. Biel's female mentor Mikkran, an unobtrusive protector and educator throughout her quest for self-awareness, is fully as important an element in this young woman's self-integration (if not a more important one) as encounters with characters or events representing different components of the traditional animus. Through this more balanced presentation of human interaction and growth, Staton consistently validates her characters' pronouncements about androgyny (the "one hundred per cent manifestation of potential" for each individual [B, p. 300]) in ways that Bryant does not. These and other significant differences between these two novels of speculation about non-sexist selfhood and societies are reflected in their respective treatments of language, legend, and written discourse.

The opening section of *From the Legend of Biel* is structurally closest to *The Kin of Ata* in the presentation of the psychic dissatisfaction solely of a male character. Howard Scott rejects a civilization "dying of gluttony and comfort" (B, p. 18), a home planet that is "just another group of systems in conflict... encourag[ing] [people] to be less than human" (B, p. 59). In this section, though, Staton displays a greater awareness than Bryant of language's complexity and of her own paradoxical reliance on its traditional, written forms to convey radically different ideas. Scott's sense of psychic incompleteness, and of the need to quest for greater self-awareness and another way of life more conducive to such psychic integration, occurs during years of suspended animation in space flight. Dreaming, he apprehends the fallacy of dichotomizing masculine and feminine, knowledge and ignorance, distance and immediacy, dream or fantasy and reality:

> Inside, beneath the stillness, he learns the other side of himself. The familiar is distant and meaningless. Perspective has been reversed. He dreams of the dreamer dreaming of the dreamer dreaming the dream. He is concentric and simultaneous selves, and none of it is a dream.   (B, p. 8)

Staton presents this category-breaking awareness, stemming from dream experience/analysis and redolent of Jungian theory, in ways that simultaneously represent her character's evolving consciousness and force the reader to recreate that dialectical process. Scott's next thoughts are depicted in split column format, and then as shape poems. Later events are similarly rendered in different typefaces. Comparable to June Arnold's brief typographic experiments in *Applesauce,* such innovations reinforce and integrate Staton's beliefs about the power of language to shape individual and social consciousness and the resultant need for language change throughout the novel. Unlike Bryant, who creates a unifying, non-sexist, non-hierarchical language for her Kin but generally limits these innovations to Ata, an experience still "waiting" for the reader, Staton's techniques continually demand immediate reader involvement. We are not permitted any of the illusory distance of the conventional "readerly" text. (In contrast, Bryant's infrequent neologisms and her dramatization of the Kin's non-hierarchical language through commensurately simple diction do frequently permit the reader to retain such illusions.) As Staton herself writes in the forwarding note to this novel, "some kind of real life takes place between . . . [the] reader's eye and the page of the book. I am interested in making the distance between that reader's eye and the surface of the page disappear" (B, unpaginated).

Staton continues this explicit call for interaction between reader and text through consistent references to the modes of communication we too often accept as authoritative. The insidious impact of verbal and written discourse on our perceptions and mental structures is reflected in discursive metaphor throughout the novel. Scott is "concealed in featureless parentheses" (B, p. 11), while another member of his exploration team is "a fat comma" (B, p. 12); later, Mikkran resembles "a natural exclamation point" (B, p. 135), "birds look like colored question marks" (B, pp. 274-75), and "flowers blink and nod like asterisks" (B, p. 275). This reliance on traditional typographical signs to order and explain experience becomes totally paradoxical for Scott after he apprehends an alien presence on MC6, the planet under investigation. This presence seems to "speak" to his own emerging personal needs, but it uses neither spoken nor written discourse. While there are "no metaphors for him— only the thing itself" (B, p. 29) in his growing attraction to MC6 and its artifacts, Scott paradoxically must use metaphor (as must Bryant himself) to articulate new insights for himself and others. Trying to analyze in conventional terms the large, geometric structures found on seemingly uninhabited MC6, Scott and the other astronauts have employed "words and ideas . . . [flying] back and forth like rice at a wedding. But the bride and groom had gone off, and the guests had left, and the rice lay where it had fallen" (B, p. 31). The failure of these explorers to recognize and articulate the forces still operant on the planet has two causes. Scott's own quest for self-awareness is still relatively new, and the other astronaut researchers, instead of being on comparable quests, are actually resistant to psychological or social change.

The others see and prosaically report on MC6 only a "wheatcolored lawn, flat as a table, stretch[ing] out to a perfectly defined horizon line . . . so clear it hurts [the] eyes. . . . [N]o clouds" but wind and a sea that is "brilliant blue and absolutely waveless" (B, p. 29). Scott, however, experiences a mystical rapport with the planet that is described lyrically and contrapuntally. Short, offset, and italicized litanies of praise alternate with extended metaphoric descriptions; synaesthetic imagery is employed throughout:

> *The hatch of Skimmer Colonus opened like an eye.*
>
> There are victories which have no violence in their beginnings or their ends. And if these victories bring with themselves a death of past and silly dreams, it is not felt as death, but as the falling of a scab. Inhale, because it heals.
>
> *Howard Scott stood paralyzed at the threshold, looking out.*
>
> There is an instant when pieces fit together, interlock their disparate knuckles and become a whole. It is almost unbearable. Such victories and such interlockings redefine our language. Inhale, because this air will make you whole.
>
> *His jaw fell in slow motion and an invisible song rolled out.*
>
> There are landscapes which, when apprehended, reduce the carbonation in the brain to stillness. Thought steps aside to let the senses bathe and cleanse themselves. Inhale. Inhale and become simplified.
>
> *His eyes became a mouth.*
>
> There is beauty which can make the genes remember reverence. When the lid of the coffin of culture is opened there is a moment when all things are possible and good. In that moment pieces fly together, kiss, and interlock in stillness with no violence as the human being kneels before himself. Inhale. Inhale, and bring your body home.
>
> *Howard Scott felt the planet rise up and meet his descending feet.*
>
> The landscape is divided in half horizontally. It is only two colors, and background for a score of sounds, and smells, and touch of wind, and taste of long, sweet grass. Step down, inhale, and bring your body home. One color is the blue of a sky which is somehow brighter than it was expected to be. It is frankly shocking—a rich and vital blue. The other color is the golden tan of long grass which has no gloss, but somehow shines.

His weight settled on the planet and was no burden at all.

The sweet smell of long gold grass glides up the nostrils, settles in a cloud around the soft palate, and floods the tastebuds on its way to the brain. Each individual step of perception is isolated in a slow train of events, and can be enjoyed as it passes.

He could not move.

The high-pitched hum of the dry wind ceaselessly combing the single blades of grass into long, even manes, is faint, but close—inside the ear. As the wind passes through the long fields it is the sound of some lost tuning fork, or some ancient glass instrument which has yet to be discovered. It is an unbroken string of sound which winds around the planet and insulates. It is a soft hand, protecting the planet from death.

Howard Scott became devout.

The surface is dry, dry and undulating—as if done with mirrors and heat. But it is not too hot. It warms the skin. The body is buffeted by the dry, slight, musical wind which ribbons up the brain and cleans it, so that the inside of the body assumes the characteristics, and the music, of the landscape.

He closed his eyes and the landscape was tattooed on his brain.

The sky rises cleanly from behind, from below the horizon line. It lifts up, lusts up, thrusts up, and domes perfectly above, with a white sun exactly in its center.

There were no metaphors for him—only the thing itself.   (B, pp. 26-29)

The contrast between Scott's described experience of the planet and that of his colleagues displays the potential duplicity of words and is thus itself one of the "interlockings" that "redefine[s] our language" (B, p. 27). Other, more literal "interlockings" include the synaesthetic images ("*eyes became a mouth.... smell... floods the tastebuds*") throughout Bryant's third person account of Scott's apprehensions and the recurring images of fusing opposites ("wind ... a soft hand, protecting the planet.... the inside of the body assumes the characteristics... of the landscape ... sky ... horizon [and] sun....). The very strangeness of MC6 attracts this character so recently galvanized by his dreams to "search for the other side of himself" (B, p. 8). "[T]he landscape ... as disconnected from the familiar as a dream—an ideal ... opens its arms and says 'Come. You are home. Come. You have been unhappy needlessly, senselessly. Come, be awake, and be whole'" (B, p. 29).

By thus positing a "home" in this life (if not this galaxy) rather than the next, *Biel* rejects *Ata*'s assignment of ultimate psychic fulfillment to the non-material plane; however, the two novels are alike in depicting a male questor's growing attraction to the earth (if not, in *Biel,* our own Earth) as representative of the search for his anima. Echoing stereotyped associations of woman with passive, fecund nature,[48] Scott feels "MC6 curl up next to his body like a woman. He felt her warm breath on his skin" (B, p. 30). Later in the novel, Bryant herself as temporarily omniscient narrator describes meadows "with all the gradual contours of a woman's body, lying like a woman asleep on a long, green, swollen carpet and covered with a quilt of yellow, lilac, rose, and green...." (B, p. 274). Such stereotypes are revised and reclaimed, however, through the unconventionally positive connections Scott perceives between MC6's generative landscape and its massive, high-technology domes. Unlike the narrator in Bryant's novel, whose spiritual growth is fostered by an (actual or imagined) technology-shunning society, Scott's quest is facilitated by the scientific advances of MC6. Entering the highest, clear-paned chamber of the central dome, Scott experiences the constructed space that Arnold's androgyny-seeking protagonist could only fantasize—an

> endless room which enclosed nothing, and kept nothing out . . . where the wall between inside and outside had been wiped away, where he was not estranged. . . . if he could stay . . . in this room, he would come together with that in himself which was not realized. What was lost would be found. The pieces of the shattered mosaic which was himself would come naturally, easily together, matching edge to edge, and click into a whole.   (B, p. 46)

In a later trip to this room, Scott sleeps and has mysterious dreams. Staton arranges these dreams spatially as shape poems, and she uses the imagery of the "new physics" to convey their disturbing content. Scott feels "molecules . . . becom[ing] eccentric" (B, p. 57) and apprehends a small hand touching his, "all in a dream and out of a dream, all in the soft events which have no sequence and no clues. . . . coherency disappear[ing]" (B, p. 58). Staton's introduction of technology, stereotypically the province of "male-produced" culture, into the male Jungian quest for undistorted selfhood is yet another "interlocking" in this text. Along with this author's emphasis on spoken and written discourse, this interlocking of technology and psychological quest forces the reader to revise conventional definitions and expectations. Women, representatives of the anima, may unconventionally be producers of technology; or, alternatively, this male quest may be resolved through encounters with another technology-producing male. The frequent description of technological items in organic terms ("The hatch . . . opened like an eye" [B, p. 26]) further confounds conventional categorization. Such "cognitive dissonance" or "estrangement"— the actual definition given to science fiction by some theorists[49]—permits Staton to introduce and reinforce polemical assertions in this work of speculative fiction. It prepares the reader for the initial incongruity of Staton's own hybrid feminist vision of Jungian theory, androgyny, and gynocentrism.

The final pages of the novel's first section unite these diverse strands and prepare the reader for its major focus, the journey of self-discovery undertaken by Biel. Scott locates within the alien dome a card which functions as a stereo cassette; after "what sound[s] like a very loud, long orchestral chord," he hears "records which had been made in some other age, some other space. . . ." (B, p. 68):

F R O M   T H E   L E G E N D   O F   B I E L...

...A S   R E C O R D E D   B Y   T H O A C D I E N...

...C A R D   ONE: THE   PARADOX.   (B, pp. 68-69)

This cassette disc's auditory format disenfranchises written discourse as a medium at the same time that the term "legend" paradoxically disavows this disc's own spoken or taped communication. A "legend" is by definition an overextended truth or outright falsehood. Nonetheless, this card and its message cause Scott to scream protractedly (the sound "erupt[s]" from him and becomes an *"aurora borealis"* [B, p. 69]) as the other astronauts attempt to communicate with him. Two typeset lines are devoted to this scream's crescendo:

AAAAAAAAAAAAAAHHHHHHHHHHHHHHHHHH
GGGGGGGGGGGGGGGA AAAAAAAAAAAAAAAAAA   (B, p. 69)

Scott's reaction, like the card's message, is conveyed by Staton through unconventional typography; offset, widely or narrowly spaced capital letters are separated by overextended ellipses and alternate with italicized narrative. As Scott listens to and comprehends more of this message, its "white spaces" (both figurative and literal) gradually decrease; this more conventional spacing recreates for the reader Scott's experience of growing comprehension. Ironically, his understanding blossoms just as a paradox is announced. Scott again realizes that *"[t]here [are] no metaphors for any of them. All [is] removed but the thing itself"* as this "PARADOX" is revealed (perhaps) to be life itself:

...C A R D   ONE: THE   PARADOX.

A sperm and an ovum collide, blend together, subdivide, and float in liquid to become a whole which coincides and flutters on its long, inevitable ride into complexity.   (B, p. 69)

The next section of the novel begins, not with Scott but with THOACDIEN,[50] unknown recorder of the legend of Biel, and leaves the reader with the mystery of Scott's fate unresolved. This mystery is alluded to, a paragraph or at most a page or two at a time, in only about twenty five pages of the text's remaining two hundred and sixty two. It is thus an enigma whose suspense we must live with, and may ultimately piece together and resolve, before the last pages' denouement. In this way, Staton's narrative strategy as well as her metaphoric and typographical innovations invest significant textual authority in the reader. Bryant also poses mysteries in *The Kin of Ata* (the initial murder, the nature of Ata itself, and the narrator's ultimate reliability or unreliability); however, these do not figure as prominently in her comparatively linear narrative and indeed—except for the question of reliability—are resolved by characters within the text itself. *From the Legend of Biel* is far more dissonant, *estranged* from textual and ideological convention, and hence speculative in its analyses of personal identity, relationships, and social structure.

Opening with an official, capitalized communication from THOAC-DIEN, Part II of Staton's novel abruptly places the reader within a seemingly disjunctive, overtly alien situation. Only gradually does one realize that THOACDIEN is a form of computer, called by some "a machine," by others "an entire technology" or "the dynamic combination of all possible media... information" (B, p. 82) and that Biel is neither the creator of this technological marvel nor one of this alien society's adult mentors. These mentors, such as Mikkran, wander to and from the "Hall of One Thousand Chambers" (B, p. 73) waiting for a charge, one of the embryos to be artificially birthed. "Biel" is actually one of these nameless embryos, Infant 187-A, 0037, recently emperiled by THOACDIEN's unprecedented, experimental decision to have the "Chembryo Lab" inject them with a massive amount of "Binol," a liquid form of THOACDIEN or information. The reader's confusion about the focus and relevance of this portion of Staton's text is both mirrored and gradually resolved by the confusion of Infant 187-A, 0037. Her mental processes, artificially stimulated in this traumatic way, are represented by increasingly unconventional forms of written discourse:

```
.................................me..............

.........yes............you....................

...........................yes.......you......

......and.....I....................yes...........

....................¢.....................yes.......

..........⌣.......

..........yes......

......◯.........

......yes.........
```

... ⌀ ...

...yes...

... 1D...

...yes...

... 2D...

...yes...

... 3D...

...yes...

... 4D...

...yes...   (B, pp. 76-77)

Mikkran, this infant's mentor, is responsible for permitting her charge to mentally "explore, verify, and be free" (B, p. 79) until the child calls her. She is therefore attuned to the embryo's mental processes and assimilation of ever-increasing amounts of information. This rapid mental growth is signaled by commensurately complex, narratively dissonant semes:

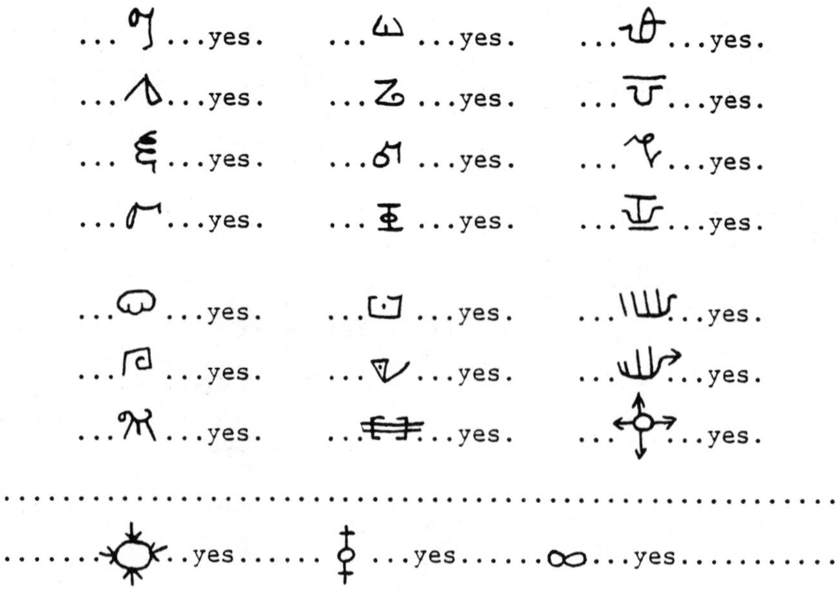

...ᠣ⅂...yes.	...ⱳ...yes.	...⅄...yes.
...∧ᗡ...yes.	...Ⱬᗅ...yes.	... �...yes.
...Ɛ...yes.	...ᑯ...yes.	...∿Ƴ...yes.
...ᶆ...yes.	...ⰾ...yes.	...ⵡ...yes.
...ꙩ...yes.	...⌐⌐...yes.	...⊪ⷞ...yes.
...ᖀᑯ...yes.	...▽...yes.	...ⵡᒃ...yes.
...ᎧᏒ...yes.	...⊞⊞...yes.	...✛⃗...yes.

. . . .

. . . . . . ☀ . . yes . . . . . . ♀ . . . yes . . . . ∞ . . . yes . . . .

(B, p. 81)

Through this narrative emphasis on Infant 187-A, 0037's atypical, evolving consciousness, the reader deduces that she is both the sperm and ovum "become a whole" (B, p. 69) at the end of Part I and the title character; Biel does not indeed name herself until almost halfway through the text. Staton here again functions, as Mikkran does with Biel, as unobtrusive mentor to the reader, permitting us to "have [our] time alone...to explore, verify...and know for [ourselves] before we can know [her]" totally (B, p. 79). Following Infant 187-A, 0037's quest for self-identity is thus—given its mysterious relevance to the novel's title, as well as its proliferating typographical innovations[51]—yet another assertion of textual authority for the reader. We must actively seek answers to these mysteries just as we must discover Howard Scott's connection with this character and her "legend." *From the Legend of Biel* is metaphorically an injection of Binol, of massive information, with which Staton hopes to expand *our* human awareness.

A woman-centered, overtly feminist context for Jungian theory is a significant part of the information Staton injects into readers of this novel. The relationship between Biel and Mikkran is of equal or greater importance in the younger woman's psychic maturation, her metaphoric rite of passage through the "Hall of One Thousand Chambers," than her literal or symbolic encounters with characters more directly representing her animus. (The Hall's name, an allusion to Joseph Campbell's labelling, in *The Hero with a Thousand Faces*, of the variations of the archetypal male quest is a further reminder of the theories Staton is reworking.) Biel's mysterious connection with Scott results in the transtemporal and spatial merging of their gene patterns as both experience intense pain. Hers is from the massive dose of Binol given prenatally, while his is from the cerebral hemmorhage induced by the flood of alien information in THOACDIEN's message. This merger, however, functions more as "red herring" in Staton's plot than as central dramatic event. Unrecorded and consequently untreated by THOACDIEN's medical technology, the merger precipitates Infant 187-A, 0037's inexplicable seizures and resultant need to wander from the dome, traditional home of children and their mentors; nonetheless, its specific effects on Biel and resultant discovery are described relatively briefly. She and Scott experience terror and pain; then, when this mystery is fully revealed and resolved in the text's final pages, they experience a "dancing unity" (B, p. 322) before resuming their separate identities. This "unity" is literally a life-saving experience for the moribund astronaut because it enables THOACDIEN to reproduce his genotype in a sperm and ovum awaiting union; it is not, however, as significant for Biel. Her later advisors view her psychological strength in merging with Scott as merely a portent of the unusual and varied psychic strengths Biel will develop as an adult.

Biel does not, then, in terms of Staton's plot, "need" this merging with a male figure to develop psychologically in the same way that Bryant's narrator in *The Kin of Ata* needs to confront and merge with Augustine, representative of his anima. Even Biel's encounter with Nyz-Ragaan, warrior-leader of the patriarchal Higgites who continue to resist alliance with THOACDIEN, further demonstrates this independence. Although this encounter is described in traditional psychological language as Biel's "exploration into [her own] primitive brain and the violence it contains" (B, p. 327), it is delineated solely in terms of its effects on Mikkran and their relationship. Despite overt reference to Jungian theory, then, this nurturing, feminist bond between two women remains the primary one in this female protagonist's quest for self-awareness. It is Mikkran who acts against THOACDIEN's dispassionate advice, the closest corollary to law in her civilization, to free the suffering, impatient 187-A, 0037 from the dome. When 187-A, 0037 begins her journey of self-discovery, Mikkran honors the toddler's self-integrity and her own moral code by not interfering with the child's undifferentiated wanderings into the hostile desert. There, Mikkran risks her own life as she unobtrusively follows, secretly tending at night to the unaware child's needs.[52] When 187-A, 0037 finally discovers Mikkran's ministrations, the mentor not only helps her to articulate an identity separate from the external world, to name herself, but also validates her diffuse anti-social rage. This rage, born of socially-engineered, Binol-induced seizures, has impelled the child into the desert. The toddler's terror at the dissolution of their images in an oasis pool is calmed by Mikkran's solid presence and her "relaxed coherence." The child's continued fascination with the contrastingly disturbed water prompts Mikkran to search her vocabulary for a word that "embraces the concept. She finds one which means pure thought disturbed, clarity agitated—turbulence. . . . Biel" (B, p. 155). Recognizing her own emotions in this concept, Biel adopts the word as her name. Mikkran accepts this choice.

Such validation of female anger is an essential component of feminist theory, regardless of its particular ideological underpinnings.[53] The assertion of female sexual autonomy which Mikkran implicitly demonstrates to Biel through unselfconscious masturbation is similarly important. Her relationship with Biel, that of "two persons of relaxed and curious mind who learn and share together, who confront the unknown . . . creat[ing] joy" (B, p. 22), is devoid of the power imbalances of traditional mothering within a patriarchal framework. The patriarchal Higgites, whom the pair encounter after they inadvertently violate Higgite territory, do not understand this relationship. Their elders maintain that "[t]o live without a mother to care for you is brutality" (B, p. 220). But they also believe that "[w]omen are made to serve men and bear children" (B, p. 164); that their own militaristic hierarchy based on male physical prowess and the ability to kill barehandedly is a valid, viable one; and that Mikkran's attraction for Nyz-Ragaan, their leader, is purely from her being "dark" (B, p. 214) in contrast to uniform Higgite blondeness. Pre-adolescent Biel recognizes the fallacies in all these assumptions, particularly the last, declaring that Nyz-Ragaan "is drawn to [Mikkran] because she lives a different and . . . superior morality—one he hopes is worthy of" (B, p. 214). Her mentor continues to educate Biel non-didactically through the example of this relationship with Nyz-Ragaan and its painful failures.

Unlike Bryant's narrator in *Ata*, Nyz-Ragaan does not succeed in transcending the patriarchal social and psychological structures that fragment him, until "[o]ne eye, which feeds half his body, sees what it wants to see—and is fire. The other eye, which feeds the other half of his body, sees what it cannot avoid—and is ice" (B, p. 202).[54] He breaks with Higgite law to free Mikkran, Biel, and another pair of Thoacdien mentor and youth whose failed rescue of the women has resulted in their own imprisonment, yet he cannot firmly decide whether he wishes to join Thoacdien civilization. His vacillation is ended abruptly by Logana, his new Higgite bride, awarded to him as a "prize" for Mikkran and Biel's capture. This male-oriented woman, so attuned to stringent Higgite concepts of femininity that she seems inhumanly to "float, an image on wheels" (B, p. 200), is enraged by his attraction to Mikkran. She follows the fleeing strangers and their "traitorous" rescuer and kills first Mikkran, then Nyz-Ragaan. This act reinforces Biel's apprehension that the "love of a good woman" will not necessarily transform or rescue the psyche of a man (regardless of her typecasting, in Jungian terms, as the mysteriously "dark" other of his dreams), and that women are not necessarily human repositories of compassion, goodness, and devotion. Bryant omits such qualifications about male-female relationships and distinctions between physiology and psychology from her more traditional fictionalization of Jungian theory.

Mikkran's death also introduces Biel to a previously-unknown dimension of human suffering. Unlike Bryant's narrator, who comes to accept Augustine's (and his own) impending death as a form of going "home," Biel experiences only loss: "She is no more. Mikkran. Is. No. More. This stillness will be with me always. I have no center and no edges. Only Mikkran's absence" (B, p. 251). Biel's grief is then expressed in an entire page of irregularly sized and spaced ellipses, with the letters "M.I.K.K.R.A.N." appearing, three to a typeset line, only toward the bottom of the page (B, p. 259). The next page visually recreates the sense of overwhelming absence that the mentor's death has left in her life. The significance of this diamond-shaped pattern is revealed only several pages later, when Biel remembers and silently addresses the dead woman:

> Now, Mikkran, there is only silence by the stream where we
> used to live and you gave me words
> and you bathed glistening like a *brown diamond* in the
> sun and I slept
> secure in the warmth of your neck.   (B, p. 262, my emphasis)

Staton, through this sequencing of information, continues to insist that the reader adduce the meanings of her text.

```
MikkranMikkranMikkranMikkranMikkranMikkranMikkranMikkran
MikkranMikkranMikkranMikkranMikkranMikkranMikkranMikkran
MikkranMikkranMikkranMikk    MikkranMikkranMikkranMikkran
MikkranMikkranMikkranMik     ikkranMikkranMikkranMikkran
MikkranMikkranMikkr          anMikkranMikkranMikkran
MikkranMikkranM              ikkranMikkranMikkran
MikkranMikkran               ranMikkranMikkran
Mikkran                      kranMikkranMikkran
Mikkran                      nMikkranMikkran
MikkranMi                    MikkranMikkranMikkran
Mikkra                       ikkranMikkran
Mikkr                        kranMikkran
Mikk                         anMikkran
Mikkr                        kranMikkran
Mikkr                        kkranMikkran
Mikk                         ranMikkran
Mikkra                       anMikkran
MikkranM                     kran
MikkranMik                   ikkran
MikkranMikkra                nMikkran
MikkranMikkranMikkr          kkranMikkran
MikkranMikkranMikkran        MikkranMikkran
MikkranMikkranMikkranMi      ranMikkranMikkran
MikkranMikkranMikkranMikk    kranMikkranMikkran
MikkranMikkranMikkranMikkran    ranMikkranMikkranMikkran
MikkranMikkranMikkranMikkranMikkranMikkranMikkranMikkran
MikkranMikkranMikkranMikkranMikkranMikkranMikkranMikkran
MikkranMikkranMikkranMikkranMikkranMikkranMikkranMikkran
```

(B, p. 260)

After Mikkran's death, the grief-stricken Biel is taken by Biteus and Xitr-Meede, her previous would-be rescuers, to Lir, a village which deliberately veils its presence from purportedly all-knowing THOACDIEN. There, her significant association with the mentor continues through encounters with Grolen, Mikkran's former charge, and Kaj-Palmir, Wizard of Time and Weaver, Mikkran's own "elder."[55] Grolen, a "sculptor of light" (B, p. 294), shares his experiences of Mikkran with Biel through a medium—holography— that obverts the ambiguities of both written and spoken discourse. He tells Biel that his hologram of his own first, adolescent love-making with Mikkran is an experience which he must share with her: "It is important for you to know her sexually. That is part of your relationship, your love" (B, p. 296). This implicit validation of woman-oriented relationships, of homosexual experience extending even into "mothering" relationships, does not exist in Le Guin or Bryant's more ideologically traditional texts.[56]

Kaj-Palmir next helps Biel to identify the cause of her seizures and her present state of being "caught between consciousness and...oblivion... unawake." This cause is the presence of "something in [her] which fights against her instinct for balance—the other...." (B, p. 310). This metaphoric description of Biel's physical dilemma, the still-unknown merging of genes with a (to her) alien male, strongly suggests an archetypal schema of the still unexplored, undifferentiated individual psyche. Biel is persuaded by Kaj-Palmir to return to THOACDIEN, where technology will permit her and Scott to understand and be reconciled to their strange unity before being separated— "[r]eleased" (B, p. 323) into psychic and physical wholeness. Their shared impressions of the surgery that accomplishes this "truce" and subsequent genetic disengagement is reminiscent of Bryant's use of light to symbolize both psychic wholeness and beneficient, universal law in *The Kin of Ata:*

> —...Beyond measurement we are sinking without motion through no motion at all, toward a horizon with a light beneath its edge—although there is none, for it is us...
> —And we are synchronized.
> —We are equilibrium.
> —...the beginning and the end—but only a small part.
> —I have been afraid of nothing.
> —Everything which terrified me was nothing at all.
> —...Only you, my friend.
> —...look...
> —There!
> —It rises, there.
> —Or the horizon falls.
> —...Is wiped away by the same hand that removed the fear.
> —The horizon becomes a ring.
> —A circle.
> —An eye.
> —...Looking at us.

—And the light source is not here.
—. . . Only the reflection of the light source is here.
—The source cannot be known.
—But we must turn around and try to get there.   (B, pp. 322-23)

Biel "awakens" from this experience—presaged in Scott's first contact with MC6, when he *"remembered a day imprinted on the genes of his race, when the first human being stepped out of the long, terrifying subterranean night into a very simple day"* (B, p. 29)—to find herself within the dome, specifically the Hall of One Thousand Chambers, being welcomed by THOACDIEN.

Staton's account of Biel's brief stay in Lir serves as commentary on both the preceding, major portion of the text and the few, somewhat mystifying pages that remain following the "help" THOACDIEN provides Biel and Scott. Staton describes this help in psychological terms as the "[r]elief that is one personality in one body" (B, p. 322). The preadolescent's encounters with Grolen, Kaj-Palmir and other inhabitants of Lir confirm and extend Mikkran's earlier teachings, which themselves echo the multiple emphases on discourse in this novel. Mikkran had told her charge that Thoacdien civilization, precipitated by the "bloodless and thorough" First Revolution, "evolved around two accomplishments: [the] discovery of the infinite capacities of any given human brain system [as opposed to holding technology in awe], and [the] destruction of the syntax of despair" (B, p. 175). According to the mentor, humanity had been sick, a "sickness manifest

in and encouraged by the way . . . people used the language . . . The essential thrust of their language was control and ownership where control and ownership were not possible. Their syntax implied one thing and reality denied it. So they continually lost the battle to control and own. The result was despair.

. . . [T]hese ill people spoke of owning each other, of owning land, ideas, animals, everything. They permitted governments and systems to try and control nonexistent entities like The People, Education, Health, even Death. They could not seem to understand that it is impossible to own mates, progeny, land, knowledge or emotions. States cannot control events. They cannot prevent change. They cannot be the stewards of The People because there is no such thing as The People. There are only persons.   (B, p. 176)

This emphasis on the particular rather than the abstract echoes June Arnold's observations about the destructiveness of such abstract categories as "apple" (woman) as well as Dorothy Bryant's focus on langauge change within Ata itself and equation of materialism with psychic disorder or incompleteness.

The inhabitants of Lir articulate further category-breaking ideas. They are systemless, living "in benevolent chaos" (B, p. 297), and their successful "absence from systems proclaims that no system has or may assume the prerogative to determine what is appropriate human behavior. . . . Systems and manifest potential are mutually exclusive realities" (B, p. 300).[57] And, unlike Bryant's Kin, who shun complex technology as a manifestation of a psychologically disturbed world, these villagers believe that "[t]echnology and systems are not the same. Technology does not depend on a system for its creation and use, but on the free imaginations of a very few persons. Historically, systems have only financed technology" (B, p. 297). This statement articulates Howard Scott's apprehension of the dome not as an artifact alien to his own inner quest but responsive to it and also reflects the actual positive uses (audio messages and holography, as well as nurturing domes) that Thoacdien civilization has made of technology. Affecting the lives of all one hundred villagers, these concepts are a "manifesto" simultaneously for Staton's own discursive innovations; the androgynous vision expressed through Mikkran's, Biel's, and the villagers' stereotype-free actions; and the text's "revisions" of conventional Jungian theory in its primary depiction of a female questor. Staton further develops this deviation from the patriarchal essentialism of traditional Jungianism through her portrayal of Nyz-Ragaan's and Logana's failed attempts at self-actualization. These characters fail to develop psychologically despite their adherence to roles traditionally assigned to men and women by such archetypal analysis. Through such revisions of traditionally androcentric theory, Staton's novel seems ideologically close to the androgynous feminist viewpoint. Certainly, her inclusion of active male as well as female characters and use of Jungian theory, however much revised, separate *From the Legend of Biel* from the more clearly gynocentric vision of another recent speculative work, Monique Wittig's *Les Guérrillères,* which employs similarly unconventional typography and narrative structures.[58]

Staton's text becomes even more complex and more self-reflexive in its last ten pages. Awakening to THOACDIEN's "Welcome" after this separation from Scott, Biel indicates no awareness of a trip from Lir back to the dome. When she asks how she had been transported back to this center, THOACDIEN replies that she never left, that she has always been in the "Hall of a Thousand Chambers." Biel expresses outrage and confusion:

> —But...the walking, the Higgites...the meadows. My friends...? Where are they?
> —Waiting.
> —You cannot tell me the journey was a dream....
> —Did you experience it?
> —Yes.
> —Then it was not a dream.
> —Did it happen?
> —Very much so.   (B, p. 324)

THOACDIEN explains further:

> —You experienced a large and prematurely administered dose of Binol. It prolonged and intensified your journey through the Hall.
> —Am I awake now?
> —Fully. You are released.

—Does this happen to everyone?
—Yes. You have experienced the journey through The Hall. The journey was different only in the amount of time it took and in the details created by your distinct brain.
—But how did I experience all that?
—Your brain designed the journey and the technology of The Hall expressed it. The nature of the journey was your creation.   (B, pp. 324-25)

By suggesting that advanced technology can facilitate the merger of psychological or dreamed experience with physical or perceived reality, Staton moves beyond Bryant's depiction of psychic renewal through dreams. *From the Legend of Biel* extends the inner quest for self-awareness and integrity from a rarefied individual or limited communal plane to a complex societal given. What is still the exception in Bryant's fictional world, particularly outside Ata, is the rule in Staton's galaxy-wide, "alien" future. While Biel is both particularly troubled and gifted due to the prenatal Binol injection, a similar process of growth "happen[s] to everyone . . . [her] journey is different only in the amount of time it took and in the details created by [her] distinct brain" (B, p. 325). This apparent democratization of the archetypal quest for complete selfhood, traditionally reserved for outstanding or "heroic" figures, is a further radical departure from the hierarchical constructs of patriarchy and a further reflection of the contrasting egalitarianism proposed by varied feminist ideologies.

Biel is then informed that Lir and the meadows "were the exploration of her own ideas and potential . . . the first articulation of changes she will make" (B, p. 327), and are therefore the only portions of her journey that she will not remember clearly. She is next reassured that Scott does indeed exist, has survived their prolonged interaction and recent separation, and will be born within the year from the sperm and ovum traced from his gene pattern. Staton's typography and visual layout consistently adumbrate these rapid surges of information and shifts in Biel's—and the reader's—awareness: lines of separated ellipses are replaced by uninterrupted linear waves (B, p. 323); single exclamation marks occupying entire typeset lines alternate with diagonally placed verbal exclamations (B, p. 323); and Howard Scott's potential adult presence in Thoacdien time and space is reflected by the parentheses in which he has habitually visualized himself and his previously unrealized potential.

He will be born soon.
. . . . (. . . . .). . . . .   (B, p. 326)

Biel then joins Mikkran, whose "death" at the hands of the Higgite Logana has enabled the young woman to know she can "survive the death of that which means most in all [her] life. . . . [to be] released . . . free to love and be loved with sovereignty" (B, p. 326). Standing beside her mentor in the clear-paned dome chamber that had once captured Scott's imagination, Biel observes the sea as she had once wonderingly observed and learned from an oasis pool. She now realizes that the ultimate catalyst for knowledge and growth is within herself: "—The sea. . . . It seems so long ago that I stood there. My hand is reaching into a pool inside my brain. Open. Closed. Grasp, Unclasp. Release" (B, p. 329). This image symbolizes the multiple outcomes of her quest.

While the convention of deploying a dream within a traditional narrative to explain shifting or improbable events is a time-honored, even hackneyed one,[59] Staton's ultimate revelation of the "unrealistic" nature of many of the events in her fiction is not such a mere narrative convenience. Instead, this rapid dislocation of the reader's expectations and understanding of the text is closely allied to the novel's modes of discourse and to the specific ideology Staton incorporates into this work. Staton's use of a speculative fiction whose premises create "cognitive dissonance" in the reader through their "fantastic" or improbable nature merges with her radical experimentation with typography; these modes of discourse engage active reader involvement with the text and thus to some extent prepare us for its unconventional revisions of Jungian theory. *From the Legend of Biel* stresses the importance of active self-analysis and dream to the personal growth of women as well as men. The reader has been introduced to such disjunctive shifts before this final revelation of Biel's having lived a "dream" experience through Thoacdien technology. Such shifts occur in Scott's unexplained absence from and then growing intrusion into the final three quarters of the novel and in Staton's counterpointing of Biel's lived experience with Scott's actuality. Biel develops from embryo to preadolescent in the fifteen minutes that transpire from Scott's first contact with THOACDIEN's recorded message to his ultimate incorporation into Thoacdien time and space. This disjuncture and suggestion of temporal simultaneity is comparable to Bryant's depiction of time through simultaneous Atan and non-Atan realities. Scott's fellow astronauts' attempted rescue of his damaged body, which ends in their destruction of MC6 with an atomic bomb after they discover his mysteriously inert form, is far more estranging to the reader than the improbabilities or disjunctures of Staton's text.

Staton reminds the reader again of our own responsibility for navigating these ambiguities and connecting the disparate elements in this novel in its last pages. THOACDIEN not only initiates reconstruction of devastated MC6 but penultimately concludes the "legend" of Biel by pronouncing, in a context that no longer has any relevant clear temporal or spatial referents, that

THE REPORT YOU HAVE
EXPERIENCED. . . . MUST LOSE MUCH OF ITS
COLOR IN TRANSLATION.
WHAT WE WERE ABLE TO GIVE
YOU IS NOT AN IMITATION, OR A
RECREATION OF EVENTS—BUT
AN OUTLINE.

```
FROM DISEQUILIBRIUM TO
EQUILIBRIUM IS A CARPET RICH
IN COLOR, INTRICATE IN DESIGN.
WHAT YOU HAVE EXPERIENCED
IS NOT THE CARPET, NOT EVEN
THE LOOM, OR THE DIZZY
WEAVER—BUT THE FIBERS,
STILL ON THE PLANTS IN THE
FIELDS.     (B, p. 331)
```

This statement's lack of referents suggests that it is directly addressed to the reader. The impact of this text's unconventional format is then referred to, and our active involvement with it and its ideas is urged:

```
THIS IS BINOL, THE HALL OF ONE
THOUSAND CHAMBERS—LIQUID
THOACDIEN: INFORMATION.
IF SOMETHING CAN BE
CONCEIVED IT CAN BE
ACCOMPLISHED.
WILL YOU JOIN US?
FROM THE LEGEND OF BIEL
AS RECORDED BY THOACDIEN—
END CARD ONE: THE PARADOX     (B, p. 331)
```

The final lines in *From the Legend of Biel* reflect its continued emphasis on discourse, the inscription and decoding of meaning, as Staton concludes with

```
STOP.

END TRANSMISSION.........................
```

If we are as adult as Biel has become, having received this transmission it is now our responsibility to create and transmit one of our own. For, as Biel learns in Lir, "[p]ersons who have been released" can—among other things—"perform *three* basic functions: creation, transmission, and reception of information" (B, p. 310, my emphasis). A reader must employ some of the concepts *Biel* advocates *beyond* the reading of this text—must "transmit" or "create" as well as "receive"—in order to be fully human or "released." With such incremental layering of theme, image, and structure, Staton strengthens her final imperative to the reader in ways that Bryant does not.

By asserting that reading can be a political as well as a philosophical act, involving the assumption of "authority" by the conventionally passive individual (reader), Dorothy Bryant and Mary Staton rebut Ursula K. Le

Guin's self-deceptive separation of artistic truth from feminist politics and poetics. *The Kin of Ata Are Waiting for You* and *From the Legend of Biel* both present, although to varying degrees, revisions of the questions about Jungian theory, androgyny, and traditional discourse raised by Le Guin's watershed *The Left Hand of Darkness*. Bryant's depiction of a non-sexist society remains closer to the androcentric essentialism implicit in traditional Jungianism, while Staton's vision of a non-sexist future is closer to feminist androgyny in its focus on an active female questor. Staton's depiction of Biel's development towards mature, caring self-reliance moves beyond the traditional version of androgyny that Le Guin inscribes. While Le Guin's hermaphroditic characters perpetuate this tradition's misleading literalization of symbol, Staton's human(oid) characters suggest that androgyny is *not* biologically determined. Instead, it is accessible to female as well as male characters (such as Genly Ai) and is not (as in traditional Jungianism) significantly dependent upon interaction with a member of the opposite sex. Staton's vision of androgynous human potential thus avoids heterosexist as well as essentialist and androcentric biases.

Bryant and Staton also differ in the extent of their formal innovation. Bryant experiments with a gender-neutral pronoun and generally questions the efficacy of conventional written and spoken discourse; Staton, however, is even more radical in her incorporation of feminist poetics into her novel. She not only poses questions about discourse similar to Bryant's but also consistently employs many alternative discursive structures. The differences between these novels' "revisions," like the varied treatments of classical metamorphosis in chapter 1, reflect the scope and complexity of current feminist ideology and the ability of feminist speculative fiction to be more than ideological tract.

3

The Battle of the Sexes: Things to Come

It is not . . . that woman is the new "victor"; rather, we have come to an age in which heroes look foolish, and truths, shallow. And, perhaps, we have grown wise enough to realize the new Heroes and new Truths can only perpetuate the oppression which men and their mighty words have created.

It is the age of woman: the ironic hero.[1]

In this introduction to a scholarly journal's recent issue on "Feminist Interpretation," Mary Edwardsen employs the metaphors of ironic heroism and questionable truths to convey contemporary feminism's multiplicity and diverse resistances to duality and hierarchy. Her metaphoric summation of feminism is also an apt introduction to another significant theme in contemporary women's speculative fiction. The "war" waged on patriarchal convention by individual protagonists in such works as *A Sea Change*, *Applesauce*, and—symbolically or psychodramatically—in *The Kin of Ata* and *From the Legend of Biel* is often depicted on a larger, social scale. Alluded to in *Call Me Ishtar*'s references to historical patriarchy and matriarchy's ancient rivalries and battles and satirized in *The Passion of New Eve*, this literal as well as figurative "war between the sexes" is a prominent plot element in a number of recent feminist works. Unlike their androcentric chronological predecessors, however, which almost uniformly posit the reestablishment of the "natural" order of male dominance,[2] Rochelle Singer's *The Demeter Flower* (1980); Suzy McKee Charnas's *Motherlines* (1978); Joanna Russ's *The Female Man* (1975); Sally Miller Gearhart's *The Wanderground: Stories of the Hill Women* (1978); and Marge Piercy's *Woman on the Edge of Time* (1976)[3] do not indicate which "camp" is or will be victorious. Indeed, Charnas has written that she is postponing completion of her trilogy of post-holocaust novels *(Walk to the End of the World* [1974] preceded *Motherlines)* until current events yield greater insight into this matter.[4]

Without clear victors, these novels also omit or subvert this tradition's focus on a single, conventionally heroic protagonist.[5] Like Staton's Biel, whose formative experiences are "legend" precisely because they illustrate, rather than exceed or contradict Thoacdien norms, these novels' protagonists are extraordinary to us because of their very ordinariness, their seemingly "unheroic" qualities within their fictional (and our own) milieus. The focus of this chapter is on three of these texts—Russ's *The Female Man,* Gearhart's *The Wanderground,* and Piercy's *Woman on the Edge of Time*—which further subvert the traditional power relationships of warring, solitary heroic leadership by depicting such leaders in fragmented, multiple, or doubled protagonists. These novels' ironic treatment of heroism, removing the power to effect social change from a rarefied, hierarchically-established individual plane, parallels the tenets of current grass-roots feminist activism.[6]

This "democratization" of heroism through challenging modernist or post-modernist characterization[7] is not the only juncture between feminist theory and fictional practice in these texts. Prolific writers of theory and criticism as well as of fiction, Russ, Gearhart and Piercy create visions of the future that range the continuum of current feminist ideologies.[8] At their most hopeful, Russ and Piercy are advocates (albeit to different degrees) of androgyny, while Gearhart speaks for gynocentric essentialism. Each employs plots, devises structures, and experiments with language in ways that allude to and reinforce the possibility, the desirability of her own feminist goals. Moreover, each of these futuristic depictions of the political struggle for social equity between the sexes continues to require the kinds of active reader involvement—the grass-roots activism, so to speak—that some contemporary critics see as the definitive, preeminent strength of science fiction itself.[9] Thus, by writing science fiction, in which the "protocol of reading"[10] requires an audience to construct the world of the story from each sentence, each unit of meaning, rather than merely assume that this fictional world is just like its own, these authors are able to counteract the implicit androcentric biases in much mis/reading of fiction according to so-called "universal" truths.[11] As Teresa de Lauretis observes, the reader must "wander" through whatever "cultural unit or galaxy of semantic traits corresponds to /female man/ as opposed to /masculine woman/ or /effeminate man/...."[12]

Russ, Gearhart, and Piercy all even further prepare for the non or anti-feminist reader's wanderings through their narratives by their inclusion in these texts of self-referential discourse which reinforces their ideological messages. These interpolations include cartoons, children's stories, and satirical skits; songs, rituals, and aphorisms; even hostile "official" accounts of subjectively narrated events. In this further preparation for the reader who may mis/read their work, these authors create a shared context with their audience that includes an awareness of feminist theory and controversy, and of women's social and literary history, still commonly omitted from general education. As Gayatri Spivak has wryly noted about some contemporary critics' objections to feminist or other activist readings of literature, "What is one man's 'intertextuality' can, alas, be diagnosed as another woman's 'moralism'."[13] Didactically, *The Female Man, The Wanderground,* and *Woman on the Edge of Time* provide glosses or mini-texts to shape the subjective intertextuality of the reader.[14] And, by emphasizing the cooperative processes of active readership rather than the static products of patriarchal law and immutable text, this interpolation of incremental and contrapuntal discourse within these works casts even the "new Truths" of contemporary feminism(s) into the subjunctive rather than the imperative mode.[15]

Acknowledged as a classic of feminist polemical literature, "the truest, most complete account available of what it feels like to be alienated as a woman and a feminist,"[16] Russ's *The Female Man* employs humor or irony both thematically and structurally in its "new conjugations" of heroism and truth.[17] Rather than one protagonist, this disjunctive text has four, each of whom is genetically identical to the other three but resides in a separate, parallel universe. Timid Jeannine, who comes from a 1930s-like America; harried Joanna, who lives in the late 1960s; enraged Jael, the assassin from a future polarized into two warring camps, Manland and Womanland; and genial Janet, the visitor from the all-female universe of Whileaway: all demonstrate through their marked contrasts with one another the significant impact that environment can have on human potential. Their characterization thus tacitly places Russ's fiction towards the androgynous end of the ideological spectrum of feminisms.[18] These characters have been perceived variously as a "montage of partial selves"; as "a cluster protagonist represent[ing] the divided consciousness of contemporary women" in patriarchal society; and as simultaneous exemplars, situated spatially rather than temporally, of the stages of woman's heroic journey towards psychic wholeness.[19] But the parallel universes of *The Female Man* are linked by the actual and possible uses of humor as much as by the shared genetic makeup of its four protagonists, and the entire novel (rather than just the sections describing warring Manland and Womanland) may be viewed as ironic commentary on the ongoing, multidimensional, "battle between the sexes" in androcentric society.

Russ employs humor on several levels in this novel. She plays with conventional prose form by interpolating satirical litanies to "The Man"(FM, p. 29) and allegorical dialogues in which women's expertise is always denigrated by the retorts of men, however ignorant. She also departs from novelistic decorum by including a digressive parody, based on her own experiences as a literary scholar, of how the critical establishment may phallocentrically respond to this work.[20] But beyond these interpolations, ironic in their unexpected form as well as their content, Russ demonstrates the ways in which humor has been used as a weapon against women. As is scathingly evident throughout *The Female Man,* the gravity of women's predicament and our attempts to question or alter our status have been defused by being treated as humorous ploys, while male violence against women has been socially condoned under the guise of goodhumored fun. Russ's protagonist Joanna makes this point explicitly several times. She recounts being told by hostile men "that [she's] joking, that [she] can't possibly mean what [she] say[s]" (FM, p. 202) and reproduces the jocularly disguised misogyny of such lines as "A pretty girl like you doesn't need to be liberated twinkle har . . . I never take a woman's advice about two things: love and automobiles twinkle twinkle har. . . ." (FM, p. 49).[21]

Jeannine, Joanna, and Jael all live in worlds in which humor is thus deployed as an anti-woman device. Only Janet, the visitor from the female universe of Whileaway, a continuum in which all males died nearly a thousand years before as the supposed result of plague, has freely experienced and created a different kind of humor, one that does not wound or function to maintain a hierarchical status quo.[22] Sparks fly when dimension-travelling Janet appears in the universes most like our own, and sparks are kindled in the reader's mind when the humorous sensibility of Whileaway is juxtaposed with ours. Shocking us into a recognition of the absurdity of patriarchal law, Russ's ironic interpolations enable the reader to achieve distance from unexamined experience or belief, to recognize the "foolishness" of patriarchal heroes and "shallowness" of patriarchal truth. This subversive use of humor "as a deflator of patriarchal order"[23] echoes a significant element of feminist theory—Hélène Cixous's joyful assertion of the potential of feminist texts "to blow up the law, to break up the truth with laughter"[24] much as the Medusa's glance was once feared capable of destroying the onlooker. As in Cixous's reclamation of the Medusa myth, this destruction of patriarchal law and "truth" is life-giving, not life-denying.

We laugh *through* the pain of self-recognition in Russ's satiric litanies to "The Man," her compilation of androcentric maxims unexpectedly offset in poetic form: "[B]ut I . . . all I did was

> dress for The Man
> smile for The Man
> talk wittily to The Man
> sympathize with The Man
> flatter The Man
> understand The Man
> defer to The Man
> entertain The Man
> keep The Man
> live for The Man.   (FM, p. 29)

And we laugh through her similar compilation of androcentric "statistics": "It's very upsetting to think that women make up only one-tenth of society, but it's true. For example:

> My doctor is male.
> My lawyer is male.

My tax-accountant is male.
The grocery-store-owner (on the corner) is male.
The janitor in my apartment building is male.
The president of my bank is male.
The manager of the neighborhood supermarket is male.
My landlord is male.
Most taxi-drivers are male.
All cops are male.
All firemen are male.
The designers of my car are male.
The factory workers who made the car are male.
The dealer I bought it from is male.
Almost all my colleagues are male.
My employer is male.
The Army is male.
The Navy is male.
The government is (mostly) male.
I think most of the people in the world are male.

Now it's true that waitresses, elementary-school teachers, secretaries, nurses, and nuns are female, but how many nuns do you meet in the course of the usual business day? Right? And secretaries are female only until they get married, at which time they change or something because you usually don't see them any more. I think it's a legend that half of the population of the world is female; where on earth are they keeping them all?   (FM, pp. 203-04)

We smile in pain at the allegorical party dialogues, presented complete with playwright's parenthetical stage directions, which stress the ritualized artificiality of our discourse:[25]

A ROUND OF "HIS LITTLE GIRL"

Saccharissa: I'm Your Little Girl.
Host (wheedling): Are you really?
Saccharissa (complacent): Yes I am.
Host: Then you have to be stupid, too.

A SIMULTANEOUS ROUND OF "AIN'T IT AWFUL"

Lamentissa: When I do the floor, he doesn't come home and say it's wonderful.
Wailissa: Well, darling, we can't live without him, can we? You'll just have to do *better*.
Lamentissa (wistfully): I bet *you* do better.
Wailissa: I do the floor better than anyone I know.
Lamentissa (excited): Does he ever say it's wonderful?
Wailisssa (dissolving): He never says *anything!*   (FM, p. 35)

And we laugh through Joanna's, the 1960s protagonist's, literalization of metaphor, her maddened and self-mocking declaration that she *is* a female man because she has been told so often that "man," "man-kind," and "he" refer to *all* of us. "If," as she says, "we are all mankind, it follows to my interested and righteous and right now very bright and beady little eyes that I too am a Man and not at all a Woman. . . ." (FM, p. 139). And, having recognized the folly of such scenarios and of patriarchal humor in general, we distance ourselves from them in defense of self-integrity. As Jael notes towards the novel's conclusion, "[B]oys throw stones at the frogs in jest. But the frogs die in earnest" (FM, p. 196).[26]

Russ indicates the psychological violence such humor perpetrates against women through twenty-nine year old Jeannine, the 1930s character who smiles weakly in responses to misogynistic jokes about "Menopause Alley" as her family urges her to marry—anybody (FM, p. 116). Russ subverts Jeannine's seeming compliance to social expectations by having the disembodied Jael "hear" what Jeannine is really thinking, perhaps really saying to the brother who no longer listens to his embarrassingly unwed sister. Does she say "I know" in response to his righteous tirade, or "Oh no"? Is she waiting "For a man," as he believes, or "for a plan" (FM, p. 113)? Russ mocks self-delusion— theirs and, possibly, ours—at the same time she suggests alternative strategies to such brow-beating.

One such strategy is to cultivate indignation rather than docile good-humoredness. Another, concomitant one is acceptance of possible change in self-concept and world-view. By the conclusion of *The Female Man*, it is Jeannine, the most acculturated, docile and self-doubting of the "four J's" who has altered the most. She unhesitatingly agrees to permit Jael to use her continuum as a way-station in Womanland's war against Manland and to act herself as Jael's emissary in this cause. Russ describes this transformation:

> Jeannine, one cheek bulging like a squirrel's, looks up as if surprised that we could hesitate to do business with Womanland. She nods briefly and then goes back to building mashed-sweet-potato mountains with her fork. Jeannine now gets up late, neglects the housework until it annoys her, and plays with her food.
> "Jeannine?" says Jael.
> "Oh, sure," says Jeannine. "*I* don't mind. You can bring in all the soldiers you want. You can take the whole place over; I wish you would."   (FM, p. 211)

It is Janet and Joanna who still demur, who wish to think more about possible cooperation in gender warfare, or—as Jael drily says—"[g]o home and find out [more] about it" (FM, p. 212) before they finally decide.

Russ indicates the necessity for *some* change in women's perceptions and demeanor most clearly in the 1960s episodes, where women are physically as well as psychologically constrained by patriarchal forms of humor. Denying her own emotions, an unhappy young woman on a bus is forced to smile at a strange man before he will go on his way; when she gives in, "people laugh" (FM, p. 65). Because young women are stereotypically supposed to be carefree, this passerby's violation of authentic female experience is perceived as a comically gallant readjustment of disorder rather than the forcible intrusion it is. Similarly, Joanna recalls having to lock herself in her car in order to cry because the world thinks the howling of a woman "comical" (FM, p. 134). At thirteen, she had been forcibly kissed by an uncle; when she tried to escape his embrace, "everyone laughed" (FM, p. 66). Women's rights and women's anger are invalidated as jokes, leading to situations in which, whenever a woman says something contradictory to the status quo, it can be shrugged off as coyness, a ploy, an appeal for attention. Russ "blows up" this so-called "truth" through the actions of Janet, the Whileawayan emissary to our own culture.

Detained by a man who will not believe her when she says she wishes to leave his party, who physically insists she stay and have another drink, Janet refuses to heed the explanations of Wailissa, Lamentissa, and Saccharissa, who insist he is being "good-humored in the only way he can" (FM, p. 43). Disregarding the rule book for male-female interaction (a book Russ has her less-developed characters literally page through during this exchange), Janet breaks his arm in order to free herself. It is an action that shocks Joanna, even though the 1960s protagonist had moments before relished the "divine relief of female irony and female teeth" (FM, p.41) in telling this man that Janet, who settles family quarrels professionally on Whileaway, is not the social worker he had assumed but a cop. Joanna is not ready for Janet's assertive action because her society—mimetically closest to the 1970s and 80s reader's—has not prepared her for it. Whileaway's ethos and institutions are too different from her own.

Rather than being an exemplar of Whileaway's achievements, Janet has been chosen to visit our universe because she is expendable; with her 186 I.Q., she is considered stupid and will not be missed if she fails to return (FM, p. 146). The logic of this selection process and of this value system is so antithetical to our own rigid concepts of hierarchy and accomplishment as to be breath-taking; Russ gives it life through Janet's favorite expression, uttered "with massive dignity and complete naturalness, 'Huh?'" (FM, p. 10). For while humor and jokes are an essential element of Whileawayan life, they are rooted in different values than those of patriarchy; they are used to acknowledge and maintain the healthy flux of life rather than to artificially, imperfectly stabilize it into a polarized status quo. For example: when Janet, newly materialized in the 1960s, is uneasy, she sensibly takes out a piece of string and begins to play Cat's Cradle. When she offers the cradle to the astounded bureaucrats who surround her, one nervously laughs, another hides his eyes, a third backs off in fear, while the fourth asks, "Is this a joke?" (FM, p. 23). It is, but not in the destructive, foolish way he intimates. Rather, it is a communication which, because of its non-threatening, truly good-humored nature, none of them is capable of recognizing. Similarly, just prior to this, none of them has recognized her first statement, "Take me to your leader" (FM, p. 23), as the deliberately playful remark it is meant to be.

In Whileaway there is, according to Russ, "incredible explosive energy, the gaiety of high intelligence, the obliquities of wit, the cast of mind that makes industrial areas into gardens and ha-has . . . that strews across a planet comic nude statuary . . . and the best graffitti on this or any other world" (FM, p. 54). It is a place where children laugh, knowledgeably, while contemplating great art (FM, p. 59); in which the litanies of "WHAT WHILEAWAYANS CELEBRATE," offset in triple-sized capital letters, include "[j]okes," the seasons, "[d]ivorces" as well as "[b]irth," "[n]othing at all," as well as "[a]nything at all" (FM, pp. 102-03). Contraries are accepted enthusiastically, and the statue of God is "a jumble of badly matching planes, a mass of inhuman contradictions . . . a constantly changing contradiction" (FM, p. 103). This avoidance of polarization between human and divine, the acceptance of multiplicity and mockery of abstract ideals, occurs on the personal as well as institutional level in Whileaway. Women "roar" in shared laughter at their own attempts at deception, such as the public rationalizations they give for prolonging their vacations after childbirth (FM, p. 50). Whileaway is *not* utopic in a number of ways,[27] but its humor is neither deceptive nor divisive. It is not used to subjugate.

Acknowledging and revelling in the uncertain multiplicity of existence, and in the wry deflation of personal and institutional pomposity, this humorous Whileawayan sensibility also assaults the new "truths" of feminism. Its credo of self-mockery rebuffs ideological intransigence of any kind but, given the context of an all-female society, seems particularly acerbic when contrasted with the often solemn spiritual certainties of extreme gynocentric essentialism. Such certainties are even rebuffed in its community rituals, so often the focus of essentialist theory and praxis.[28] Describing "HOW WHILEAWAYANS CELEBRATE," Russ rhetorically asks, "If Indian dancing says I Am, if ballet says I Wish, what does the dance of Whileaway say?" The amused answer is that "It says I Guess" (FM, p. 102). Similarly, Janet describes the pronouncements of Whileaway's philosophers in ways that suggest her culture's comprehension of these sages' fallible human motivation. Philosopher Dunyasha Bernadetteson's declaration that "Humanity is unnatural" is immediately followed by the pun-revealing information that she "suffered all her life from the slip of a genetic surgeon's hand which had given her one mother's jaw and the other mother's teeth—orthodontia is hardly ever necessary on Whileaway" (FM, p. 12). Dunyasha's seemingly profound observation about "humanity" is thus revealed as a probable comment on her own physical predicament. Janet further illustrates her continuum's skepticism towards the mythologizing of ideology in an anecdote that highlights the extent to which some feminist beliefs still mirror the dualistic, hierarchical thought processes of patriarchy.

Her tale of "the old Whileaway philosopher . . . a folk character" (FM, p. 153) is precipitated by impatience with Joanna and Jeannine's stories about enchanted frogs turning into princes:

The Old Whileawayan philosopher was sitting cross-legged among her disciples (as usual) when, without the slightest explanation, she put her fingers into her vagina, withdrew them, and asked, "What have I here?"

The disciples all thought very deeply.

"Life," said one young woman.   .

"Power," said another.

"Housework," said a third.

"The passing of time," said the fourth, "and the tragic irreversibility of organic truth."

The old Whileawayan Philosopher hooted. She was immensely entertained by this passion for myth-making. "Exercise your projective imaginations," she said, "on people who can't fight back," and opening her hand she showed them that her fingers were perfectly unstained by any blood whatever, partly because she was one hundred and three years old and long past the menopause and partly because she had just died that morning. She then thumped her disciples severely about the head and shoulders with her crutch and vanished. Instantly two of the disciples achieved Enlightenment, the third became violently angry at the imposture and went to live as a hermit in the mountains, while the fourth—entirely disillusioned with philosophy, which she concluded to be a game for crackpots—left philosophizing forever to undertake the dredging out of silted-up harbors. What became of the Old Philosopher's ghost is not known.   (FM, pp. 153-54)

The abstractions with which these "disciples" respond echo not only the focus of patriarchal philosophy ("Life," "time," and "truth") but also some buzzwords ("Power" and "Housework") of contemporary feminism. That each young woman associates these concepts with female physiology is a further ironic link with excessive gynocentric essentialism. That the disciples specify seemingly dichotomous abstractions may be a comment on the infiltration of patriarchal dualism into feminist theory. Janet rebuts theory which ignores daily actuality in her analysis of this folk tale:

Now the moral of this story is that all images, ideals, pictures, and fanciful representations tend to vanish sooner or later unless they have the great good luck to be exuded from within, like bodily secretions or the bloom on a grape. And if you think that grapebloom is romantically pretty, you ought to know that it is in reality a film of yeasty parasites rioting on the fruit and gobbling up grape sugar, just as the human skin (under magnification, I admit) shows itself to be iridescent with hordes of platelets and swarms of beasties and all the scum left by their dead bodies. And according to our Whileawayan notions of propriety all this is just as it should be and an occasion for infinite rejoicing.   (FM, p. 154)

Returning to the original stories of enchanted princes and princesses, she goes on to demolish comparable patriarchal myth:

After all, why slander frogs? Princes and princesses are fools. They do nothing interesting in your stories. They are not even real. . . . Frogs, on the other hand, are covered with mucus, which they find delightful; they suffer agonies of passionate desire in which the males will embrace a stick or your finger if they cannot get anything better, and they experience rapturous, metaphysical joy (of a froggy sort, to be sure) which shows plainly in their beautiful, chrysoberyllian eyes.   (FM, pp. 154-55)

Given her "low" I.Q. of 186, Janet herself may be viewed as such a contented, unheroic Whileawayan frog, dismayedly coping with the expectations of Laura, her 1960s lover, and assorted non-Whileawayan officials that she must surely be a prince/princess in disguise. This embedded self-referential discourse is thus a multiple comment on the possibilities of "misreading" the social "texts" of experience.[29]

Janet's encounters in non-Whileawayan society provide further comic insight into the possibilities of mis/reading experience according to internalized cultural expectations. Given a bunch of chrysanthemums at a woman's club luncheon, she holds them—according to the audience and narrator's perceptions—"upside-down like a baseball bat" (FM, p. 59). This unwitting confusion of decorative with functional "object" is emblematic of the graver, converse misreadings of "woman" by patriarchal societies as detailed by Jael. This emissary from a future continuum actively involved in gender warfare, like Liza Durach in *Applesauce,* is continually perceived as representative of a purportedly uniform class rather than as an individual. Ceaselessly queried about her "Brand Name" (FM, p. 19), Jael finally kills a Manlander who refuses to see her as anything other than such a generic sexual toy.[30] This individual's misreading of "woman" is only one instance of Manland's androcentrism, its inability or unwillingness to revise its own cultural expectations. Each year Manland's cosmetic surgeons accept "wilder and wilder" (FM, p. 161) specifications for their production of transsexuals. The concept of woman as totally alien other underlies this credulity; Manlanders force the weakest boys to undergo sex-change operations in order to obtain the "women" who will become their simultaneously adored and despised "wives." Jael believes that most Manlanders would not recognize an authentic woman if they saw one.

Jael details the same kind of cultural blindness in her account of an earlier sojourn in a feudal continuum resembling Western Europe's Middle Ages. There, winning a high military and political position as a supernaturally gifted warrior believed to be a male representative of "Faeryland," she fulfills her mission to misdirect important patriarchal leaders. When she reveals her true gender, her devoted followers can only exclaim, *"If the women of Faery are like this, just think what the MEN must be!"* (FM, p. 191). By embedding this seemingly parenthetical account within her overall narrative of the four J's, Russ reinforces the reader's awareness of sexual stereotypes' impact on cultural and personal perceptions of reality. Jael's "vassals" immediately translate the unknown into known elements, however distorted. Janet, again functioning as a "key" to Jael's enraged experience, comments upon such faulty communication soon after her first appearances in Jeannine and Joanna's worlds. Interviewed on a television talk show, she impatiently notes, "Evason is not 'son' but 'daughter.' That is *your* translation" (FM, p. 18). The interviewer has erroneously translated Janet's matronymic into terms that reflect his own partriarchal world-view.

Aimed at recognizedly diverse classroom audiences at different levels of theoretical and practical feminist awareness, feminist pedagogy as such a mode of "simultaneous translation" is a concept only now gaining recognition.[31] Yet Russ's *The Female Man,* through its didactic embedding of narratively intrusive but self-referential discourse, functions as such simultaneous translation for its presumably heterogeneous audience. As Nelly Furman notes, "there is no reason to believe that, as readers, men and women impart identical connotations to words,"[32] and one might add there is no assurance that a non- or anti-feminist audience will read a text in the same ways that a feminist or proto-feminist one will. Indeed, Russ's rendition of the phallocentric, *ad feminim* criticisms that this novel may be subject to indicates her apprehension of reading as a form of authorship, potentially destructive as well as constructive. These criticisms range from stereotyped views of women ("shrill"; "vituperative"; "twisted, neurotic") and of woman-produced art ("this shapeless book"; "some truth buried in a largely hysterical...."; "the ladies'-magazine level"), including pseudo-scientific rebuttals ("denial of the profound sexual polarity which"; "inability to accept the female role which"; "the predictable fury at anatomy displaced..."), to attacks on feminism and outright misogyny ("selfish femlib"; "another of the screaming sisterhood"; "those who cuddled up to ball-breaker Kate will"; "needs a good lay"). Russ's awareness of readers' constructive (or destructive) perceptions of a text antedates the critical establishment's growing interest in reception theory since *The Female Man*'s original publication.[33]

The embedding of other, even more overtly disjunctive asides, litanies, and choral commentaries further highlights the polemical continuity of this unconventional text. Often set off typographically by large or italicized print, or made prominent through internal chapter divisions and spatial arrangements customarily reserved for poetry or dramatic literature, these interpolations are associatively rather than linearly connected to the dominant narrative of the four J's. As such, they reflect the "discursive, conjunctive style" some linguists associate with feminist discourse.[34] Early examples of such interpolations occur during Janet's stay with a "typical," All-American family of the 1960s. An unidentified persona—perhaps Joanna or possibly a vehement Russ herself—unexpectedly voices one of the informal norms operating in this society:

VI

A beautiful chick who swims naked and whose breasts float on the water like flowers, a chick in a rain-tight shirt who says she balls with her friends but doesn't get uptight about it, that's the real thing.   (FM, p. 60)

This passage's slang suggests the extent to which this contemporary concept of "true womanhood" has permeated all social levels. This definition of womanly "perfection" counterpoints the self-doubts, unhappiness, and frustration of this family's bright teenage daughter, Laura. Although phrased more neutrally, the interpolated passage immediately following this one further comments on her socially-undermined ambition and curiosity:

VII

> There are more whooping cranes in the United States of America than there are women in Congress.   (FM, p. 61)

A later, more virulent commentary is interspersed in the older Joanna's account of her own, earlier adolescence. Again, Joanna-the-character or Joanna-the-author is probably the fragment's source; however, the remark applies equally to Russ's depiction of Jeannine and Jael's similarly sexist upbringings and therefore it resonates beyond these limits of narrative probablility:

V

> Learning to
> despise
> one's
> self   (FM, p. 207)

Such mysteriously interpolated discourse, to some extent validated by the text's science fictional premises of transtemporal and spatial travel, reinforces the feminist or proto-feminist reader of the novel at the same time that it *forces* the non or anti-feminist reader to confront possible androcentric biases. Such interjections foster interpretation of the four J's narrative from a woman-oriented rather than a conventionally androcentric viewpoint.

The further possibility of feminist readers' mis / reading of social or literary texts is also alluded to in this multidimensional novel. Ironically, the vehicle for this possibility is a literal "shaggy bear" story told by a playful Whileawayan child to Joanna when the 1960s character is transported to Janet's continuum. This picaresque account of the adventures of an apocryphal Whileawayan wild child raised by bears is laboriously concocted for Joanna's amusement. Leaving her adoptive family, this "heroine" arduously seeks, finds, and then amicably parts from her human mother for further adventure. But Joanna needs help to discover and interpret the tale's relevance to her own life. Vittoria, Janet's wife, voices the significance of this absurdly complex story for the woman accustomed to living in patriarchal society: "Anyone who lives in two worlds," (said Vittoria) "is bound to have a complicated life" (FM, p. 99). But, according to Russ, there is hope: "Whileaway," she writes, "is the inside of everything else" (FM, p. 95); for, as Rachel Blau Du Plessis has noted,

"Whileaway exists in one's mind more than anywhere else."[35] One can alter one's perceptions, learn to read rather than misread. Russ points this out in her text's first "shaggy bear" story, immediately preceding and setting the stage for the other. The author notes that *The Female Man* is a book written in blood and tears. But, she goes on, as the bear swore in the Pogo cartoon after "having endured a pot shoved on her head, being turned upside down while still in the pot, a discussion about her edibility, the lawn-mowering of her behind, and a fistful of ground pepper on the snoot," there is recourse open to us. We can swear, just as the bear swore "on the ashes of her mothers (*i.e.,* her forebears)

OH, SOMEBODY ASIDES ME IS GONNA RUE THIS HERE PARTICULAR DAY. (FM, p. 95)

That the bear in the original Pogo cartoon is male, not female, is relevant to this fictional analysis of human potential as affected by diverse societies and cultures. The ability to transcend and transform experience, to take what has been male-identified and make it female-identified or gender-free is intimated by this superficially insignificant literary transformation. In a work in which humor is the focus and force of so much injustice, of so much righteous female anger, it is appropriate that a cartoon is used as a metaphor for feminists' changing consciousness. Previously victimized or coopted by patriarchal humor, we learn from *The Female Man* to step outside the frame of the "cartoon" of our lives, just as Jeannine and Joanna step outside of their lives into different realms of possibility. Whileaway offers insight into possible options, into other forms of female life and female humor within a feminist version of the future.[36] Russ's observation that "the way into Whileaway is barred neither by time, distance, nor an angel with a flaming sword, but by a cloud of gnats. Talking gnats" (FM, p. 104) refers both to past failures and complicity in not transforming experience, in not reading actively into social and literary "texts," and to the possibility of altering these non-productive patterns of behavior. Swatting gnats is a disagreeable but not impossible task.

   The Female Man's envoi embodies both Russ's themes and the structures she has employed throughout this text to communciate her polemical concerns to a varied audience. Situated after the conclusion of the four Js' interlocking stories, it is thus itself an apparently extraneous narrative element. Nonetheless, it is voiced by the distinct narrative persona that, separately and at times merging with the protagonist Joanna, has previously interjected telling associative asides and remarks to the reader. But this envoi is ironically addressed to the text itself:

    Go, little book.... Live merrily, little daughter-book, even if I can't and we can't; recite yourself to all who will listen; stay hopeful and wise. Wash your face and take your place without a fuss in the Library of Congress, for all books end up there eventually, both little and big. Do not complain when at last you become quaint and old-fashioned, when you grow as outworn as the crinolines of a generation ago . . . do not mutter angrily to yourself when young persons read you to hrooch and hrch and guffaw, wondering what the dickens you were all about. Do not get glum when you are no longer understood, little book. Do not curse your fate. Do not reach up from readers' laps and punch the readers' noses.

   Rejoice, little book!

   For on that day, we will be free.   (FM, pp. 213-14)

Conveying the possibility of a radically altered future; interlaced with humorous, often self-mocking illustrations; and concerned with the possibilities of mis/reading, this conclusion reflects the nexus of ideology and aesthetics in this text. Just as the mis/adventures of the four J's incite reader response in relation to personal or social injustice and reform, the disjunctive, associative structures of *The Female Man* require such active reader involvement in order to construct its meanings. This envoi also captures much of the novel's wry tone. The ruefully intimate relationship the author/narrator assumes towards this text (little daughter-book. . . . Wash your face . . . .)is a further reminder not only of Russ's personal involvement with the issues it addresses[37] but of the intimacy the reader has just "enjoyed" with it and the parental responsibility one may now feel towards the ideas nurtured in it. That the possibility of misreading is, at the conclusion of *The Female Man,* a positive rather than a negative act, illustrative of a productively altered future rather than the continuation of a sexist society which regularly produces phallocentric misreadings, is Russ's final, bittersweet irony. Ultimate victory in the gender warfare this novel alludes to will occur not as the result of any one decisive battle but when its feminist author's strongest weapon, her text, no longer functions on any front.

   Sally Miller Gearhart's *The Wandergound: Stories of the Hill Women* differs markedly from *The Female Man* in the feminist vision of the future it presents. Gearhart's outlook in this collection of discrete yet interlocking stories is essentialist rather than androgynous; her depiction of a future in which "Mother" Earth (W, p. 140) has revolted against the destructive excesses of patriarchy is predicated upon the concept of innate psychological and spiritual differences between the sexes. This author, a radical cultural feminist,[38] inverts and extends the patriarchal culture/nature paradigm historically used to elevate biological man and his achievements at the expense of biological woman. Overzealous adherence to cultural feminism is satirized in *The Passion of New Eve,* but Gearhart's treatment is a serious, respectful one. In Gearhart's schema, women *are* in closer rapport with nature than men, but this relationship yields greater insights and more power, rather than less. Theoretical writings of the current women's spirituality movement provide the ideological framework for this text. Moving beyond the reclamation of matriarchal history and myth, such works as Ann Rush Kent's *Moon, Moon* and Z Budapest's *The Feminist Book of Lights and Shadows* detail ways in which contemporary women may practice new versions of the ancient, goddess-centered religions. Such religions are not only rooted in the concept of women's innate, special rapport with nature but affirm women's arcane powers as the result of this bond. While these particular works are not necessarily direct sources for *The Wanderground,* they illustrate the theoretical climate from which it springs.[39]

Set on the North American continent in a recognizably near future, *The Wanderground* describes the rural lives of descendants of women who, some eighty years before, had escaped epidemic "Purges" and "New Witch Hunts" (W, p. 152). During this period, precipitated by reports of virgin births in women's communes,

> state laws were . . . revised to require every woman to be married. . . . Curfews on women went into effect. . . . Any woman caught wearing pants went to a behavior modification unit. . . . Women became more and more divided. All the freaky-looking ones were rounded up . . . the kind that would rather be with women than with men, or the kind who gave their husbands any taste of a hard time. . . . Only the ones who looked and behaved like ladies had a chance. . . .
>
> Then the misfit women began leaving the cities, heading for the hills, going towards rumors of country women who lived off the land. Some found those women. Others probably didn't. All of them had to get away from police and state militia. All of them had to hide.
>
> If they were caught, they didn't get a trial.   (W, pp. 152-53)

Escape was only possible because these and other ecological barbarisms finally precipitated the revolt of "Mother Earth." Then and in *The Wanderground's* fictional present, that revolt causes men's machinery (both technological and sexual) to malfunction once outside city limits and also causes all animals to refuse men's commands. (This animal revolt parallels the dogs in Bryant's *Ata* whose "natural" response is refusal to kill Augustine.) As a result of such "sanctified" separation of rural lands and lifestyle from technological centers and culture, the surviving women have developed agrarian communities geographically distinct from the cities. A routinely patrolled "Dangerland" separates these particular characters' safe "Wanderground" from the City's terrors.

In addition to these patrols, the Hill Women and their sister communities routinely send volunteers, disguised as men, in rotated shifts to live within the City itself to further observe its politics. There, an underground minority of non-violent, homosexual or asexual men, "gentles," aids them in their surveillance. As one critic has noted, Gearhart's text differs from traditional depictions of gender warfare in its portrayal of these women as "resisters and watchers . . . as defensive observors" rather than as warriors.[40] Certainly, such seemingly "passive" defense contrasts markedly with the "masculinely" explosive rage of Russ's female assassin Jael and with both Womanland's active battles with Manland and its aggressive attempts to infiltrate patriarchal worlds. And yet, despite this and other significant ideological differences observable between *The Wanderground* and Russ's works,[41] Gearhart's *Stories of the Hill Women* and *The Female Man* are alike in their manipulation of literary form to arouse reader involvement towards specific feminist goals.

Humor is a benign and pervasive element in *The Wanderground*. The possibility of laughter's "constitut[ing] some irreverence ... at the center" of the Hill Women's cavernous "Deep Cella," their ritual place of birthing and worship of chthonic power, is "[a]n obsolete response" (W, p. 49). Yet this Wanderground is *not* Whileaway. Lacking the omnipresent but conservatively used high technology of Russ's androgynous female future,[42] *The Wanderground* is narrative space in which the musings of gynocentric essentialism are given fictional life. In Teresa De Lauretis's words, this text contains its own specific "signs of w$_a^o$nder"[43]—both for its hopeful author and its readers. We "wander" through this landscape which emphasizes biological woman's innate psychological differences as positive, rather than negative traits and "wonder" about the implications of this value system for our own lives. One of the fictional techniques Gearhart employs to focus and engage reader involvement or "wonder" about her ideological concerns is the reconstruction of language.

Believing in women's psychic potential, Gearhart endows the Hill Women with what dominant society now considers extrasensory or "witch-like" powers.[44] They can communicate among themselves and with other living organisms telepathically, can transport objects mentally, can ride the winds and can heal psychically. Gearhart designates each of the these abilities with a neologism. Telepathy has many names, depending on the purpose and quality of the communication: "short stretch" (W, p. 5), "long stretch" (W, p. 53), "enfoldment" (W, p. 7), "listenspread" (W, p. 1), "care/curl" (W, p. 21), and "love glow" (W, p. 35) are but a few. Teleportation is termed "toting" (W, p. 41), while psychic healing depends on and is thus called the gift of "sisterblood" (W, p. 33). Gearhart similarly creates such new words as "lonth" (one's untapped reservoir of physical strength, including control of the autonomic nervous sytem), "carjery" (unreasoning distaste or lack of harmony), and "learntogether" (one's first sexual and affectional playmate) to describe accurately those aspects of the Hill Women's existence that are conceptually alien to her own (and, presumably, the reader's) dominant cultural experiences (W, pp. 12, 34, and 3, respectively). While these linguistic innovations are comparable in kind to ones in *The Kin of Ata,* they are more precise, varied, and numerous than Bryant's use of "Kin," "nagdeo," and "donagdeo." Rather than universalizing language, Gearhart is interested in exploring its potential nonsexist complexities—particularly in relation to feminist discourse. Her telepathic characters' use of spoken language is a metacommentary on both the positive and negative aspects of such verbalization for the writer of feminist theory and speculation:

> They were speaking aloud, the three of them. . . . That was a discipline they frequently used for the refining of present images and the generation of new ones. Still it created a far less vulnerable state, even a less honest one, than their usual stretch-communication [telepathy].   (W, p. 60)

Through frequent neologisms interspersed with simple diction, this author similarly refines "present images" and generates "new ones"; however, the paradoxical possibility of being misunderstood, of a "less vulnerable... less honest" communication still remains. Gearhart counteracts this possibility through typographical innovation and interpolated discourse which function as "simultaneous translation" to reinforce her polemic. Unlike Russ, Gearhart adapts these techniques to a specifically gynocentric, essentialist ideology.

Fluted leaves rather than ellipses separate passages in this text which celebrates physiological woman's spiritual rapport with Mother Earth (W, pp. 142, 143, 146, 148, 149, 150, 157, 158, 166, 183, 184, 91, 81, 66, and 67). The appropriateness of these demarcations becomes even more apparent as *The Wanderground* depicts the dailiness of the Hill Women's "fantastic" communion with nature. A shoreline tree succors an exhausted swimmer with its mobile roots, and another woodland one offers its leaves as a cup for a medicinal potion, while a fern agrees to "exchange" its energy for that of a tired child. Paralleling current "nature" feminist theory, Gearhart repudiates the separation of animate from inanimate life as she simultaneously rejects the anthropocentrism of conventional patriarchal (and some rationalist feminist) attitudes towards nature.[45] Cats, dogs, ponies, and even fish are all sentient allies in *The Wanderground*. Such characterizations incrementally prepare the reader for the Hill Women's more far-reaching, mystical communion through the sentient full moon with other free women half-way around the world.

In "Diana and the Full Moon," the appropriately named protagonist and her companions experience orgasm under the full moon's influence. Naked and supine on the ground, Diana

> forced open her eyes, the better to see a lover full in the face and she gasped at the intimacy there. A searing whiteness was wrapped in bright metallic tendrils, starshot and rain washed. They fell in an ecstacy of silence across her open body, they plunged into the earth and bent within it to encircle her shoulders, her spine, her legs. She was drowning in light, drummed by pellets of quickening silver, swept and pushed back, pulled and released, drawn and expelled. Her breath, when it at last let go, escaped in a long, cascading cry. It was not her cry only.   (W, p. 98)

Redolent of the moon worship of some matriarchal religions, this sexual and emotional rapport sensitizes Diana's whole body until it becomes a channel for world-wide communication:[46] "She was transfixed. Her eyes closed with the warm kiss of cold light and she smiled in an expectant contentment. She could listen now, her whole body attuned, her whole body the ear, the channel of meaning" (W, p. 99). What she discerns is another, geographically distant but spiritually close community of women dedicated to the worship and preservation of nature:

> The rejoicing was upon them all. Shapes began to form. She saw them with the eyes that her viscera had become—dark brown women, wild black hair, white teeth smiling in the joy of the together listening and knowing. They lay holding together, some eight of them, each open and turned toward a pale rising light. Strange colorful birds clucked and squawked among them, climbing over their bodies, occasionally joining the listening. The sounds of the women were no longer a cacaphony but a practiced enfoldment now of their own, sent forth to the moon, their high lover and draped through her over the women of the hills.
>
> Diana scarcely breathed. She understood that the messages were passing through her, understood even some of the messages themselves: that these faraway women had no need to hide, that the melting mountain had taken many of them, that only a few hundred of them had survived and some of the gentles with them. She knew in her tiniest cell how these women spent their days, of the tasks they had set for themselves in the girdling of the globe, of the healing mineral springs in their mountains, of the passing into food each of them for the others. They shared secrets about the moon that strode the sky between them; how she lifted up the tides and set them down again, how she drank from mothers' milk to whiten her face, how even when she seemed darkened and shy still she sought the caresses, the passings through and over her, of her earth daughters. For their part in their listening, the hill women shared the textures of their lives, the boundaries of their fears, and the importance of the work they took to be their own.   (W, pp. 99-100)

It is easier to accept the moon's sentience and power, a concept integral to earlier matriarchal cultures, when one has accepted the sentience and psychic strength of other "inanimate" objects. Such incremental characterizations also prepare the reader for the disembodied voice at the text's conclusion, purportedly that of Mother Earth herself, which good-naturedly and patiently responds to a puzzled child's interruption of an old Hill Woman's death ceremony.

Many such rituals are interpolated throughout *The Wanderground*. Each emphasizes female physiology and elemental forces in its imagery; each also employs rhythmic, contrapuntal repetitions which convey the choral, communal quality of this discourse. Gearhart places actual choral responses (rather than individual "arias") in italics. The Women's ritual for soothing distress, called "sharing earth" or "earth touch" (W, p. 15), literally involves two or more characters breathing in harmony with one another as at least one touches the ground. Between Hill Women Alaka and Evona, it concludes:

> "...Thank you. Fully given and well taken. Soon,
> Alaka."
> "Or deep, Evona," chanted Alaka.

"Soon."
"And deep."
"Red waters."
"Deep."
"Deep."
"Deep."
"Deep."
They spoke together: "Deep. Soon."   (W, pp. 8-9)

This refrain, with its references to menstruation and other natural currents and its association of these elemental experiences with intensity of experience and immediacy of involvement, is repeated several times throughout the narrative. The chant to comfort and honor the dying is also repeated several times:

Easy. Long.
Easy. Long.
Leaning back upon the sea.
Leaning back upon the earth.
She will bear you.
She will bear you.
Easy. Long.   (W, p. 191)

The integration of these rituals and their rhythms into the Hill Women's daily experience is indicated not only by their reoccurrence in the text but through their assimilation, apart from such ceremonies, into commonplace discourse. Prior to her own ceremonial honoring, old Artilidea speaks of her chosen way of death:

"I'll lie open to the wind. The weather and the wolves may have whatever of me is good for them. Yelena and Voki will go with me tomorrow to the upland scree to a place I have seen in my early morning dreams." Artilidea reached down to touch the goat at her feet. "Thelma wishes to go, too. We'll be companions as good in death as we have been in life. Yelena and Voki will hold us there, hold us into our passing. They will lean us back upon the earth, lean us back upon the sea, easy and long. Then the earth will bear us. Then the sea will bear us. Easy. Long. Easy. Long. Yelena and Voki will leave us there."   (W, p. 191)

The Hill Woman's words incorporate the phrases of the as-yet unspoken ritual chant, as do the narrator's comments about the community response immediately following this ceremony: "There was another time of no words. Easy and long" (W, p. 191).

This interfusion of psychological experience and social practice is typical of Gearhart's fictional future; it reflects her belief that, despite differences of individual temperament, women are psychologically allied through our very "nature." She states this belief explicitly in her description of the "gatherstretch," the telepathic communion among all Hill Women to reach consensus on a significant political decision:

Gradually the presencing grew stronger again. Some unity, some bonding on a fundamental level struck an ultimate sense in every gatherstretching woman. It went as deep as their female nature and spread as wide as their infinitely varied temperaments. All leaned together toward the image of woman-on-woman, women-on-women, toward the sameness and toward the differences that mark any two or any two thousand women. All moved toward the gentle holding of two calm lakes, each of the other.   (W, p. 129)

In her theoretical writing, Gearhart elaborates on this image of "women-on-women" or "two calm lakes" as a paradigm of women's non-intrusive sexuality—a sexuality distinct from the partriarchal "sexual model which uses male-female genital differences to justify active-passive roles."[47] Conversely, Gearhart uses women's genital and other physiological similarities to justify her extrapolation of a future society without such roleplaying. This negation of roles, the ability or willingness of individuals to assume different postures according to discrete situations, is translated into a social context through the voiced ritual that concludes the gatherstretch:

I embrace the possibility: I may yield.
I may not. Yet I may.
I embrace the possibility: We may not be together always.
We may not. Yet we may.

I may not. Yet I may.
We may not. Yet we may.   (W, p. 130)

This choral refrain holds the ability to separate over disagreement in equilibrium with the ability to yield on disputed points.

This freedom of choice, particularly in constrast to the literal as well as figurative rape of women by patriarchy, is a dominant theme in *The Wanderground*. It is given further emphasis by extended interpolated discourse which, unlike Russ's litanies satirizing androcentrism's absurdities, seriously highlights the reclamation of matriarchal history and myth. Even in these didactive reinforcements of the main narrative, Gearhart is more explicitly gynocentric than Russ. Early in the narrative, a Hill Woman, Seja, is maddened with rage and grief at the experiences of a raped City woman who has escaped to the Wanderground. Her lover sees in Seja's rage the Amazon, the free, rather than cloistered, "virgin" of matriarchal history:[48]

Seja was a warrior—strong, righteous, brave, committed. She rode bare-breasted under a brilliant helm of crescent horns and flanked by bold and bright-clad sisters. Stonefaced, powerful, beautiful, highly-trained and self-disciplined, she was the virgin, the one-unto-herself, the spirit of the untrodden snow, whose massive hands were as unflinching in battle as they were gentle in love. And her sword rang on the shields of men who dared to violate the sanctity of womankind. Here was no passive damsel, here none of the forgiveness of the soft supine woman. "He who rapes must die." A simple maxim by which to live your life, by which to die yourself if that is necessary. Now there was the fighter, flushed with valor, sworn to death or triumph and now here was the calm victor, not rejoicing in the kill but looming over her vanquished enemy at this very moment about to let fall the fatal blow.   (W, pp. 25-26)

Later in the text, the Kore/Demeter myth is sung, with the resistance and triumph of divine mother and daughter against Dis, Lord of the Underworld, emphasized. While lustful Dis is able to abduct Kore from her mother Demeter, this enraged goddess's control of the harvests forces him to relinquish Kore for at least six months of the year. The refrain of this chant, "Never may I enter where the way is not open, never can I take her if she does not choose to go," (W, p. 75) is an explicit reference to the fruitlessness of rape. The chant concludes with a feminist revision of this myth, weighting its ultimate significance towards matriarchal triumph rather than defeat:

Giving love and fealty to the mother-lover,
Giving love and fealty to the lover-daughter,
Finding the love and fealty from the daughter-mother,
They knew in their bodies that the gods were doomed.   (W, p. 75)

At the same time that matriarchy and its religions are being overthrown by patriarchy (an event symbolized, for some theologians, in the Kore/Demeter myth[49]), Demeter's continuing influence over the harvest portends patriarchy's ultimate demise. In the Hill Women's chant, Hecate and Kore, wise through their very femaleness, instinctively recognize this eventual triumph "in their bodies." This knowledge parallels, for Gearhart, the Women's own innate psychic gifts.

Extrapolating the seeds of their own culture from past, mythologized experience, Gearhart's characters heal the wounds of historical brutalization. The demarcations between history and myth, culture and nature, material and psychological experience so often stressed by patriarchy at the expense of women's lived and perceived realities are erased.[50] As one Hill Woman concludes at the beginning of the gatherstretch, "She had found a vision in the deep returning rhythms of that final joining—or was it a memory?—a vision of that green world filled with laughter far beyond the stars" (W, p. 125). This conflation of the future with the past, lived with imagined or imaginable experience, is indicative of the visionary power of memory in *The Wanderground.* The Hill Women reclaim not only the extraordinary or archetypal experiences of their mythic, heroic past but also the particular, daily experiences of ordinary women. The Remember Rooms, the subject of one of Gearhart's "stories" or chapters, are places where her characters psychically relive the previous experiences of women under patriarchy. Told from the perspective of Clana, a child making her first pilgrimage to the rooms, this story contains both extended vignettes of flight from the New Witch Hunts and a montage of sentence-long, disparate female experiences in twentieth century America.

This passage indicates Clana's glimpses of conventional heterosexual romance; the unreleased anger of an overworked female short order cook; the exhilaration of women athletes; the frustration of a woman caring for an aged in-law; a wife waiting late at night for her errant husband; a contented mother and one despairing of her child's soiled diapers; women protesting for abortion and other rights; exuberant women at a concert; and newspaper headlines both proclaiming women's political advances and indicating some prominent women's rejection of feminist activism ("Rhodes Scholars Say Women's Lib Didn't Help Them a Bit" [W, p. 141]). These interpolated "mundane" details, like the "folk wisdom" Artilidea imparts before her dying ("Beans planted when the moon is Leo-borne will speck and rot. Scrapings from a cow's horn can clot wasting blood. The wind won't turn the barrels when clouds are in the east...." [W, p. 191]) counterpoint the more traditionally heroic accounts of Kore/Demeter and the Virgin Warrior. Through this balanced glossary of female experience and achievement, interpolated throughout the ongoing *Stories of the Hill Women,* Gearhart dramatically reconfirms one of her fictional community's prime maxims: "What we are not, we each could be, and every woman is myself" (W, p. 63).

Gearhart also implicitly conveys this cultural axiom through her text's narrative structure. Like *The Female Man,* also a rendition, albeit from a different perspective, of the potential of "Everywoman" (FM, p. 213), *The Wanderground* contains not one, classically heroic protagonist but many, ordinary ones. Each of its stories features different Hill Women as protagonists; ancillary characters or others merely alluded to in one story reappear later in the text as central figures, while protagonists in some stories reemerge as background characters in others. *The Wanderground* is not episodic in structure, though, because each story is discrete; moreover, it does not fall easily into other conventional categories of fictional structure. As Barbara Bowman notes, its design is well-suited to its particular feminist polemic: "[R]eject[ing] the structural expectation that each part is causally-connected to every other part and that part by part the action will rise to a climax and then fall off and congeal into a tidy resolution... the interweaving of many stories eventually creates the texture of a dynamic community."[51] While Bowman does not comment on the possibility of sequential publication having influenced *The Wanderground*'s narrative form (some of the stories originally appeared individually in periodicals[52]), her comments on the unconventional, non-patriarchal unity among these stories remain apt. The concluding story, "The Telling of the Days of Artilidea," illustrates the alternative narrative strategies that Gearhart employs.

While this story recounts the death of an old Hill Woman who has chosen this particular time to "return to the Mother," its resolution of Artilidea's final days, of the women's sad willingness to accept her decision, and indeed of *The Wanderground* itself does not convey a sense of closure.[53] Instead, the chanting of "the story of Artilidea" becomes "the weaving of an intricate narrative that [will] now belong to each one there" (W, p. 190). This communal continuity and explicit sense of non-closure are reinforced by Artilidea's dispensing of her own folk wisdom and the lulling, ritualized death chant (both previously discussed) and by the other ritual that Artilidea then invokes. After *"the closing of sorts"* the women experience "while all rest on some shared plateau listening to the passing words, the passing influence of Artilidea" (W, p. 192, my emphasis), they begin this final voiced chant in response to a ritual question about the earth's and the human race's future. This collective response, despite the Hill Women's strength and determination, can of course only be phrased in the subjunctive mode:

> *To work as if the earth, the mother, can be saved.*
> *To work as if our healing care were not too late.*
> *Work to stay the killer's hand,*
> *Helping him to change*
> *Or helping him to die.*
> *Work as if the earth, the mother, can be saved.*   (W, p. 195)

With the same degree of equilibrium, poised between hope and resignation, Artilidea, one of the women who had escaped the original Purges, bequeaths her responsibility in this task to the younger women: "Yours is the task, then. Mine the passing. And, although I may, I may not come again" (W, p. 196). As before, her words presage those of communal ritual:

> *If you so believe, then so it is:*
> *Ours is the task,*
> *Yours the passing.*
> *And, although you may, you may not come again.*   (W, p. 196)

In this exchange, uncertainty or narrative non-closure is reinforced as an integral component of the Hill Women's ethos. This ethos is portrayed as a hopeful rather than an anxiety-ridden belief system, one that acknowledges the interplay of individual will and consciousness with social goals and institutions. Such interplay, encompassing non-human as well as human life and negating distinctions between material and psychic reality, is metaphorically rendered in the text's final paragraphs:

> So the holding began with Ara and Artilidea as they embraced and rocked together in the soft light. Yelena drew Voki to her and together they leaned in upon Artilidea and Ara.

Slowly, others gathered, encircling, enwombing each other. Clana and Gynia rode the shoulders of bigger women. Layer upon layer, fold upon fold, the holding began. All the women leaned each on others, yet nowhere was there a burden—closely fitting, closely entwined, Artilidea at the center held by all. A low level of humming came from everywhere; it seemed literally to support the mass of women. Animals crowded inward, mixing sometimes in the circle, more often providing a circumference beneath the suspended glow lobes. Their wild, domestic and barnyard noises blended into a concert of women's sounds.

   The circle of humming rocking bodies held Artilidea, held each other, far into the darkest hours. Some left when the night was deepest, some stayed till dawn, holding and rocking; most were still there when three women and a white nanny goat walked into the sunrise toward the upland scree.   (W, p. 196)

This "enwombing," which provides support but not "burden[s]," is a gynocentric paradigm for the social structures of learntogether, non-possessive intimacy, sharemothering, and rotational representation that the Hill Women have developed. Its ritual humming, "seem[ing] literally to support the mass of women," is emblematic of the antimaterialistic world-view, expressed in ritual song, that permeates this community and fosters its development of individual and collective psychic potential beyond the boundaries of twentieth century materialistic convention. According to one punning Hill Woman maxim, "Once you know something... it becomes immaterial" (W, p. 107). This maxim merges these characters' innate, extrasensory skills ("immaterial knowledge") with the unthinking, habitual performance of acquired, long-practiced ones. Similarly, this passage's integration of "wild, domestic and barnyard noises" into a significant ceremony reflects the author's nature feminism which opposes specieism. That Artilidea walks "into the sunrise" towards her death, rather than towards a more conventional sunset, is a reminder that death for these characters is but one part of an endless cycle, that this "ending" is also the beginning of another part of that indeterminate cycle. And, finally, Artilidea's confluence with the process of life rather than her position as one of its terminal products is celebrated with her reminder that, "although [she] may, [she] may not come again" (W, p. 196).

   Process is also a key to *The Wanderground*'s depiction of gender warfare. Like *The Female Man, The Wanderground* is open-ended in its presentation of possible outcomes to a future "battle of the sexes." The defensive, observing Hill Women may succeed in "Helping [patriarchy] to change/ Or helping [it] to die" (W, p. 195), but only their determination is certain. Gearhart's gynocentrically essentialist text differs surprisingly from Russ's androgynous vision inasmuch as *The Wanderground* at least broaches the possibility of women's coexistence with men in some non-sexist future. Unlike Whileaway, which obviates the issues of feminist separatism, cooperation, or cooptation through its convenient absence of men,[54] the Wanderground "borders" Dangerground and the City. Physical proximity precludes Janet's representatively Whileawayan indifference to patriarchal custom; the Hill

Women have learned from their rotated shifts in the City and their experiences of patriarchy in the Remember Rooms that while "[i]t is too simple... to condemn them all [men] or to praise all of us [women].... [F]or the sake of earth and all she holds, that simplicity must be our creed" (W, p. 2). This distrust emerges clearly in the story titled "Meeting the Gentles."

Even through the psychic communion of the gatherstretch, the Hill Women cannot reach consensus about participating in the meeting that these non-violent men have urgently requested. And so, adhering to their own agreement to disagree among themselves, only individual women, not representatives of the entire community, travel to this Dangerland meeting. But even these politically moderate characters distrust the gentles' insistence that the constant, increased presence of Hill Women in the City is needed to balance its destructive psychic energies and immobilize its machinery. Even these moderates are appalled by the gentles' revelation of their own developing psychic powers. The men reveal these powers when, aligned in a row, four of them are able to read the minds of the women's nearby bird companions. This communication is not like the individual or collective "enfoldment"(W, p. 178) that Gearhart's female protagonists practice; rather, it is in the gentles' terms "like a bridge, not a circle... [l]ike a bridge between two people. [They] build a track to come to another's space—" (W, p. 178). But the Hill Women are horrified by this power, whose necessary linear configuration (the men must stand in a row in order to communicate telepathically) symbolizes for them "a sword... another fancy prick to invade the world with" (W, p. 179).

By depicting her female and male characters' psychic abilities in situations and language that reflect their physiological differences, (vaginal "enfoldment" vs. phallic "bridge" or "sword"), Gearhart reinforces her suggestion of ineluctable psychological differences between the sexes. These differences exist however well-meaning individuals may be. Evona, one of the Hill Women, voices the negative implications of such difference to the gentle Labrys:

> "I am not scorning any one of you or your discovery," she said, "or even your intent. My mistrust is of a deeper thing."
> Labrys spoke. "Our maleness."
> Evona nodded.
> "Then only time will tell," he said.
> "Yes." She met their eyes one by one.   (W, pp. 180-81)

Some of the gentles themselves voice anger and resentment at the Hill Women's mistrust. Their comments further echo the discord in some feminist theory and practice about women and men's cooperation and ultimate coexistence:[55]

> "You still want it all, don't you? Just like every woman since the dawn of time. You demand your holy isolation from men so you can develop your unique female powers, but you are

threatened to the core by the suggestion that we have equally unique powers—don't even whisper that they might be equally valuable. You want us out of your life so you won't have to deal with our so-called violent energy, but you'd perish tomorrow on your rotation if gentles were not in the City aiding you.... Face it, Amazon woman. We're not just your protectors anymore. We begin, just barely begin, to live without violence, to learn what you started learning long ago. Very slowly we are following a healthy hope, a life-giving possibility, a pathway that will make us your strong allies when the day of reckoning comes. You have to trust us now, lady. You may sicken at that thought, but you've got no choice."   (W, p. 180)

Gearhart captures in this diatribe some of the arguments and tone of male liberation polemic.

These particular characters conclude their heated meeting amicably, if somewhat uneasily, which provides a degree of emotional resolution to this story; however, the long-range possibilities of extensive cooperation between their communities remain moot. Again, Gearhart avoids more traditional narrative closure. Furthermore, her depiction of the gentles removes the Hill Women's possible victory in gender warfare, the success of their resolve to "help" man to change or "help" him to die (W, p. 195), from war's clear-cut metaphors of "heroism" and moral "truth." The gentles' undeniable bravery and virtues cloud the definitions of such propagandistic terms. The Hill Women's mixed responses and the men's own ambivalent attitudes towards coexistence are an extension of the composite view of feminism in conflict which Russ provides through the four J's and their encounters with one-dimensional men and Manland. Ironically, Gearhart creates more rounded male characters in her gynocentric polemic than Russ does in her speculations aobut androgynous human potential. Thus, even this overtly essentialist feminist fiction retains an element of ideological complexity.

Marge Piercy's *Woman on the Edge of Time* develops the possibility of coexistence between women and men in a non-sexist future more fully and hopefully than either Russ's or Gearhart's texts. This fictional account of welfare mother Connie Ramos's experiences in twentieth century America and in two disparate, alternative futures is, however, similar to these works in a number of ways. Like *The Female Man* and *The Wanderground,* it employs narrative structures that embody its feminist themes and demand active reader involvement to construct textual meaning(s). These structures include a multiple, atypically heroic protagonist, dialectical plots and settings, and interpolated "translations" of the narrative's didactic messages. And, like these works, *Woman on the Edge of Time* examines the issues and outcomes of possible gender warfare speculatively rather than definitively.

Connie Ramos's social position removes her from the realm of classical heroism. A poor Chicana, she has experienced economic and ethnic discrimination as well as the sexual stereotyping which confronts women of other social backgrounds. Rape, illegal abortion, on-the-job sexual harassment, and confinement for inappropriate or "insane" behavior are all part of this character's gradually revealed past.[56] The novel opens with Connie's latest unjust confinement in a state asylum for "insanely" attacking her niece Dolly's brutal pimp and then alternates between life in this asylum and the future societies to which this character's special telepathic powers give her access. For Connie, like some other women and men whose unconventional perceptions or behavior lead to their forcible confinement, is not the powerless person her society believes; instead, she is a powerful telepathic "catcher" (E, p. 41), capable of receiving the mental impulses of time-travelling Luciente and similarly receptive Gildina. These characters provide the confined woman with access to two possible, conflicting futures: Luciente is from the egalitarian New England community of Mattapoisett in 2137, while Gildina, whom Connie contacts only once, is herself a woman literally as well as figuratively confined. She lives within the purdah-like seclusion and rigid sex roles decreed for women by a second, dystopic future.

Piercy's investiture of power in the conventionally powerless figure of Connie gives fictional life to radical critiques of psychiatric theory and institutions, particularly in relation to women.[57] It also suggests the power the conventionally passive reader may exert in constructing this text's meanings. We may synthesize concepts emerging from the dialectic Piercy establishes through this novel's structural alternation among grim present and disparate, possible futures,[58] or—as Connie has in the past—we may unproductively fragment our perceptions. As Connie tells Luciente,

> in a way I've always had three names inside me. Consuelo, my given name. Consuelo's a Mexican woman, a servant of servants, silent as clay. The woman who suffers. Who bears and endures. Then I'm Connie, who managed to get two years of college—till Consuelo got pregnant. Connie got decent jobs from time to time and fought welfare for a little extra money for Angie [her daughter]. She got me on a bus when I had to leave Chicago. But it was her who married Eddie, she thought it was smart. Then I'm Conchita, the low-down drunken mean part of me who gets by in jail, in the bug-house, who loves no good men, who hurt my daughter. . . .   (E, p. 122)

This character's inability to "claim" under one name the different aspects of her experience reflects the strength of society's wildly conflicting stereotypes for women.[59] The reader may similarly conventionally disown or unconventionally claim the doubled or tripled manifestation of characters in this text. This doubling or tripling does not occur solely within Connie's twentieth century self-fragmentation but in similarities between Connie's contemporary experiences and those of twenty-second century Luciente and Gildina.

These similarities suggest that Connie's visions of Mattapoisett and Gildina's caged existence may just be hallucinations, and that Connie actually *is* mad and merely clothing her hopes and fears in mental fantasy. Regardless of their origins, however, these visions or hallucinations depict society's impact on human potential in ways that make them effective narrative polemic. Thus, an attempt to categorize these chapter-long, futuristic episodes as *either* madness or vision is distortingly irrelevant; these possibilities are complementary rather than mutually exclusive. As in *Applesauce,* the possibility of narratorial unreliability does not invalidate the text's insights. Instead, it is further evidence of their affective authenticity.

Like Russ's four J's, genetically identical but greatly dissimilar in personality, outlook, and ultimate physical development, Piercy's 1970s characters have superficial "doubles" in the futures she depicts. "Violent" Connie; homosexual, at times suicidal Skip; and angry, witchlike Sybil are termed insane and incarcerated by their own society, but their parallels in Mattapoisett—Luciente, Jackrabbit, and Diana—lead happy and productive lives.[60] Luciente, whose "Indio" face (E, p. 33) resembles Connie's, rather than being constrained by femaleness, moves with the "air of brisk unselfconscious authority Connie associated with men" (E, p. 67) and has both family and a respected profession; Jackrabbit's sexual ease, reflected in his name, is relished rather than punished by his associates and is merely one dimension of his life as an artist; while Diana is honored rather than condemned for her psychological strengths and astuteness as a healer. Even Connie's daugher Angelina, taken away when her mother is deemed unfit, and Connie's lover Claud, killed in a prison medical experiment, have Mattapoisett correspondences in Luciente's daughter Dawn and lover Bee. Piercy has Bee explain this strange congruence to Connie on one of her psychic "visits" to Mattapoisett: "I'm not Claud. Maybe I look like Claud did. Maybe I move like [him]. You feel so.... Maybe I am potentialities in [him] that could not flourish in your time. But I am also me, Bee, friend of Luciente, friend of yours" (E, p. 189). This observation, upholding the androgynous vision in its suggestion that nurture is more important than nature, is reinforced by still other correspondences within the novel. These further ironic parallels among differently raised characters are foreshadowed early in the novel by thirty-eight year old Connie's resentful amazement at her social worker's age. Although middle class Mrs. Polcari is at least thirty-six, unlike Connie she looks at least ten years younger.

Society's impact on women's appearance and attitude is most dramatically displayed in the character of Gildina. Originally "just a chica" like Connie, her niece Dolly, or Luciente, Gildina has been "cosmetically fixed for sex use" (E, p. 299) until she seems a "cartoon of femininity, with a tiny waist, enormous sharp beasts" and "hips and buttocks ... oversized and audaciously curved" (E, p. 288). This "gilding" of natural femaleness, reminiscent of Manland's grotesque expectations for womanliness in *The Female Man,*[61] is but an extension of the cosmetic ordeals that prostitute Dolly inflicts upon herself to achieve a prized "Anglo" look (E, p. 218). Gildina's degraded connection to Luciente is also implicit in the resonance of their names. Conditioned by her dystopic society to live vicariously, attached each day to a "Sense-All" unit for stimulation (E, p. 292) much as twentieth century women (including Connie) depend upon television for entertainment and companionship, Gildina is "gilded" or falsely glittering. Luciente, though, who is active, purposive, and productive, glows with the inner "light" her Spanish name denotes. It does not seem coincidental that Mattapoisett's ritual greeting is a beneficent invocation of "Good light" (E, p. 72). Instead, this greeting is a further link between social norms and individual development.

Healthy individuals, much like the plants that plant geneticist Luciente creates, flourish in the "good light" of a non-sexist, egalitarian society; Gildina, on the other hand, lives in a windowless cubicle in a society where pollution has literally destoryed all good light. She confides to Connie that she had thought the "sky was yellow" until she attained enough social status to secure an apartment on the 126th floor, and that even this elevation is not high enough to obtain "light from outside" (E, p. 295). While Piercy's protagonist is shocked by this revelation, Piercy reveals earlier in the novel that Connie's own barren walk-up studio, all that she can afford on a subsistence welfare income, has only a tiny "airshaft window" (E, p. 11). Connie, unlike Luciente, cannot "create" greenery in this dark place but only preserve "dried flowers and grasses, from a rare picnic" (E, p. 16). Her other option is to tend plants artificially in her brother's chemical-ridden Long Island greenhouse—a further product of a society where it is "a crime to be born poor ... born brown," where it is criminal to cause "a new woman to grow. ..." (E, p. 62). Connie Ramos, whose last name is the Spanish word for "flowering branch," has herself never had the opportunity to flower. Good and bad light and their effects are thus metaphors that further unite these three characters.

Through these and other specific comparisons among the three societies she details,[62] Piercy makes apparent the seeds of both alternative futures within our own time. Indeed, the intrusive corporate control and psychosurgical monitoring of all individuals in Gildina's society are direct outgrowths of the behavior-modifying psychosurgery Connie herself as a mental patient is forced to undergo. As Luciente tells this character, "We are only one possible future.... Yours is a crux time. Alternative universes coexist. Probabilities clash and possibilities wink out forever" (E, p. 177). What occurs in Connie's time—our own era—will shape the future. During one of this character's later telepathic visits to Mattapoisett, Luciente discusses the war her society is engaged in and once again indicates twentieth century complicity in its undecided outcome. Unlike the conflicts envisaged in the futures of *The Female Man* or *The Wanderground*, this is not gender warfare but a war of ideologies. Power and greed rather than sexual identity characterize Mattapoisett's enemy in this conflict:

> The enemy is few but determined. Once they ran this whole world, they had power as no one, ever the Roman emperors, and riches drained from everywhere. Now they have the power to exterminate us and we to exterminate them. They have such a limited base—the moon, Antarctica, the space platforms—for a population mostly of androids, robots, cybernauts, partially automated humans, that the war is one of attrition and small actions in the disputed areas, raids almost anyplace. We live with it. It's the tag end. We fear them, but we've prevailed so far and we believe we'll win . . . if history is not reversed. That is, the past is a disputed area.   (E, p. 267)

By making the past "a disputed area," Piercy heightens the significance of Connie's choices within this narrative and the reader's involvement with the text both during and after the process of reading. There is no definitive resolution to Mattapoisett's conflict—only disparate speculative ones, each of which depends on the concerted actions of many individuals rather than the special, heroic leadership of one. Thus, the responses of "unknown" readers to this work and its themes are as significant as those of the politically or socially prominent reader. Luciente explains this vision of decisive collective action, a vital component of feminist theory, to a puzzled Connie:

> Connie smiled, poking the fire idly with a stick that charred at the end. "I ask you about I and you answer me about We."
> "Connie, we are born screaming Ow and I! The gift is in growing to care, to connect, to cooperate. Everything we learn aims to make us feel strong in ourselves, connected to all living. At home."   (E, p. 248)

As Connie perceives the connections between her own predicament and the alternative possibilities of Mattapoisett or Gildina's future, she rejects her solitary status "to care, to connect, to cooperate" with Mattapoisett's goals in the only ways she can discern. With, appropriately enough, herbicide from her brother's greenhouse, she poisons the medical researchers who are experimenting with psycho-surgery on her and other mental patients. She has realized the possible long-range impact of their attempts to chase "feeling . . . the crouching female animal through the brain with a scalpel" (E, p. 282). Through this assassination, she hopes not only to rescue the remaining inmates from surgery but to prevent the development of new techniques that may ultimately lead to Gildina's controlled, monitored society.

Some Marxist or feminist readers, noting the sacrificial and seemingly isolated nature of Connie's rebellion, object to Piercy's conclusion of *Woman on the Edge of Time* with this act. They suggest that this assassination is a futile individual response when—as Piercy herself notes through Luciente—only collective action can significantly influence the course of social development. Rachel Blau Du Plessis, in particular, maintains that Connie's act "creates problems for the very thesis which [Piercy] wants the book to state" because "Connie leaves no evidence that this is a planned . . . chosen . . . political act. Naturally, it will be interpreted as mad, only confirming the diagnosis of

Connie Ramos as hopelessly violent.... if this tactic is chosen, political education to make others understand the dire necessity for such an act could be its only viable complement."[63] But Du Plessis herself misreads the politically educative coda to this novel. She views the social workers' and physicians' reports on Connie which follow this assassination and her implied criminal conviction, recited as they are in the "unbearable and sickening jargon of 'normal' discourse," as a "distancing device."[64] Rather than distancing the reader, though, this flawed "translation" of Connie's aptitude and experience may further involve us in her predicament and in the construction of textual meaning.

Connie, once more incarcerated, may no longer have choice of action, but these reports, which flatly contradict the previous "realities" of this fiction, *require* evaluative choice from the reader. Has Connie been "crying without cause" (E, p. 378)? Can one "respond well to medication" if there are "pronounced side effects" (E, p. 379)? Are "[n]egativism" and the claim to have completed two years of college when "[w]elfare records indicate only 1 yr., 3 mths. in community college" (E, p. 381) symptoms of committable mental illness? Is Connie's brother a concerned, reliable informant about his sister's mental health merely because he is a "well-dressed man (gray business suit)...and has a confident, expansive manner" (E, p. 381)? Finally, can Connie's ultimately foiled but laboriously planned and executed escape from the asylum towards the relative freedom of anonymity in Hispanic Nueva York rationally be described as a "patient wander[ing] out of the hospital and [being] lost in the woods for two whole nights and days ... very confused and uncertain where she was trying to go" (E, p. 380)? These reports, which also contain factual contradictions about Connie's age and ethnic background, indicate that "official" observors may be as biased, as narratorially unreliable as a potentially insane character. Like Jeannine's brother in *The Female Man,* these observers may perceive only those remarks or events which conform to their rigid preconceptions.

This further subversion of traditional authority not only heightens reader awareness of Connie's past mistreatment and contrasting brief happiness in Mattapoisett but directs the reader beyond the text itself. Connie's fictional fate is, at this point in the novel, already sealed; we must take the questions and emotions this faulty translation of her life raises and direct them elsewhere— towards the issues rather than the characters of this novel. Piercy thus succeeds in her attempt "to write beyond the ending" of her text.[65] Despite the defeat of her protagonist, the possibility of the collective success of her vision of Mattapoisett remains.[66] This author's depiction of the future as disparate possibilities rather than as an inevitability is thus as much reassuring as threatening. Furthermore, the official reports about Connie Ramos which close *Woman on the Edge of Time* provide the reader with a narrative bridge to both future possibilities. Rejecting the validity of these reports, we move closer to Mattapoisett; accepting their worth, we draw closer to Gildina's society. While it is still possible to hold both interpretations of this coda in mind, to seek the grace of narrative ambiguity, the increasingly overt disjunctures and ironic parallels between this conclusion and the rest of the narrative make such readerly neutrality problematic. We are led by this novel's incomplete narrative closure to join Connie "on the edge of time" and decision.

Piercy intensifies the significance of such decision by delineating Mattapoisett and its neighbors in comprehensive and inviting detail. In contrast to twentieth century America's general rootlessness and apathy, each community in Luciente's time has adopted "the flavor" (E, p. 153) of an earlier, cohesive ethnic group. Mattapoisett itself retains some of the customs and values of the Wamponaug Indians once indigenous to its New England locale; other near-by communities, regardless of the racial or ethnic makeup of their inhabitants, similarly cultivate the flavor of Azhkenazim (Middle European Jews) or of Harlem Blacks. Shared world-view rather than similar physical heritage unites villagers, and individuals may move freely from one community to another.[67] This rationale for social grouping or regrouping is a logical, collective correlative to the androgynous vision of individual human potential.

In addition to voluntary, communal cohesiveness, Luciente's time frame fosters active, participatory community life. Mattapoisett celebrates "Thanksmaking" (E, p. 174) rather than the twentieth century's Thanksgiving. Our own often empty holiday is implicitly satirized in Connie's outpatient visit to her brother Luis. Rather than as a relative to share Thanksgiving, Luis wants and treats her as an unpaid cook. In contrast, Mattapoisett celebrates this holiday with rituals, songs, and pageants that are representative of its many joyful gatherings. Piercy interpolates a number of such rituals and songs throughout *Woman on the Edge of Time*. Offset as poetry, they emphasize the reverence for nonhuman as well as human, inanimate as well as animate life shared by this village and its neighbors:

> "Only in us do the dead live.
> Water flows downhill through us.
> The sun cools our bones.
> We are joined with all living
> in one singing web of energy.
> In us live the dead who made us.
> In us live the children unborn.
> Breathing each other's air
> drinking each other's water
> eating each other's flesh we grow
> like a tree from the earth."   (E, pp. 181-82)

The reverence for all, interconnected life ("one singing web of energy") expressed in this ritual song leads Mattapoisett and its neighbors to include an Earth Advocate as well as an "Animal Advocate" (E, p. 151) on their rotating planning committee. These representatives, rather than being elected, volunteer on the basis of their dreams. Emphasizing mystic communion with nature, this aspect of Mattapoisett's culture is reminiscent of the nature feminism of such gynocentric visionary works as *The Wanderground* and *The Kin of Ata.*

Mattapoisett's holiday ceremonies are adumbrated in its ritual songs and poems for the dead, during which characters express sentiments in comparable nature imagery:

> "A hand falls on my shoulder.
> I turn to the wind.
> On the paths I see you walking.
> When I catch up
> person wears another face.
> In dreams I touch your mouth.
> When new friends ask me of my life
> I speak of you
> and words turn to pebbles
> on my tongue.
> I turn from them
> to the wind...."   (E, p. 309)

As in *The Wanderground,* the indeterminate cycle of life rather than its finite conclusion is emphasized in communal mourning. All those gathered at the graveside of Jackrabbit, killed while on defense, join in a child's lullaby to comemmorate the painful, mysterious flux of life:

> "Nobody knows
> how it flows
> as it goes.
>
> Nobody goes
> where it rose
> as it flows."
>
> ....
>
> "Nobody knows
> how it chose
> how it grows...."   (E, p. 317)

They then make plans for the child that will ultimately "replace" their dead comrade:

> "I am dreaming of a baby
> floating among others
> like a trout in a stream.
> I am dreaming of a baby

> whose huge eyes
> close over secret promises.
> I am dreaming of a baby
> who drifts in the throbbing
> heart of the brooder
> growing every day
> more beautiful,
> closer to me."   (E, p. 321)

Even this unborn child is conceived of in metaphors ("a baby/floating... / like a trout...) that connect human with non-human life.

Piercy's use of embedded discourse in passages describing Connie's and Gildina's societies heightens the impact of these interpolated fragments of Mattapoisett's lore and culture. Instead of reinforcing "messages" about the unity, sanctity, and continuity of all life, Connie is bombarded by out-sized newspaper headlines proclaiming.

GIRL SHOOTS M.D.
IN L.A. LOVE SPAT   (E, p. 60)

and by crudely typewritten notes from Dolly:

```
Dear Connie,

   I got yr messag, how do you like my new machine? Isn't it
something? I almost fell off the chair, I hear your voice
come out. Save me loosing calls when I am bussy!
Saves $$$$ too.

Nita is prettier every day, wait till you see her.
I am ok. Gerado that no good punk left me stuck with the
hospitia bill, my operation, I am still paying on it.
I have a new man, trickly bussyness.  This one is ok,
you will like him.  He is call Vic, he used to be a real pro
baseball player.  I will ask him to bring me up there this
Sunday. Can't come Saturday do to bussyness. Sunday will
come with Nita. Will go by Daddy's and get yr things. You
don't say what you want, I will pick out what I think. If
you think of something call me back and put it on the
machine so I bring it.

                    XXXX
                    Love, your Dolly   (E., p. 169)
```

This note indicates the *lack* of communication between Connie and Dolly, whose drug-reinforced self-centeredness leaves her little appreciation for Connie's plight. Habitual drug-user Gildina is similarly uninvolved with her (possibly dead) mother's situation while being enthralled by a Sense-all catalogue for violent and pornographic programs:

"Sorrinda 777": Story of a love never suppose to be, between a low-level medimat swab and a doctor in service to a nuke fission family; her faithfulness, her suffering, her shining love: will she give the ultimate sacrifice of her heart to replace his legal contracty's coronary dystrophy? FD 15.

"Good Enough to Eat": Top-level bulger ignores warnings from family and romps in Roughlands. She is captured by mutes. Mass rapes, torture, (inch-by-inch close-up with full Sense-all). Ultimate cannibal scene features close-ups. DD 25.

"When Fems Flung to Be Men": In Age of Uprisings, two fem libbers meet in battle—kung fu, tai chi, judo, wrestling. Stronger rapes weaker with dildo. SD man zaps in, fights both (close-ups, full gore), double rape, double murder, full Sense-all. HD 15.

"Contract Null and Void": A dud woman blackmails a re-op technician into a series of beauty-ops, enters career of social scramble from level to level (costumes by Rang-up, full Sense-all) till she falls for Dirk, Assassin to Spaceport Mobilgulf. FD 15 (E, pp. 293-94)

These plot synopses demonstrate that Gildina's society is a projection of the worst misogynistic elements of the twentieth century. Their emphasis is on women's traditionally subservient and self-sacrificing roles ("her faithlessness, her suffering, her shining love"; "career of social scramble") as well as the punishment of women who transgress against patriarchal convention ("ignores warnings from family...mass rapes, torture"; "two fem libbers...rape... murder").[68] As Connie dispiritedly observes, thinking of Times Square, "Men and women haven't changed so much" (E, p. 294). Gildina, like most "contracties" or middle-class wives-for-hire, is locked into her cubicle each day by her employer/spouse; this caged existence is a nightmarish conjunction of Connie's 1970s experiences as an "insane" woman and those of "normal" housewives similarly incarcerated in "[l]ittle houses" like "appliance[s] on legs" (E, p. 254). The lack of change or change only for the worse that Connie perceives in Gildina's society is dramatic confirmation of Mattapoisett's utopic dimensions.

In Luciente's time, insanity is perceived not as a commitable offense but as evidence of the individual's laudable desire to get "in touch with the buried self and the inner mind" (E, p. 66). It is a "time to disintegrate, to reintegrate [one]self" (E, p. 66). Luciente regards her own personal inexperience with madness as a lack of vision; she tells Connie that "[I've] never gone down [my]self, [I'm] too...flatfooted...earthen somehow, so it's beyond [my] experience" (E, p. 65). But Jackrabbit and Diana have both been mad—Diana several times—and are gifted, valued members of their communities. This difference in social values between twentieth and twenty-second century America is paralleled by differences in naming customs.

Consuelo Camacho Álvarez Ramos trails a string of irrelevant fathers' and husbands' surnames to her introductions in Mattapoisett, but she is astonished to learn that each person there has only one, individual name. Furthermore, they may alter their names to express periods of growth or change in their lives without being made to feel that this process is one of instability or non-productive madness. The young Swallow becomes Bolivar; the young Peony ultimately becomes Jackrabbit "for [his] long legs and . . . big hunger . . . big penis and . . . jumps through the grass of [their] common life" (E, p. 77). One old villager called Sojourner jokes about the whirlwind period of name changes that adolescents routinely undergo in Mattapoisett: "They're always trying out fancy new labels every week till no one can call them anything but Hey you or Friend. It slows down by and by" (E, p. 77). To signal adult status after a survivalist rite of passage, everyone in this community undergoes at least one name change. This sense of evolving selfhood, mirrored and reinforced by culturally accepted, fluid name change, differs dramatically from the destructive self-fragmentation that Connie experiences in the twentieth century. There, her doubts find expression in despairing, simultaneous existence as "Consuelo," "Connie," and "Conchita." She is never permitted to mature, either by merging these personae or by abandoning the least desirable one(s). Her former boss embodies society's simultaneous reinforcement of and disdain for such perpetual female adolescence. Rather than identifying his Latina secretaries as separate, responsible adults, he calls each of them "Chiquita" (E, p. 50). As Arnold notes in *Applesauce,* women are often labelled and treated as indistinguishable members of a consumable class ("apples" or "bananas") instead of as individuals.

Gender is irrelevant to personal names in Mattapoisett. Some names— like Sojourner, Bee, or Connie's own nickname "Salt and Pepper"—are gender-free, while others have lost their twentieth century sexual connotations. As Connie exclaims confusedly about the male Jackrabbit's former identification, "Peony sounds like a girl's name" (E, p. 77). None of Mattapoisett's names, moreover, is used for "namecalling": in the twentieth century Connie is ridiculed for her erratically colored hair, undyed since her forcible confinement, but in Mattapoisett "Salt and Pepper" is a term of affectionate badinage. Piercy, like Gearhart and Russ, incorporates a gentle, non-judgmental humorous sensibility into her fictional, non-sexist society and its customs. But these transformations are only some of Mattapoisett's linguistic innovations. Like Bryant's Ata, this community employs a sex neutral pronoun—"per" (E, p. 321)—and uses "person" instead of woman or man, girl or boy. Luciente responds to Connie's inability to consider seriously the possibility of communicating with non-human species with the maxim that "[p]erson must not do what person cannot do" (E, p. 99). This development of androgynous rather than sex-specific language use is counterpointed by linguistic change that emphasizes sensual or material experience. When

Luciente is pleased, she is "feathered" (E, p. 103); one must "suck patience" (E, p. 42) rather than acquire it; rash criticism, like unproductive stone-throwing, is "slinging" (E, p. 42). Some linguists identify such intensified deployment of sensual metaphoric language with feminist attempts to reclaim women's traditional, daily linguistic experience. According to Julia Penelope Stanley and Susan J. Wolfe, in much consciously woman-centered writing "[l]abels and abstract nouns as viable perceptive categories give way to active, process verbs and concrete nouns, the language of touch...."[69] In this sense, Piercy's depiction of language use in this future society incorporates both androgynous and gynocentric versions of feminism.

Other aspects of life in Mattapoisett reflect a similar incorporation of disparate feminist ideologies. As noted earlier, this community integrates the concern for non-human as well as human, inanimate as well as animate life often characteristic of gynocentric nature feminism into its social organization and rituals. This concern is fostered, however, by a society that is actually closer to the androgynous end of the spectrum of feminist ideologies. Women and men coexist without sex stereotyping or prescriptive roles in Mattapoisett and its neighbor communities. While its gender free language use abets this egalitarianism, the judicious use of technology is an even greater factor in the development and maintenance of this integrated, non-sexist society. Routine domestic and production chores, in the past the province of Western society's least valued, female members, are performed by machines, and children are artificially conceived, nurtured, and born in mechanical "brooders" (E, p. 101). Luciente explains the significance of this technological development to Connie:

> "It was part of women's long revolution. When we were breaking all the old hierarchies. Finally there was that one thing we had to give up too, the only power we ever had, in return for no more power for anyone. The original production: the power to give birth. Cause as long as we were biologically enchained, we'd never be equal. And males would never be humanized to be loving and tender. So we all became mothers. Every child has three. To break the nuclear bonding."   (E, p. 105)

Embodying some Marxist feminist theory about the importance of developing technology to an androgynous, non-sexist future,[70] this aspect of life in Mattapoisett nonetheless acknowledges gynocentric tradition and values. Men as well as women become "mothers" rather than fathers or parents, and hormone supplements enable male as well as female "mothers" to nurse their children. Conversely, women as well as men defend Mattapoisett's values in the ongoing war against "the enemy" who would eradicate them.

There *are* personal and ideological disagreements in Luciente's time frame beyond this major conflict. Individuals who cannot coexist amicably undergo appropriately designated "worming" sessions (E, p. 124) to analyze and resolve their friction, while first time criminal transgressors agree to periods of isolated, distasteful, or dangerous labor before returning to the community.

(Habitual violent offenders are executed.) During Connie's visits, she also learns of an on-going political disagreement between "the Shapers" and "the Mixers." The former "want to breed for selected traits" (E, p. 226), to shape human development much as twentieth century psychosurgeons wish to shape human response, while the latter—including Luciente and most of Mattapoisett—believe that they cannot "know objectively how people should become." Luciente thinks that the Shapers' movement is "a power surge" (E, p. 226). Connie first learns of this long-standing debate by reading the community bulletin board, which contains the "newest notices, poems, proposals, and complaints":

> *With you*
>
> Well coupled: I could wade
> in warm water
> and melt like a sugar cube.

ANYONE WHO DOESN'T CLEAN DIVING GEAR DESERVES TO DROWN!

Do you value yourself lower than zucchini? Vote the SHAPERS!

Class starting in bacterial fertilizers, Tuesday 8 P.M., Amilcar Cabral greenhouse.

Cellist wanted, antique music quartet. See Puccini, Goat Hill.

WANDERING PLAYERS: Goose Creek players visiting this week. Thursday: THE ROBBER BARONS (historical satire); Friday: WHO KNOWS HOW IT GROWS (Shaping drama); Saturday: WHEN TIME FRAYED (drama of battle at Space Station Beta).   (E, p. 226)

Within this warm and humorous melange of communications (itself quite a contrast to the interpolated "bulletins" of her own or Gildina's time) Connie finds an announcement of a political play ("WHO KNOWS HOW IT GROWS") and the self-mocking polemic "Do you value yourself lower than zucchini? Vote the SHAPERS!" This element of humor, the ironic recognition that human disagreement is inevitable and therefore secondary to the on-going, mutual enjoyment of life, also differs profoundly from the attitudes towards disagreement or non-conformity Connie experiences in the twentieth century. This comparatively tolerant attitude also characterizes the other major feminist disagreement between socialist and radical critiques of society which Piercy alludes to in this text. By focusing this argument on a work of art, novelist/poet Piercy adopts some of Mattapoisett's rueful self-mockery.

Luciente criticizes a hologram for its emphasis on traditional gender identity rather than materialist greed as the cause of past oppression:

In their recent holi, the image of struggle was a male and a female embracing and fighting at once, which resolved into an image of two androgynes. Yet the force that destroyed so many races of beings, human and animal, was only in its source sexist. Its manifestation was profit-oriented greed.   (E, p. 210)

Another villager agrees, adding that "the holi should have related the greed and waste to the political and economic systems" (E, p. 210). Bolstered, Luciente then states that she furthermore "can't see male and female as equal to blame, for one had power and the other was property. Nothing in what [was] made speaks of that" (E, p. 211). This critique echoes the twentieth century's longstanding, still current controversy between socialist and feminist theorists, and also captures the flavor of past ideological critiques of art for "flawed" or "inappropriate" didacticism.[71] As old Sojourner reports with impatient good humor, "Every piece of art can't contain everything everybody would like to say! I've seen this mistake for sixty years. Our culture as a whole must speak the whole truth. But every object can't! That's the slogan mentality at work, as if there were certain holy words that must always be named" (E, pp. 210-11). Tellingly, Piercy places this aesthetic and ideological debate within a subjective context: Luciente is not criticizing the work of unknown artists but the joint creation of her "sweet friend" Jackrabbit and his long-time lover Bolivar. As all the participants in this discussion come to realize, however valid her objections, Luciente's ambivalence towards Bolivar must be seen as a factor in her criticism. Piercy thus reminds the reader that aesthetic or political objectivity is as much a myth as the scientific objectivity that Connie's physicians smugly assume.

By incorporating this complex, self-reflexive debate within her novel, Piercy not only demonstrates the importance of art to her vision of a better future society but also ruefully acknowledges some of the criticism that her text (like any other art work) may draw from committed ideologues. Her own stance may be voiced in the combined ambivalence of this fictional hologram's creators: Jackrabbit ultimately concedes the possible relevance of Luciente's remarks, while Bolivar continues to insist that a powerful "image radiates many possible truths." It need not, therefore, explicitly or solely communicate a community's "common politics" (E, p. 211). Whether or not this analysis will satisfy readers of *Women on the Edge of Time* whose perceptions of the present and aspirations for the future do not resemble Piercy's own hybrid feminist vision remains moot. Her positing of questions without final answers to this disagreement is consistent, however, with the novel's dominant theme of the future as malleable, alternate possibilities rather than a single inevitability. And, through the subjective framing of Luciente and Bolivar's particular disagreement, Piercy further reminds her readers to reexamine closely the possible motives for such aesthetic or political debate.

Joanna Russ's *The Female Man,* Sally Miller Gearhart's *The Wanderground: Stories of the Hill Women,* and Marge Piercy's *Woman on the Edge of Time* are alike in their questioning, open-ended depiction of the future and its possibilities for women's and men's non-sexist co-existence. Russ is most skeptical of this possibility, while Gearhart is painfully doubtful and Piercy affirms it through detailed fictional representation. These novelists are not committed to the same feminist ideology: Russ and Piercy affirm the androgynous concept of human potential while Gearhart emphasizes essential psychological differences between the sexes. Despite these ideological differences, though, these authors do employ similar literary techniques, including dialectical and associative narrative structures, atypically heroic or multiple protagonists, and embedded discourse which emphasizes their particular didactic aims both incrementally and contrapuntally. Demanding active reader involvement to construct textual meaning, these techniques challenge the reader's traditional passivity. In this encouragement of audience "grass roots activism," the narrative forms (as well as the content) of these texts embody feminist theory and foster feminist praxis. Finally, regardless of the contrasts in their aspirations for a feminist future, these authors all include a different, non-combative humorous sensibility in their works. While each envisions a non-sexist society that is still struggling to obtain or preserve its rights, humor is not depicted as one of its destructive weapons. Russ employs savage satire and irony in *The Female Man,* but—as she herself observes in that novel's envoi—the realization of her feminist ambitions will make her text incomprehensible. While this remark refers primarily to the ravaging sexism her work depicts, it may also be interpreted as a comment on the ultimate anachronism of its (currently) justifiably scathing tone. Beyond their commitment to sexual equity, one of the few, underlying "new Truths" these diverse feminist texts share is the desire and respect for the potential healing powers of humor.

4

The Futures of Feminist Discourse

The universe is made of stories,
not of atoms.

....

I am working out the vocabulary of my silence.

....

Who will speak these days,
if not I,
if not you.[1]

This excerpt from Muriel Rukeyser's poem "The Speed of Darkness" metaphorically conveys the transactive nature of much contemporary feminist speculative fiction.[2] Writing within a genre whose very reading protocols may prepare the reader to distance her or himself from conventional realities, the authors discussed in the preceding chapters employ SF's potential to "defamiliarize" the known towards some overtly polemical ends.[3] They not only question sex roles, gender identity, and sexual stereotypes in their "re/visions" of traditional literary motifs but also extend their analyses of the "constructed" nature of human identity to include more encompassing social and epistemological critiques. For example, the communal social structures of *The Kin of Ata, From the Legend of Biel*'s Lir, *The Female Man*'s Whileaway, *The Wanderground*'s Hill Women, and *Woman on the Edge of Time*'s Mattapoisett subvert both the patriarchal nuclear family and the capitalist work ethic; *Call Me Ishtar* and *The Passion of New Eve* question the traditional divisions between history and myth. Premised on conventionally "fantastic" events, all of the texts I have examined in this study suggest that the immutable laws of nature, often cited in support of sexual bias, may themselves be fictive constructs subject to revision.[4]

This suggestion allies these texts with implications currently being derived from new research in physics; to paraphrase Rukeyser, we have indeed begun to realize that the universe is figuratively made of changing stories *about* atoms, rather than literally *of* such illusory, discrete particles themselves. Furthermore, the biases of the "teller" may influence the scope and proportions of any multi-galactic paradigm or "tale." Commenting on post-Einsteinian physics, itself a field premised on the "fantastic" speculations of a few individuals, Fritjof Capra notes that the expectations of researchers have often affected their results. Seeking the basic building-blocks of sub-atomic particles, such researchers have observed wave-like behavior when they *expected* to discover waves; however, they have found discrete particles when those were their goal.[5] Or, as another post-Einsteinian scientist has written, "What we observe is not nature itself, but nature exposed to our method of questioning."[6] According to current scientific theory, then, the physical universe is composed not of waves *or* of particles, but of something "more than both."[7] This "undifferentiated reality," like the Eastern mystical states of "enlightenment" to which some avante-garde theorists compare it,[8] is difficult (if not impossible) to verbalize for several reasons: first, it is conceptually antithetical to the West's classically logical, "either-or" mentality; secondly, lanaguage, a symbolic system, is necessarily at odds with such non-dualistic lived experience; and, finally, any understanding or model of a system implicitly involves giving up some other ways of conceiving of it.[9] (Within this vision of the new physics of flux and uncertainty, the discipline of physics itself is merely another necessarily limited and distorting symbolic system.[10] It is, in Rukeyser's words, a "vocabulary of... silence" rather than of adequate or eloquent expression.)

This fluid reconfiguration of perceived physical reality, validating temporal simultaneity and spatial relativity, is redolent of the "feminine consciousness" deliberately articulated by such earlier twentieth century women writers as Virginia Woolf, Dorothy Richardson, and Rosamund Lehmann.[11] Significantly, it also parallels the dynamic challenges that (among other alternative gestalts) current feminist theory and praxis offer to "phallogocentric" Western thought.[12] This dominant tradition, which posits biological or phallus-bearing man as the locus of a world fully comprehendable through linear logic and its symbolic representation in the word ("logos") is a static and hierarchical one.[13] Many of the texts I have examined deny the capability of this tradition to convey their meanings; for their authors, such conventional discourse is merely another "vocabulary of... silence." Advocates of feminist androgyny, however, most forcefully challenge this phallogocentric tradition. While proponents of gynocentric essentialism invert the ontological premises of androcentric essentialism, they too accept the dualism, the "either-or" mentality, of such physiological premises. They implicitly work within a comparably circumscribed and therefore distortingly symbolic model of reality. Rather than promulgating a dynamic, phenomenological view of the universe comparable to that of the new physics, such theorists as Hélène Cixous and Luce Irigaray valorize a woman-centered but nonetheless ontological—and hence symbolically re-presentable— framework. Such conflation of symbolic with lived experience has also characterized Western patriarchy's similarly essentialist, androcentric versions of androgyny, posited in necessarily hermaphroditic or epicine figures. It is the ability to separate (or hold in equilibrium) symbol and "incongruous" actuality, to move beyond both fictive categories of human experience (wave or particle, male or female) to something potentially "more than both" that characterizes the viewpoint I have designated "feminist androgyny."

My study of diverse speculative fictions has confirmed my perceptions of feminist androgyny as a literary force as well as a philosophical construct. It has also, however, surprisingly indicated some ways in which this viewpoint and its seeming ideological opposite, gynocentric essentialism, are allied through common feminist praxis. (The opposition of gynocentric essentialism to feminist androgyny is, after all, yet another inherently misleading symbolic model.) The connection between these theoretical poles of this particular spectrum of ideological feminisms occurs within the narrative techniques employed, albeit to different degrees, by each of the authors whose works I have discussed. Each of these authors challenges the traditionally static, hierarchical relationship among author, text, and reader fostered by our dominant, phallogocentric Western tradition. They replace the one-directional, linear exchange of a "finished product" from knowledgeable, active writer to uninformed, passive reader with a fundamentally different and dynamic *process*.

Regardless of the particular feminist ideology she advocates, each of the authors I discuss employs narrative techniques that engage active reader involvement in the de/construction of textual meaning. These techniques include complex, at times unreliable narration; plot devices and metaphoric systems that invert "fact" and "fiction"; unconventional typography and graphic design; dialectical and associative narrative structures; and atypically heroic or multiple protagonists. They also include neologisms (both gender-free and gender-specific); subversive humor; interpolation of incremental or contrapuntal embedded discourse to reinforce didactic aims; and omission of narrative closure. Rather than privileging themselves as author/ities whose works contain inviolable, immutable "truth," these writers of diverse speculative fictions posit themselves as collaborators—along with the reader—in the creation of a potentially "multiple" literary work. This authorial stance merges the feminist politic of "grass-roots activism" with the original meanings of text as a "woven" fabric or structure.[14]

A significant number of contemporary, overtly political women writers work within this radical definition of textuality, in which warp and woof are formed by socially-conditioned reader as well as "interested" author.[15] Perhaps coincidentally, several of the texts I discuss actually employ the metaphors of weaving to convey the complexities of constructing "truth" or "reality": in *Call Me Ishtar*, Rhoda Lerman describes the ways in which the "polyester" fiber of patriarchal technology has obscured women's myth, folklore, and matriarchal religions—memories of "the luminous threads . . . of the legendary white mare of Ireland" (I, p. 2). Ursula K. Le Guin in *The Left Hand of Darkness* peripherally terms Faxe, the humanoid locus of psychic energies, a "Weaver" (LH, p. 67). In *From the Legend of Biel,* the wise elder Kaj-Palmir is both "Wizard of Time" *and* "Weaver," and the reader is warned that, while "EQUILIBRIUM IS A CARPET RICH/ IN COLOR, INTRICATE IN DESIGN," what we have experienced while reading this narrative "IS NOT THE CARPET, NOT EVEN/ THE LOOM, OR THE DIZZY/ WEAVER— BUT THE FIBERS,/ STILL ON THE PLANTS IN THE/ FIELDS" (B, p. 331, my emphasis). It is therefore our responsibility as active readers to "weave" these fibers into the coherent, stable, and potentially luminous whole that is our lives. Similarly, in *The Wanderground* the Hill Women's shared stories become "the weaving of an intricate narrative" that ultimately "belong[s]... to each one there" (W, p. 190). This common metaphoric system allies these works with other contemporary feminist fictions, such as E.M. Broner's utopian novel *A Weave of Women,* which similarly suggest that the fabric of our lives is in our own hands rather than those of the gods.[16] Furthermore, in light of previously-noted correspondences among the open-ended mental patterns promulgated by the new physics, Eastern mysticism, and some feminist theory, it is interesting—if highly speculative—to note yet another metaphoric correspondence among these three superficially diverse fields: the practice of Buddhism, its *tantra,* literally means "to weave" in Sanskrit.[17] And yet, there are significant differences in the degree of feminist praxis (the *tantra,* if you will) as well as in the kind of feminist theory deployed in the works I have examined.

Some of these texts are more unconventional than others. The ones that are most innovative in their narrative strategies, that call most strongly upon the reader to de/construct their meaning(s), are also among those which most forcefully advocate feminist androgyny: June Arnold's *Applesauce,* Mary Staton's *From the Legend of Biel,* and Joanna Russ's *The Female Man.* These novels *consistently* violate sequential chronology, subvert discrete characterization, defy linear or authoritative narration, and question typographical and design conventions. In contrast, the other works analyzed in preceding chapters adhere more frequently to phallogocentric narrative norms: they may contain extended passages in which sequential chronology *is* observed *(The Kin of Ata, Woman on the Edge of Time);* present characters who are *not* questionably doubled or multiple *(A Sea Change, The Wanderground);* employ narration which *is* seemingly reliable, if not linear *(The Wanderground);* or only *minimally* question typographical or layout formats *(A Sea Change; The Passion of New Eve; Woman on the Edge of Time).* While I do not wish to overgeneralize from my observations, the "volatile" text which lends itself readily to de/constructive readings seems particularly well-suited to the presentation and inculcation of "undifferentiated" human potential—in other words, of feminist androgyny.

Jacques Derrida, a leading exponent and practitioner of deconstruction, in fact describes this method of literary analysis in terms that might also characterize the theoretical construct of feminist androgyny. According to Derrida, the deconstructor's

> task is to dismantle the metaphysical and rhetorical structures at work in (the text), not in order to reject or discard them, but to reinscribe them in another way. [These structures are usually binary opposites such as] subject/other, identity/difference, and male/female [in which] one of the two terms controls the other.... holds the superior position. To deconstruct the opposition is first... to overthrow the hierarchy.... In the next phase of deconstruction, this reversal must be displaced [by] the irruptive emergence of a new "concept," a concept which no longer allows itself to be understood in terms of the previous regime.[18]

The binary oppositions and hierarchies that Derrida locates textually are also characteristic of the polarized gender roles and androcentric biases of Western patriarchy. Thus, the first phase of de/constructive reading (and, implicitly, of texts which invite such readings) is comparable to feminism's most fundamental challenges to patriarchal sexism: "[t]o deconstruct the opposition... to overthrow the hierarchy." It is "in the next phase of deconstruction" that the specific connections between feminist androgyny and this method of literary analysis become clear.

The correction of binary imbalance *without* the subsequent instatement of its hierarchical inverse is what fundamentally distinguishes feminist androgyny from gynocentric essentialism. The latter ideology, which merely inverts the ontological premises of androcentric essentialism, remains a concept which still can "be understood in terms of the previous regime." It is equally essentialist and still defines "woman" in relationship to biologial "man." Similarly, it is the "irruptive emergence of a new 'concept'" which is no longer congruent with previous "terms" or symbols which separates feminist androgyny from traditional versions of androgyny, with their overemphases on symbolic representation and patriarchal biases. This "irruptive" disjuncture also characterizes the relationship between the new physics and the previous Newtonian, mechanistic model of the universe. The "principle of uncertainty" now predominant in our scientific world-view directly contradicts the vision of a stable, fully and precisely comprehendable universe that had existed before Max Planck's and Albert Einstein's early twentieth century speculations.[19] The universe thus can no longer be symbolically represented in traditional terms as a perfect mechanism to be objectively and *finally* known or mastered. Like Eastern mystics, scientists now maintain a dynamic vision of the universe that contradicts the pragmatic principles underlying so much of Western, patriarchal civilization.

What, then, are the implications of these observations about feminist diversity, speculative fiction (and scientific speculation), and deconstruction? Although, in writing this conclusion, I was eager to see if women writers with overtly dissimilar feminist beliefs had indeed employed literary practices and forms uniquely congruent with their own particular ideologies, I have not found strong evidence of such congruence. Some advocates of feminist androgyny do indeed write texts which foster a reading protocol that adumbrates their beliefs; however, even writers such as Sally Miller Gearhart, who militantly advocates gynocentric essentialism, and others—such as Rhoda Lerman, Angela Carter, and Dorothy Bryant—whose beliefs fall somewhere between the specified ideological poles, utilize some of the same narrative techniques. And Marge Piercy, herself a strong proponent of feminist androgyny, does not employ as many of these techniques as other feminist advocates of the androgynous vision—Arnold, Staton, or Russ. There is a difference in degree but not in kind among the transactive narrative practices of these diverse feminist authors. This finding confirms the observations of other literary critics who also identify deconstruction as a literary technique employed in the actual writings of Continental proponents of gynocentric essentialism, as well as in critical "readings" by these proponents.[20] Furthermore, while some of the authors I have discussed incorporate, in Hélène Cixous's words, efforts to "write through their bodies," to "write woman" into their texts,[21] these efforts are not made solely by those writers ideologically closest to the gynocentric vision. A comparison of the gynocentric *Wanderground* with the primarily androgynous *Woman on the Edge of Time* or *The Female Man* illuminates this point of textual pluralism.

The *Wanderground*'s cyclical, rather than linear, narrative structure, with characters emerging from and then merging back into the fabric of the text, does resemble some of the prescriptions for *"l'écriture feminine"*—that is, authentically female writing—made by such gynocentric theorists as Cixous and Luce Irigaray. This structure is closer to the ebb and flow of the pervasive female sexuality that they valorize than it is to the abrupt "rise and fall" of a phallic paradigm.[22] Gearhart's sensory neologisms also reflect an emphasis on corporeality—although not necessarily female corporeality. Cixous and Irigaray claim that phallogocentric "principles of identity, sameness, and visibility" have precluded the representation of woman both in and by conventional Western discourse.[23] Irigaray believes that these valorized principles stem directly from the dominant position of biological man in Western society; she asserts that "all Western discourse presents a certain isomorphism with the masculine sex: the privilege of unity, form of the self, of the visible, of the specularizable, of the erection."[24] Gynocentric discourse, she hypothesizes, consequently would correctively reverse this hierarchy and express authentic female physiology and experience—particularly its traditionally non-representable vulval multiplicity and diffuseness.[25] Yet Marge Piercy's vision of androgynous Mattapoisett in *Woman on the Edge of Time* fulfills some of these essentialist prescriptions. It incorporates sensory neologisms similar to Gearhart's and might, in its doubling and tripling of characters, be said to be "multiple," if not precisely cyclical in structure. *The Female Man*'s associative intertwining of four separate continuums is similarly non-linear and multiple. Thus, as manifested in feminist speculative fiction, neither feminist androgyny nor gynocentric essentialism is expressed through literary practices or formats that are *exclusively* its own. Instead, their proponents have in common elements of fundamental, empowering feminist praxis—the engagement of active individual (reader) involvement in the de/construction of meaning.

If, then, this "literature of the future" *is* an indicator of our own literary future, we may look forward to exciting textual pluralism rather than to ideological conformity—whether such conformity be to diverging feminist or traditionally patriarchal norms. And yet, any projections made for the future directions of feminist discourse must take into account marketplace factors affecting the publication and dissemination of such writing. As Hélène Wenzel notes in her critique of feminist discourse which seeks (unrealistically, she maintains) to embody a purely gynocentric vision, it is "[o]nly after women appropriate the real world" that we "will be capable of [truly] finding a woman's 'imaginary.'"[26] (This observation amplifies *The Female Man*'s ironic envoi, in which the author/narrator looks forward to the day when this radical feminist text will be obsolete.) The recent history of speculative fiction reflects the applicability of Wenzel's comment to the possibly endangered continuation and proliferation of feminist experimentation within this field.

Suzy McKee Charnas was in the mid-1970s for several years unable to find a publisher for *Motherlines* just because this novel, the sequel to an already well-received work, contained no male characters. Publishers feared that there would be little interest in such a "woman-only" future vision.[27] Subsequent reader response to *Motherlines* and the expanding sales of other overtly feminist fictions, including the reissue of earlier, "lost" or forgotten texts such as *Herland,* have confounded those first, chauvinist misgivings. But similar attitudes continue to influence some publication decisions. Two of the most innovative texts examined in this study—Mary Staton's *From the Legend of Biel* and Joanna Russ's *The Female Man*—are currently out of print,[28] while *Applesauce* and *The Wanderground* were available only due to the editorial and marketing efforts of Daughters, Inc. and Persephone Press. These two women-run small presses were specifically devoted to the publication and proliferation of women's writing; as one might imagine, they did not have the financial scope and stability of larger, mass-market publishers. (In fact, Daughters, Inc. went out of business as this study was being written and Persephone Press closed soon after.) Dorothy Bryant has "solved" the problems of publishers' rejecting or distributors' precipitously remaindering her works by forming her own publishing firm—Ata Books! She is able to support this enterprise by advertising, packing, and distributing its wares herself—*and* by drawing upon income from other, unrelated jobs.[29]

The impact of marketplace factors does not, moreover, end with a firm's rejection or early warehousing of a feminist text. As Andrea Dworkin notes in her author's afterword to *Womanhating,* a philosophical critique written in 1974 and published by the mainstream firm of E.P. Dutton, such traditional publishers are not always receptive to the additional typesetting expenses, let alone the controversial and therefore economically risky nature, of graphic innovations characteristic of such works as *From the Legend of Biel.* Dworkin ironically titles this account of her losing battle with E.P. Dutton to omit capital letters and employ idiosyncratic punctuation in *Womanhating* "The Great Punctuation Typography Struggle."[30] The implications of such editorial intrusion for possible literary experimentation are evident in the history of Samuel R. Delany's *Babel-17:* it is only in its 1982 reissue that this 1966 SF novel featuring a strong, independent woman protagonist has been printed with the interpolated split-page format that Delany had originally specified. (This format is briefly used by June Arnold in *Applesauce.*) In 1966, Delany, now a prominent writer, did not have enough "marketability" to debate his publisher's conservatism.[31] Contemporary feminist inquiry and literary innovation are thus still potentially subject to the traditional Western ethos in decisively pragmatic as well as covertly ideological ways.

However, the dynamics of the SF field itself may operate to inhibit such potential "censorship" of feminist theory and praxis. The innovative or radical SF author need not combat such prejudice alone—or necessarily make her stand within the traditional market-place arena. The contemporary SF subculture provides a concrete network of options to traditional artistic isolation and conventional avenues of publication;[32] these alternatives are still often only theoretical constructs or infrequent, isolated actualities for practitioners of other literary forms. This subculture supports interactive, actual or potentially non-hierarchical social structures that prefigure some current feminist theory. For example, Carolyn Burke, describing the transactive relationship among reader, text, and author inculcated by Irigaray in her own unconventional, theoretical writings, sees in such feminist discourse "a complicity between reader and writer not unlike that which may occur in the analytic situation, between a nonsubordinate analysand and a nonauthoritarian analyst. Reading [such discourse] is like taking part in a process in which neither participant is certain of the outcome.... Reserving a space for the reader, [such texts offer] 'the site of a listening attention,' or what the analyst provides for the analysand."[33] This analogy is an illuminating one for several reasons. First, it specifically touches upon the speculative re/visions of psychological theory and analysis made (albeit to different degrees) by such writers as Dorothy Bryant and Mary Staton; secondly, it describes the active reading protocol that SF in general and feminist SF in particular both implicitly and explicitly establish for the reader; and finally and most relevantly, it captures the interactive relationships of SF fans with the production and dissemination of this genre.

Recent studies confirm the continuation and proliferation of SF fans' interaction with writers, editors, agents, and publishers of speculative fiction. This interaction occurs not only at numerous local, national and international conferences held each year but through SF publications ("fanzines") as well as through commercially-subsidized magazines ("prozines") devoted to this field and its multi-media offshoots. Each year in the United States writing workshops are held at which aspiring authors may meet established ones, and a significant number of professional SF writers were originally fans active in this SF subculture.[34] At Worldcon, a yearly international fan conference, enthusiastic readers of speculative fiction vote Hugo Awards for the best SF works of the year. (The other major award for creative work in SF is the Nebula, bestowed annually by the Science Fiction Writers of America, a professional writers' organization.) According to sociologist Linda Fleming, there is more interaction between consumers and producers of SF—whether artistic or commercial—than in any other literary field today.[35]

The history of specific works and authors of feminist speculative fiction during the last decade supports this observation. Readers of such woman-focused fanzines as *The Witch and the Chameleon* and *Janus* knew of *Motherlines'* inhospitable reception by potential publishers soon after Charnas began her efforts to market this work.[36] One can only wonder about the positive impact of this printed, inter/national commentary about publishers' foibles and prejudices on the ultimate editorial decision to accept *Motherlines*. More certainly, the comments and questions raised in such fanzines about the feminist directions (or lack of direction) taken by specific authors *have* directly influenced some of these writers. Marion Zimmer Bradley acknowledges that her overtly feminist novel *The Shattered Chain*—which contains discussions of celibacy, lesbianism, and conventional heterosexuality as equally viable, alternate lifestyles—developed in response to such fanzine and fan conference discussions of her work. Bradley has since collaborated with SF readers (who call themselves "Friends of Darkover," the name of her future world) in the writing of two commercially-published volumes of Darkover-focused short stories.[37] Fanzines provide an outlet for first publication of original SF as well as for exchange of information and analysis of the field; they are thus grass-roots versions of the woman-run and centered small presses that have sustained so much feminist inquiry and reclamation of women's history during the last decade. Feminist fanzines and conferences, similarly responding to this second wave of feminism, have also proliferated in the SF subculture during this period.[38]

The field of speculative fiction, then, currently supports social structures that are both implicitly and explicitly receptive to active reader involvement with the text—its artistic conception, commercial production, mass distribution, and popular and critical reception. While these structures do not control the course of speculative fiction (as the current publication status of *From the Legend of Biel* and *The Female Man* attests), they have influenced this field's development and have the potential to shape this development even further. If readers respond affirmatively to the textual and social challenges proffered by feminism, its diverse theories and common praxis, we may strengthen and expand the current outlets for visions of a different, non-sexist "reality." We may actively sustain speculative fictions that question the conventional wisdom, paradigms, and hierarchies that not only feminist inquiry but also the new physics has demonstrated to be value-laden and distortingly limited. As Muriel Rukeyser writes in her prophetic vision of a "universe...made of stories,/ not of atoms,"

> Who will speak these days,
> if not I,
> if not you.

Feminist theory validates the worth of each individual voice in such speech, while feminist literary praxis can foster such utterance. We "speak" each time we de/construct a complex, multiple text just as surely as we "speak" each time we attempt to infuse the SF subculture with even more feminist energy and goals.

Speculative fiction is thus significant "new space"[39] for the continued merger of such feminist theory and praxis for several reasons. Its generic "cognitive estrangement" of the audience from conventional reality prepares readers to question biases inherent in any dominant world-view, while its current sociological status inculcates individual and small group interaction in all phases of its production. As the works I have analyzed in this study demonstrate—and as the new physics' transubstantiation of matter and energy would attest—"[a] literary work [may once again be perceived] not so much [as] an object...as a unit of force whose power is exerted upon the world in a particular direction."[40] Feminists have much to gain by voicing the direction(s) of our choice.

Notes

Introduction

1. Monique Wittig, *Les Guérillères*, trans. David Le Vay (1969; New York: Avon Books, 1971), p. 89.

2. Speculative fiction, a term frequently used by author-critic Samuel R. Delany, subsumes both science fiction and fantasy. According to Delany, "science fiction" depicts what has not yet occurred, while "fantasy" depicts what—due to known physical laws—can never occur ("About Five Thousand Seven Hundred and Fifty Words," in *The Jewel-Hinged Jaw* [Elizabethtown, New York: Dragon Press, 1971], pp. 43-44). As women's studies research and the new physics indicate that such conventional concepts of im/possibility are limited and value-laden, I employ "speculative fiction" or the ambiguous acronym "SF" as often as I can.

3. The phrase "social science fiction" is widely used by speculative fiction historians and critics to describe the proportionately greater use by SF writers in the 1960s, 1970s, and 1980s of anthropology, sociology, economics, and linguistics. These so-called "soft" sciences replace or augment the preceding decades' focus on technological or "hard" sciences as plot elements. While some scholars link "soft" or "social science fiction" with women authors, Joanna Russ points out that ignorance of women writers' historical role in English language SF and patriarchal stereotypes are responsible for this overgeneralization: by androcentric, phallocentric definition, men are "hard" when women are "soft." See "Reflections on Science Fiction: An Interview with Joanna Russ," in *Building Feminist Theory: Essays from Quest, a feminist quarterly* (New York: Longman, 1981), p. 248.

   Doris Lessing has begun to write "social science fiction" in her "Canopus in Argos: Archives" series (to date, *Shikasta* [NY: Alfred A. Knopf, 1979]; *The Marriages Between Zones Three, Four, and Five* [NY: Alfred A. Knopf, 1980]; and *The Sirian Experiments* [NY: Alfred A. Knopf, 1980]; *The Making of the Representative for Planet Eight* [NY: Alfred A. Knopf, 1982]; and *Documents Relating to the Sentimental Agents in the Volyen Empire* [NY: Alfred A. Knopf, 1983]). This study's focus, however, is on less prominent authors who have consistently written popular speculative fictions. I concentrate on these authors because, proportionately, they have not received the critical attention that an established, mainstream author such as Lessing has and continues to receive. (For discussion of Lessing's science fiction, see Marie L. Ahern, "Why Doris Lessing's Move Into Science Fiction," Doris Lessing Session, MLA Convention, Houston, 1980; Judith Kegan Gardiner, "Evil, Apocalypse, and Feminist SF," Science Fiction Section, MMLA Convention, Oconomowoc, WI, 1981; and Betsy Draine, "Competing Codes in *Shikasta*," Doris Lessing Section, MLA Convention, Houston, 1980.)

4. See, for example, *New French Feminisms: An Anthology,* ed. Elaine Marks and Isabelle de Courtivron (Amherst: University of Massachusetts, 1980) for an overview of Continental feminist diversity, which is also relevant to the works I discuss.

5. June Singer, *Androgyny: Toward a New Theory of Sexuality* (Garden City, New York: Anchor/Doubleday, 1976), pp. 39-40 also makes this point.

6. Singer, p. 218.

7. Further specific references for the androgynous vision and for gynocentric essentialism will be given in the body and main notes of the text.

Chapter 1

1. Lucy Lippard, "Introduction: Changing Since *Changing,*" *From the Center: Feminist Essays on Women's Art* (New York: E.P. Dutton, 1976), p. 4.

2. See, for example, June Singer's *Androgyny: Toward a New Theory of Sexuality* (Garden City, N.Y.: Anchor/Doubleday, 1976); Carolyn G. Heilbrun's *Toward a Recognition of Androgyny* (New York: Harper and Row, 1973); and Julia Kristeva's *About Chinese Women,* trans. Anita Barrows (New York: Urizen Books, 1977). Much psychological research currently focuses on sex roles and sexual stereotyping. See, for example, Alexandra G. Kaplan and Joan P. Bear, eds., *Beyond Sex-Role Stereotypes: Readings Toward a Psychology of Androgyny* (Boston: Little Brown, 1976).

3. Julia Kristeva, "*La femme, ce n'est jamais ça,*" ["Woman Can Never Be Defined"], in *New French Feminisms: An Anthology,* ed. Elaine Marks and Isabelle de Courtivron (Amherst: Univ. of Massachusetts Press, 1980), p. 137.

4. See, for example, Hélène Cixous's "The Laughter of the Medusa," trans. Keith Cohen and Paula Cohen, *Signs,* 1 (1976), 875-93; Mary Daly's *Gyn/Ecology: The Metaethics of Radical Feminism* (Boston: Beacon Press, 1978); and Susan Griffin's *Woman and Nature: The Roaring Inside Her* (New York: Harper and Row, 1978).

5. Significant recent works in this area include Elaine Morgan, *The Descent of Women* (New York: Bantam, 1976); Elizabeth Gould Davis, *The First Sex* (New York: Putnam, 1971); Merlin Stone, *When God Was a Woman* (New York: Harvest/Harcourt Brace, 1976); Julia O'Faolain and Laura Martines, *Not in God's Image* (London: Maurice Temple White, 1973); Naomi R. Goldenberg, *Changing of the Gods: Feminism and the End of Traditional Religions* (Boston: Beacon Press, 1979); and Adrienne Rich, *Of Woman Born: Motherhood as Experience and Institution* (New York: W.W. Norton, 1976). Periodicals devoted exclusively to women and religion include *Woman Spirit* and *Lady-Unique-Inclination-of-the-Night;* both *Chrysalis* and *Heresies* have published issues focusing on this topic.

6. This transformation in viewpoint was the framework for Marion Vlastos Libby's discussion of *My Mother, Myself* and *Of Woman Born* at the 1979 MLA Conference in San Francisco; Mary Daly has also written of her altered perspective toward androgyny (as cited by Maurine Renville, et al., "Women's Survival Catalog: Women's Spirituality," *Chrysalis,* no. 6 [1978], p. 88).

7. Lois Gould, *A Sea Change* (New York: Avon, 1976). All subsequent references will be made parenthetically in the text.

8. Rhoda Lerman, *Call Me Ishtar* (Garden City, N.Y.: Doubleday, 1973). All subsequent references will be made parenthetically in the text.

9. Angela Carter, *The Passion of New Eve* (London: Arrow Books, 1978). All subsequent references will be made parenthetically in the text.

10. June Arnold, *Applesauce* (1966; New York: Daughters, Inc., 1977). All subsequent references will be made parenthetically in the text.

11. In this short story, a wife suddenly finds herself in her husband's body, conversing with his friends on their way to work. This experience gives the character new insight into male views of "the ladies" and also subliminally leaves her husband with new perceptions. In *The Charlotte Perkins Gilman Reader*, ed. Ann J. Lane (New York: Pantheon, 1980), pp. 32-38.

12. I omit Kafka's "Metamorphosis" here because its conflicts are not rooted in the sexual politics of a specific social milieu.

13. See, for further illustrations of this point, Alta's "Pretty" and Una Starnard's "The Mask of Beauty" in *Woman in a Sexist Society: Studies in Power and Powerlessness,* ed. Vivian Gornick and Barbara K. Moran (New York: Basic Books, 1971), pp. 35-36 and 187-203, respectively. Cixous also comments upon the past alienation of women from our own bodies if these were unconventional in any way.

14. Lippard, "Making Up: Role-Playing and Transformation in Women's Art," in *From the Center,* pp. 103-04. Recent articles in New York's *The Village Voice* confirm that this movement is still an active one.

15. Lippard, "Making Up," p. 105.

16. Lippard, "Making Up," pp. 106-08.

17. Carol Christ, *Diving Deep and Surfacing: Women Writers on the Spiritual Quest* (Boston: Beacon Press, 1980), p. 4.

18. Significant critical works on feminist SF, which has blossomed in the last decade, include Pamela Annas, "New Worlds, New Words: Androgyny in Feminist SF," *Science Fiction Studies,* 5 (1978), 143-56; Mary Kenny Badami, "A Feminist Critique of Science Fiction," *Extrapolation,* 18 (1974), 6-19; Joanna Russ, "Images of Women in Science Fiction," rpt. in *Images of Women in Fiction: Feminist Perspectives,* revised ed., ed. Susan Koppelman Cornillon (Bowling Green: Popular Press, 1973), pp. 79-94; Joanna Russ, "Outta Space: Women Write Science Fiction," *Ms.,* January 1976, pp. 109-11; Susan Wood, "Women and Science Fiction," *Algol/Starship,* Winter 1978-79, pp. 9-18; Carol Pearson, "Women's Fantasies and Feminist Utopias," *Frontiers: A Journal of Women's Studies,* 2 (Fall 1977), 50-61; Rachel Blau du Plessis, "The Feminist Apologues of Lessing, Piercy, and Russ," *Frontiers,* 4 (Spring 1979), 1-8; Pamela Sargent, "Women and Science Fiction," introduction to *Women of Wonder* (New York: Vintage, 1974); *Future Females: A Critical Anthology,* ed. Marleen S. Barr (Bowling Green: Popular Press, 1981); and *The Feminine Eye: Science Fiction and the Women Who Write It,* ed. Tom Staicar (New York: Frederick Ungar, 1982). In her recent article, "Frankenstein's Daughters: The Problems of the Feminine Image in Science Fiction," *Mosaic,* 13 (Spring/Summer 1980), 15-27, Patricia Monk treats the subject in a superficial, distorting manner. Both *Science-Fiction Studies* and *Extrapolation* have devoted issues to women SF writers; *Women's Studies International Forum* has an upcoming issue devoted to feminist SF. Moreover, feminist SF is the focus of numerous fanzines and fan conferences and is currently being offered as a course by numerous women's studies programs. See Wood's article for bibliography.

19. Judith Barry and Sandy Flitterman, "Textual Strategies—The Politics of Art Making," *Screen,* 21 (Summer 1980), 37. Barry and Flitterman further refine this classification, noting

four categories. Within the essentialist perspective, they distinguish the creators/advocates of women's crafts from the more theoretically oriented artists; moving toward the androgynous end of the spectrum, they also include non-feminist artists—"women artists who maintain that they are people who 'happen' to be women" (p. 42).

20.   Barry and Flitterman, p. 43.

21.   Elaine Hedges and Ingrid Wendt, *In Her Own Image: Women Working in the Arts* (Old Westbury, N.Y.: The Feminist Press, 1980), pp. 295-98.

22.   Elaine Showalter, *A Literature of Their Own: British Women Novelists from Bronte to Lessing* (Princeton: Princeton Univ. Press, 1977), p. 264.

23.   Heilbrun, p. 155.

24.   Virginia Woolf, *Orlando* (1928; New York: Harvest/Harcourt Brace, 1956), p. 138. All subsequent references will be made parenthetically in the text.

25.   Claudine Herrmann, from *"Les coordonnées féminines: espace et temps"* ["Women in Space and Time"], in *"Les voleuses de langue"* ["The Tongue Snatchers"], in *New French Feminisms*, p. 171.

26.   Ellen Morgan, "The Feminist Novel of Androgynous Fantasy," *Frontiers*, 2 (Fall 1977), 42.

27.   In addition to provoking Heilbrun and Showalter's disagreement, *Orlando* has been perceived variously as a parody of literary biography, a *roman à clef*, and a social comedy.

28.   In its focus on a Black man as a rapist, Gould's work is also potentially racist; Susan Griffin notes in "Rape: The All-American Crime," *Female Psychology: The Emerging Self*, ed. Sue Cox (Chicago: Science Research Associates, 1976), pp. 301-03, the exaggeration of such occurrences in the racist "white mythos" (p. 302).

29.   The classic exposition of this stereotype is Sherry Ortner, "Is Female to Male as Nature Is to Culture?" in *Woman, Culture and Society*, ed. Michelle Zimbalist Rosaldo and Louise Lamphere (Stanford: Stanford Univ. Press, 1974), pp. 67-68.

30.   Barry and Flitterman, pp. 37-38.

31.   Recent books—such as Suzy Orbach, *Fat Is a Feminist Issue* (New York: Berkeley Books, 1978)—and articles—such as Deborah Larned Romano, "Eating Our Hearts Out," *Mother Jones*, June 1980, pp. 20-30, 60-63—analyze the androcentrism that underlies current standards of beauty, which emphasize male slenderness at the expense of female bodies. According to some authors, eating thus becomes a form of rebellion. The overweight protagonist of Margaret Atwood's *Lady Oracle* (New York: Simon and Schuster, 1976) initially rebels in this way.

32.   E.M. Broner, in "The Dirty Ladies: Earthy Writings of Contemporary American Women— Paley, Jong, Schor, and Lerman," *Regionalism and the Female Imagination*, 4 (1979), 34-43 discusses Lerman's humor. This article is the only substantial discussion of the novel I have been able to locate.

33.   Other feminist revisions of women's roles in fairy tales include Anne Sexton's *Transformations* (Boston: Houghton Mifflin, 1971); portions of Olga Broumas' *Beginning with O* (New Haven: Yale Univ. Press, 1977); and Joanna Russ's *Kittatiny, a Tale of Magic* (New York: Daughters, Inc., 1978), a tale aimed specifically at a juvenile audience.

34.   I am indebted for this analysis of male and female symbols in relation to the Jungian quest for self to Annis Pratt, her courses at University of Wisconsin-Madison and her *Archetypal Patterns in Women's Fiction* (Bloomington: Indiana Univ. Press, 1981), pp. 174-75.

35. See Mary Daly's *Beyond God the Father: Towards a Philosophy of Women's Liberation* (Boston: Beacon Press, 1973) and Phyllis Trible, "Eve and Adam: Genesis 2-3 Reread" in *Womanspirit Rising: A Feminist Reader in Religion,* ed. Carol P. Christ and Judith Plaskow (New York: Harper and Row, 1979), pp. 74-83.

36. This theme of man as an unwelcome, evolutionary aberration—at times the result of harmful radiation—is current in some works of lesbian separatist speculative fiction. See, for example, Donna J. Young, *Retreat: As It Was!* (Weatherbuty Lake, Mo.: Naiad Press, 1979).

37. See *Women and Psychoanalysis: Dialogues on Psychoanalytic Views of Femininity,* ed. Jean Strouse (New York: Dell, 1974) for an overview of Freud's essentialist views on femininity and for diverse feminist commentaries on his influential theories.

38. See Stone's *When God Was a Woman* and Goldenberg's *Changing of the Gods* (both cited earlier) and Charlene Spretnak, *Lost Goddesses of Early Greece* (Berkeley: Moon Books, 1978), among others, for detailed accounts of matriarchal religions and their overthrow.

39. Again, see Stone and Goldenberg. Adrienne Rich's discussion of matriarchal religion and myth, pp. 56-127, in *Of Woman Born* (New York: Norton, 1976), similarly details the loss of mothers' autonomy and power with the advent of dominant patriarchal structure. Esther Harding, in *Women's Mysteries: Ancient and Modern* (New York: G.P. Putnam's Sons, 1971), discusses the autonomy, rather than circumscribed existence, of "virgins" in pre-patriarchy.

40. See C.G. Jung's *Psychological Reflections* (New York: Bollingen, 1953); *Psychology and Symbol* (Garden City, N.Y.: Anchor/Doubleday, 1958); *The Basic Writings of C.G. Jung* (New York: Modern Library, 1959); and *The Development of Personality* (New York: Bollingen, 1954) for fuller development of this point. See Annis Pratt's *Archetypal Patterns in Women's Fictions* and "Archetypal Approaches to the New Feminist Criticism," *Bucknell Review,* 21 (Spring 1973), 163-94 for discussions of these theories in relation to women's literature.

41. See works by Jung cited above.

42. Angela Carter, *The Sadeian Woman and the Ideology of Pornography* (New York: Pantheon Books, 1978), p. 5.

43. See R.W.B. Lewis, *The American Adam: Innocence, Tragedy, and Tradition in the Nineteenth Century* (Chicago: Univ. of Chicago Press, 1955) for a discussion of this widely prevalent cultural image.

44. It is only recently that the corresponding image of woman, "Eve" in American society, has received significant critical or historical attention. See Judith Fryer, *The Faces of Eve: Woman in the 19th Century American Novel* (New York: Oxford Univ. Press, 1976) and Ernest Earnest, *The American Eve in Fact and Fiction* (Bloomington: Indiana Univ. Press, 1975).

45. Significant treatments of these romanticized images of women and men in classical Hollywood films include Molly Haskell, *From Reverence to Rape: The Treatment of Women in the Movies* (New York: Holt, Rinehart and Winston, 1974); Joan Mellon, *Women and Their Sexuality in the New Film* (New York: Horizon Press, 1973); Marjorie Rosen, *Popcorn Venus* (New York: Avon Books, 1973); and *Women and the Cinema: A Critical Anthology,* ed. Karyn Kay and Gerald Peary (New York: E.P. Dutton, 1977).

46. Jack Kerouac's *On the Road* (New York: Signet, 1955) is the prototype of this genre.

47. Other works of feminist fantasy that explore the concept of parthenogenesis include Donna J. Young's *Retreat: As It Was!;* Rochelle Singer, *The Demeter Flower* (New York: St. Martin's

Press, 1980); Suzy McKee Charnas, *Motherlines* (New York: Berkeley, 1978); and Joanna Russ, *The Female Man* (New York: Bantam, 1975).

48. The mythic rescue of a daughter by her mother is commented on by numerous works focusing on matriarchal religions and cultures. See bibliography listed in footnote 5.

49. These definitions of "Beulah" are found in *Webster's New 20th Century Dictionary of the English Language,* Unabridged 2nd Edition, and *The American Heritage Dictionary of the English Language.*

50. See Mary Ellmann, *Thinking About Women* (New York: Harcourt Brace Jovanovich, 1968) for a discussion of current conflicting female stereotypes.

51. Samuel R. Delany's speculative fiction, *Triton: An Ambiguous Heterotopia* (New York: Bantam, 1976) depicts an interesting variation of this situation. The protagonist Bron is socially and psychologically maladjusted because, in a future society free of sex roles or stereotypes, he is implicitly chauvinistic. No woman is passive or masochistic enough for him, and so he too transforms himself—albeit through fantastic future technology—into the "woman of his dreams."

52. This passage plays upon both Jean Paul Sartre's existentialist philosophy and Simone de Beauvoir's extension of it, her analysis of woman as immanent "other" to man's transcendent self, in *The Second Sex* (Paris, 1949; New York: Bantam, 1970).

53. Carter, *The Sadeian Woman,* p. 5.

54. This allusion to Melville's novella, with its narrator's misperception of people and events, is a comment upon both racial prejudice and the illusory nature of human experience.

55. Sartre, as cited and critiqued by Tzvetan Todorov, *The Fantastic: A Structural Approach to a Literary Genre,* trans. Richard Howard (Cleveland: The Press of Case Western Reserve Univ., 1973), p. 73.

56. Carol Pearson's "Toward a New Language, Consciousness, and Political Theory: The Utopian Novels of Dorothy Bryant, Mary Staton, and Marge Piercy" (unpublished paper delivered at 1979 MLA Conference in San Francisco) is one critical work that recognizes and critiques the use of the "new physics" by writers of feminist SF. Pearson draws upon such recent popularizations as Fritjof Capra, *The Tao of Physics* (New York: Bantam, 1977). A revised version of Pearson's essay appears in *Heresies,* No. 13 (1981), pp. 84-87; the same material is incorporated into a book she has coauthored with Katherine Pope, *The Female Hero in American and British Literature* (New York: R.R. Bowker, 1981).

57. In addition to the critical works focusing on traditional images of women in classical Hollywood cinema listed in footnote 43, several periodicals concentrate on women and film, notably *Jump Cut* and *Camera Obscura.* In actuality, Merle Oberon and Laurence Olivier starred in *Wuthering Heights;* Katherine Hepburn and June Allyson starred, respectively, in the 1930s and 1950s versions of *Little Women;* Merle Oberon played George Sand to Cornell Wilde's Chopin; and Vincent Price played Roderick Usher in the American version of Poe's story.

58. T.S. Eliot, "The Four Quartets," in *The Complete Poems and Plays 1909-50* (New York: Harcourt Brace and World, 1971), p. 129.

59. This observation parallels that of Annis Pratt about "the restorative power of women's fiction consist[ing] in a dialectical relationship between novel and audience.... The synthesis [occurs] in the mind of the reader, who, having participated in the narrative reenactment, must put its message into effect in her own life" (*Archetypal Patterns in Women's Fiction,* p. 177).

60. See Cixous for a discussion of this traditionally negative image of women which woman-centered artists have begun to redefine. Annis Pratt's " 'Aunt Jennifer's Tigers': Notes Towards A Preliterary History of Women's Archetypes," *Feminist Studies,* 4 (1978), 163-94 discusses some of the ways woman-oriented artists have begun to reclaim such images.

61. Pratt's comment, in *Archetypal Patterns,* that some feminist writers are interested in a "gynandrous" approach to life (p. 112) is applicable here. In *The Sadeian Woman,* Carter controversially suggests that pornography is a tool to achieve such understanding.

62. Esmé Dodderidge's *The New Gulliver* (New York: Taplinger Publishing, 1978), whose astronaut-protagonist crashes on a matriarchal planet, similarly reverses the import of the original parody. Jill Johnston's *Gullible's Travels* (New York: Links Books, 1974), detailing her experiences as a lesbian in patriarchal society, also ironically alludes to Swift's classic.

63. Morgan, p. 41.

64. Showalter, p. 264.

65. In the mid-1960s, popularizations of the "new physics" were not readily available; consequently, Arnold's protagonist believes in a stability that Carter's no longer does.

66. Marcia Holly's "Consciousness and Authenticity: Toward a Feminist Aesthetic," in *Feminist Literary Criticism: Explorations in Theory,* ed. Josephine Donovan (Lexington: Univ. of Kentucky Press, 1975), examines the value of "authenticity" as a criterion for feminist writers and readers (pp. 38-47).

67. Morgan (p. 44) assigns these characters similar roles. Because Morgan's discussion of the sexist denigration each character experiences is thorough and perceptive, I have omitted a detailed analysis of each "marriage."

68. Adrienne Rich, pp. 218-55, discusses the ramifications of patriarchal norms in mother-daughter relationships in detail. Nancy Chodorow's *The Reproduction of Mothering: Psychoanalysis and the Sociology of Gender* (Berkeley: Univ. of California, 1978) provides further theoretical background for this phenomenon.

69. See, for example, Cynthia Secor, "Androgyny: An Early Reappraisal," *Women's Studies,* 2 (1974), 161-69, and Daniel Harris, "Androgyny: The Sexist Myth in Disguise," *Women's Studies,* 2 (1974) 171-84. Naomi Goldenberg sees androgyny as a concept that poses dangers to women not only because it is usually androcentric but because it "retains an unrealistic, otherworldly quality" (p. 80).

70. Morgan, p. 43, interprets this image similarly.

71. Arnold's *The Cook and the Carpenter: A Novel by the Carpenter* (Plainfield, VT.: Daughters, Inc., 1973), does not employ gender pronouns at all. Arnold "explains" this practice on its unnumbered frontispiece: "Since the differences between men and women are so obvious to all, so impossible to confuse whether we are speaking of learned behavior or inherent characteristics, ordinary conversation or furious passion, work or intimate relationships, the author understands that it is no longer necessary to distinguish between men and women in this novel. I have therefore used one pronoun for both, trusting the reader to know which is which." "Na" is used in place of he or she, "nan" instead of him or her.

72. In "Metaphysical Feminism," Robin Morgan calls for feminist rethinking and reshaping of language to express women's needs and goals, in *Going Too Far: The Personal Chronicle of a Feminist* (New York: Random House, 1977), pp. 290-95. Julia P. Stanley and Susan J. Wolfe's feminist analysis of current linguistic and literary practice extends Morgan's points and provides Arnold's observations with a theoretical and historical context: "Toward a Feminist Aesthetic," *Chrysalis,* No. 6 (1978), pp. 57-71.

73.   Stanley and Wolfe, p. 67, identify discursive linearity as one aspect of patriarchal writing.

74.   Ellen Morgan, p. 44.

75.   Sandra M. Gilbert and Susan Gubar's discussion of the difficulties of previous women writers in appropriating and using such "authority" in relation to the creation of art—*The Madwoman in the Attic: The Woman Writer and the Nineteenth Century Literary Imagination* (New Haven: Yale Univ. Press, 1979), pp. 3-92—seems to me also an appropriate metaphor for the acculturated, inhibited and thereby "unauthorized" reader of an aesthetically, politically radical text. I do *not* believe that the ambiguity of these works' conclusions, so deliberately interwoven with themes and form throughout each text, is evidence of the writer's inability to assume authority.

76.   The radically educative potential of SF has been receiving increasing critical attention. Most recently, to my knowledge, Barbara Emrys made this point at a panel in "Feminist SF: Shaping the Future" at the April 1981 Great Lakes Women's Studies Association meeting in Mankato, Minn.

Chapter 2

1.   Robin Morgan, "Metaphysical Feminism" in *Going Too Far: A Personal Chronicle of a Feminist* (New York: Random House, 1977), p. 295.

2.   Roland Barthes characterizes undemanding, linear texts (as opposed to "writerly" texts which require active reader involvement to construct textual meanings) in this way in *S/Z: An Essay,* trans. Richard Miller (New York: Hill and Wang, 1974), pp. 3-4.

3.   Dorothy Bryant, *The Kin of Ata Are Waiting for You,* formerly *The Comforter* (1971; San Francisco: Moon Books, 1976). All subsequent references will be made parenthetically in the text.

4.   Mary Staton, *From the Legend of Biel* (New York: Ace Books, 1975). All subsequent references will be made parenthetically in the text.

5.   Ursula K. Le Guin, *The Left Hand of Darkness* (1969; New York: Ace Books, 1974). All subsequent references will be made parenthetically in the text.

6.   Drawing upon the works of Carl Jung, such writers as Joseph Campbell, *The Hero with a Thousand Faces* (New York: World Publishing, 1970); Lord Raglan, *The Hero: A Study in Tradition, Myth, and Dream* (New York: Oxford Univ. Press, 1937); Jessie Weston, *From Ritual to Romance* (Garden City, N.Y.: Doubleday, 1957); and Dorothy Norman, *The Hero: Myth/Image/Symbol* (New York: New American Library, 1969) examine the prevalence and analyze the patterns of this motif in Western and non-Western literature and folklore. More recently, Carol Christ examines this motif from a feminist perspective in *Diving Deep and Surfacing;* Carol Pearson and Katherine Pope's *The Female Hero in American and British Literature,* published as this chapter was being completed, and Annis Pratt's *Archetypal Patterns in Women's Fiction* (Bloomington: Indiana Univ. Press, 1981) are also feminist analyses of this tradition in relation to women's fiction and fictionalization.

7.   From More's *Utopia* to such classic American works as Edward Bellamy's *Looking Backward,* this tradition has received significant critical attention. See, for example, Lyman Tower Sargent, *British and American Utopian Literature 1516-1975: An Annotated Bibliography* (Boston: G. K. Hall, 1979). More recently, women's place in utopian societies (Elaine Baruch, "'A Natural and Necessary Monster': Women in Utopia," *Alternative Futures: The Journal of Utopian Studies,* 2 [Winter 1978-79], 28-48) and utopian literature written by women have received increasing critical attention. See, for example, Margaret

Miller, "The Ideal Woman in Two Feminist Science-Fiction Utopias," *Science-Fiction Studies,* 10 (1983), 191-98, and Carol Pearson's previously cited work. Pearson, singly and in collaboration with Katherine Pope, is the only other critic who has examined *The Kin of Ata* and *From the Legend of Biel* at any length. When I am indebted to her stimulating work (*The Female Hero* appeared while this chapter was being concluded), acknowledgment will be made; however, our approaches to the texts differ significantly in my evaluation of them in relation to *The Left Hand of Darkness,* feminist ideology, and feminist speculative fictions in general, and in my more critical treatment of *The Kin of Ata* and Jungian theory's role in all three texts.

8. Le Guin does, however, overtly request personal involvement from readers of two of her critical essays, "American Science Fiction and the Other," in *The Language of the Night: Essays on Fantasy and Science Fiction,* ed. Susan Wood (New York: G.P. Putnam's Sons, 1979), pp. 97-100 (first appeared in *Science-Fiction Studies* 7 [1975]) and "Science Fiction and Mrs. Brown," also in *The Language of the Night,* pp. 101-19 (first appeared in *Science Fiction at Large,* 1976). These essays analyze the absence or distorted depictions of women in science fiction and encourage its writers to be less biased and its readers to demand more in characterization.

9. Le Guin discusses her emerging, ambivalent feminism in her essays. In "The Stalin in the Soul" she mentions the lack of awareness that led to her permitting *Playboy* to print one of her stories under the eponymous byline of U. K. Le Guin (*The Language of the Night,* p. 217; first appeared in *The Future Now,* 1973); in "Is Gender Necessary?," she analyzes negative as well as positive reader response to—and her own rationale for—the controversial depiction of "androgynous" characters in *The Left Hand of Darkness.* This essay appears in *Aurora: Beyond Equality,* ed. Vonda N. McIntyre and Susan Janice Anderson (Greenwich, Conn.: Fawcett, 1976), pp. 130-39.

    Le Guin's ambivalence may be contrasted with Bryant's commitment to feminist concerns and goals, not only in *The Kin of Ata* but in Bryant's other fictions. *Ella Price's Journal* (New York: New American Library, 1972) depicts the psychological and social changes of a woman in her mid-thirties returning to school; *Miss Giardino* (Berkeley, Calif: Ata Books, 1978) examines the continued psychological growth of a schoolteacher in her mid-sixties who chooses active solitude rather than retirement and marriage; *The Garden of Eros* (Berkeley, Calif.: Ata Books, 1978) examines the impact of pregnancy and birth on a woman; *Prisoners* (Berkeley, Calif.: Ata Books, 1980) traces the relationship of a mature woman and a prison inmate with whom she corresponds; and *A Day in San Francisco* (Berkeley, Calif.: Ata Books, 1982) examines the relationship of a mother and adult gay son. Staton, to my knowledge, has not published anything except *From the Legend of Biel,* which I believe speaks eloquently for its author's feminist commitment.

10. I am not asserting that Bryant and Staton's works are *direct* responses to Le Guin's novel but rather that they are overtly feminist reworkings of a dominant theme in SF—that of the questing or searching male protagonist—which Le Guin only partly breaks away from in her fiction. As SF fans and historians know, there are other, even earlier depictions of physiologically androgynous characters than Le Guin's—see, for example, Theodore Sturgeon's *Venus Plus X* (New York: Pyramid, 1960).

11. See, for example, *Ursula K. Le Guin,* ed. Joseph D. Olander, and Martin Harry Greenberg (New York: Taplinger, 1979), the special Ursula K. Le Guin issue of *Extrapolation,* 21 (Fall 1980), and the Le Guin issue of *Science-Fiction Studies* (November 1975). Amidst other critical acclaim, Robert Scholes has written that Le Guin may be America's greatest contemporary author (*Structural Fabulation: An Essay on the Fiction of the Future* [Notre Dame, Ind.: Univ. of Notre Dame Press, 1975], p. 80); however, I have maintained (at the

Great Lakes Women's Studies Conference in Mankato, Minn. in April 1981) that Le Guin's favorable reception by the traditional literary establishment may stem not only from her talents as a writer but from the safely "diluted" version of feminism her works contain.

12. Dena C. Bain, "The Tao Te Ching as Background to the Novels of Ursula K. Le Guin," *Extrapolation,* 21 (1980), 209-22 and Robert Galbreath, "Taoist Magic in the Earthsea Trilogy," *Extrapolation,* 21 (1980), 362-68 are among those who analyze Le Guin's use of Taoism; Peter Brigg, "The Archetype of the Journey in Ursula K. Le Guin's Fiction" and Sneja Gunew, "Mythic Reversals: The Evolution of the Shadow Motif," in *Ursula K. Le Guin,* pp. 36-65 and 178-99, respectively, analyze her debts to Jungian theory. Susan Wood, "Introduction" to *The Language of the Night,* pp. 11-18, discusses this journey motif in less ideological terms.

13. Le Guin herself, in "American SF and the Other," discusses the explicit relegation of women in SF to the alien otherness detailed by Simone de Beauvoir in *The Second Sex.*

14. I am indebted to James Bittner for his analysis of the "writerly" elements of *The Left Hand's* construction, in personal conversation and through his "Approaches to the Fiction of Ursula K. Le Guin," Ph.D. dissertation, University of Wisconsin-Madison, 1979.

15. These objections are capsulized in *The New Woman's Survival Sourcebook,* ed. Kirsten Brimstad and Susan Rennie (New York: Knopf, 1975), p. 132. Le Guin responds to these remarks in "Is Gender Necessary?," p. 138.

16. See Grimstad and Rennie, p. 132 and Joanna Russ, "The Image of Women in Science Fiction," pp. 89-91. For somewhat different views of Le Guin's feminism, see Norman N. Holland, "You, U.K. Le Guin," and Marleen S. Barr, "Charles Bronson, Samurai, and Other Feminine Images: A Transactive Response to *The Left Hand of Darkness,*" in *Future Females: A Critical Anthology,* pp. 125-37 and 138-54, respectively.

17. Le Guin, "Is Gender Necessary?," p. 131.

18. "Is Gender Necessary?," p. 137.

19. See Wolfe and Stanley, Morgan, and such recent works as Dale Spender, *Man-Made Language* (Boston: Routledge and Kegan Paul, 1980).

20. In *The Language of the Night,* pp. 141-42.

21. This is not to overlook the strong commitment to more generalized moral and ethical concerns that Le Guin makes in her fiction and essays. See, for instance, "The Stalin in the Soul," an essay in which she describes implicit marketplace censorship of "serious" literature. Le Guin herself, however, separates explicitly feminist works from this category.

22. "Is Gender Necessary?," pp. 130-32.

23. "Is Gender Necessary?," pp. 133-35.

24. "Introduction to *Planet of Exile,*" p. 143.

25. Samuel R. Delany has commented on this implicit heterosexist bias in another Le Guin novel, *The Dispossessed: An Ambiguous Utopia* (New York: Harper and Row, 1974). See "To Read *The Dispossessed,*" in his *The Jewel-Hinged Jaw: Essays on Science Fiction* (New York: Berkeley Publishing, 1977), pp. 218-83.

26. The few contemporary fictions that do assert this are structured on reversal of traditional, stereotyped roles, with males being considered the physical and social inferiors of women. See, for example, JayGee Carr's *Leviathan's Deep* (New York: Playboy, 1979), Marion Zimmer Bradley's *The Ruins of Isis* (Virginia Beach, Va.: Donning, 1978), or Judith Merril's

earlier "Wish Upon a Star," in *The Best of Judith Merril,* ed. Virginia Kidd (New York: Warner Books, 1976). Joanna Russ discusses this tradition of sex-role reversal in speculative fictions written primarily by men (usually to highlight women's dastardliness, should we ever gain power) in "*Amor Vincit Foeminam:* The Battle of the Sexes," *Science-Fiction Studies,* 7 (1980), 2-15.

27.   See Adrienne Rich's essay, "When We Dead Awaken: Writing as Revision," in *Adrienne Rich's Poetry,* ed. Barbara Charlesworth Gelpi and Albert Gelpi (New York: W.W. Norton, 1975), pp. 90-98 (originally in *College English,* 34 [October 1972], pp. 18-25), for the development of this term within the lexicon of feminist theory.

28.   Lillian S. Robinson, "Dwelling in Decencies: Radical Criticism and the Feminist Perspective," in *A Case for Equity: Women in English Departments,* ed. Susan McAllester (Urbana, Ill.: National Council of Teachers of English, 1971), pp. 33-43, is among such critics.

29.   See Andrea Dworkin, *Woman-Hunting* (New York: E.P. Dutton, 1974), as well as Mary Daly's *Gyn/Ecology* and Susan Griffin for discussions of historical gynophobia.

30.   Pearson and Pope's *The Female Hero in British and American Literature* and Annis Pratt's *Archetypal Patterns in Women's Fiction* analyze the stages of the quest in equivalents of Jungian terminology.

31.   Pearson also notes the absence of physical transportation in this narrator's and, subsequently, Howard Scott's (in *From the Legend of Biel*) travel to a different time and place, but does not elaborate on the ideological implications of such "willed" travel. See "Toward a New Language, Consciousness, and Political Theory: The Utopian Novels of Dorothy Bryant, Mary Staton, and Marge Piercy."

32.   While people are not identified by sex in Ata's language, all other animate creatures and inanimate objects are. The narrator notes that "[g]reat care was taken to pair 'masculine' and 'feminine' objects in planting and arranging things" (A, p. 50). This pairing suggests the Jungian merger of opposites. (Language use in *Ata* is briefly discussed by Robert J. Branham, "Fantasy and Ineffability: Fiction at the Limits of Language," *Extrapolation,* 24 [Spring 1983], 66-79.)

33.   Many feminist theorists have discussed the implications of having the power to name oneself, to validate one's own experience and existence. See, for example, Cixous' "The Laugh of the Medusa," Rich's "When We Dead Awaken: Writing as Revision," and Mary Daly's *Beyond God the Father.*

34.   Joanna Russ, "SF and Technology as Mystification," *Science-Fiction Studies,* 5 (1978), 250-60.

35.   See, for example, Susan Rennie and Kirsten Grimstad, "Spiritual Explorations Cross-Country," *Quest,* 1 (Spring 1975), 49-51.

36.   Christ, p. 51.

37.   Susan Rennie and Kirsten Grimstad allude to this controversy, evident in numerous texts and organizations, in their overview essay, "Does the Spirit Matter to Women?" in *The New Woman's Survival Sourcebook,* p. 191. See also *The Politics of Women's Spirituality,* ed. Charlene Spretnak (Garden City, N.Y.: Anchor, 1982).

38.   Again, see Ellmann's *Thinking About Women* for a discussion of these and other stereotypes.

39.   De Beauvoir makes use of these existentialist terms in her analysis of contemporaneous women's lives in *The Second Sex.*

40. Dorothy Bryant, "My Publisher/Myself," *Frontiers: A Journal of Women Studies,* 4 (Spring 1979), 35.

41. As explicated by Pratt in *Archetypal Patterns in Women's Fiction,* pp. 73-74 and 93-94.

42. Jessie Weston's *From Ritual to Romance* and Joseph Campbell's *The Hero with a Thousand Faces,* among others, explore the prevalence of yearly sacrifice as an actual or symbolic religious ritual. Andre Schwarz-Bart popularized the Talmudic story of ten just men in his novel of the Holocaust, *The Last of the Just,* trans. Stephen Becker (New York: Atheneum Press, 1960).

43. As previously mentioned, Esther Harding is one Jungian theorist who, in *Women's Mysteries,* at times veers from this definition. Nor Hall, *The Moon and the Virgin: Reflections on the Archetypal Feminine* (New York: Harper and Row, 1980), is similarly unorthodox on occasion.

44. Rebirth is one of the figurative stages of the archetypal journey as outlined by, among others, Campbell, Pratt, Pearson and Pope. It often occurs after such a physically as well as emotionally traumatic event.

45. See such works as Mary Jane Sherfey, *The Nature and Origin of Female Sexuality* (1966; New York: Random House, 1972), for a discussion of female sexuality.

46. Le Guin herself writes that "men, more often than women...identify...with Genly...." in "Is Gender Necesary?," p. 138.

47. Sydney Janet Kaplan, *Feminine Consciousness in the Modern British Novel* (Urbana: University of Illinois Press, 1975). See in particular Kaplan's discussion of Rosamond Lehmann, pp. 120-21, of Dorothy Richardson, p. 41, and of Virginia Woolf, p. 90.

48. In addition to Sherry Ortner's previously-cited "Is Female to Male as Nature Is to Culture?," Annette Kolodny's *The Lay of the Land* (Chapel Hill: Univ. of North Carolina, 1975) and Susan Griffin's *Woman and Nature* explore such stereotypes. It is interesting that one of Griffin's juxtaposed examples of patriarchal brutalization of woman and nature similarly involves space exploration (p. 55).

49. See Scholes's *Structural Fabulation,* pp. 46-47 and Darko Suvin, *Metamorphoses of Science Fiction: On the Poetics and History of a Literary Genre* (New Haven, Conn.: Yale Univ. Press, 1979), pp. 7-8.

50. Like Staton, I capitalize THOACDIEN when it functions as a proper noun and use lower case letters when it functions as an adjective.

51. Some of these innovations—different typefaces, juxtaposition of layout conventionally associated with poetry within a prose work, phrase-by-phrase or line-by-line interweaving of thematically related but disparate narratives, and incorporation of traditionally non-narrative semes are also employed by Susan Griffin in *Woman and Nature.* Monique Wittig, *Les Guérillères,* also employs such unconventional typography and narrative devices—for example, litanies of women's names alternating with the body of the text.

52. Pearson and Pope maintain that Mikkran herself develops psychologically through this experience, learning to reject the self-sacrifice traditionally demanded of mothers or mother-figures by patriarchy when, faint with thirst and hunger, she accepts the toddler's aid. I am not convinced that this interpretation is justified by the sequence and emphasis of the narrative's events.

53. Surfacing in numerous feminist texts, both fiction and non-fiction, this concept is dealt with at length by Griffin in *Woman and Nature.* In fact, one of Griffin's related sub-sections is

(coincidentally?) titled "Turbulence" (pp. 182-83). Mikkran's acceptance of 187-A, 0037's choice of this name also validates both her autonomy to choose at all and the importance of naming.

54. These images echo the ironic choices of Robert Frost's "Fire and Ice," in *The American Tradition in Literature,* vol. 2, 3rd ed., ed. Sculley, Bradley, et al. (New York: W.W. Norton, 1967), p. 1083.

55. Kaj-Palmir's tag-name is reminiscent of the similarly metaphoric use of weaving in Le Guin's creation of Gethenian Faxe, called "the Weaver" (LH, p. 67), whose focusing and merging of others' psychic powers enables him/her to foretell future events.

56. See *Of Woman Born,* pp. 232-33, for a discussion of the possible erotic subtext in mother-daughter relationships.

57. This view of an anarchy's total absence of systems seems a more naive one than Le Guin's depiction in *The Dispossessed* of the inevitable power structures that develop on anarchic Anarres.

58. Wittig's depiction of a future society of separatist women waging a winning war against patriarchy alternates capitalized litanies of women's names and page-sized circles, representative of women's genitalia as well as essential psychic "wholeness," with its elliptical narrative.

59. Within the recent tradition of fantasy literature, Lewis Carroll's *Alice in Wonderland* comes to mind.

Chapter 3

1. Mary Edwardsen, "Introduction," *Union Seminary Quarterly Review,* 35 (Fall and Winter 1979-80), 3.

2. See Joanna Russ's previously cited *"Amor Vincit Foeminam:* The Battle of the Sexes in SF" for an historical overview of these (generally) virulently misogynistic works in twentieth century fiction. Russ discusses ten stories and novels, ending with Thomas Berger's dismayingly recent *Regiment of Women* (New York: Simon and Schuster, 1973).

3. Sally Miller Gearhart, *The Wanderground: Stories of the Hill Women* (Watertown, Mass: Persephone Press, 1978) and Marge Piercy, *Woman on the Edge of Time* (Greenwich, Conn.: Fawcett Publications, 1976). Subsequent references to these texts and the previously cited *The Demeter Flower, Motherlines,* and *The Female Man* will be made parenthetically.
     Short stories which similarly treat the "battle between the sexes" from a feminist perspective and conclude ambiguously include Kit Reed's "Songs of War," in *The New Women of Wonder,* ed. Pamela Sargent (New York: Vintage Books, 1977), pp. 121-75 (first printed in 1974); Carol Emschwiller's "Maybe Another Long March Across China 80,000 Strong," in her *Joy in Our Cause* (New York: Harper and Row, 1974), pp. 161-70; and James Tiptree, Jr.'s "Mama Come Home," in her *Ten Thousand Light Years From Home* (New York: Ace, 1973), pp. 51-78. (James Tiptree, Jr. is the pseudonym of Alice Sheldon.) Tiptree's "Houston, Houston, Do You Read?" in her *Star Songs of an Old Primate* (New York: Ballantine, 1978), pp. 164-226, alternatively suggests that women may win such a war.

4. This third volume (to have been titled *Holdfast Harrowing*) was intended to provide a synthesis between traditional androcentric culture and feminist theory. Charnas writes: "Considering the way things are likely to go in the next decade or so, specifically with regard to the hard-won and now imperilled gains of women and non-whites in America, I don't think anybody who was not insane could actually write that book. Someday, maybe, I hope."

Private correspondence, November 6, 1980 cited by Jeanne Gomoll, in "Out of Context: Post-Holocaust Themes in Feminist Science Fiction," *Janus,* No. 18 (Winter 1980), p. 15.

5.   For a classical definition of heroism, see Norman, p. 12.

6.   The assumption and use of political power by feminists is discussed in such works as Nancy Hartsock, "Policial Change: Two Perspectives on Power"; Nancy Hartsock, "Fundamental Feminism: Process and Perspective"; and Karen Kollias, "Class Realities: Creating a New Power Base," in *Building Feminist Theory: Essays from Quest,* ed. The Quest Staff (New York: Longman, 1981), pp. 3-19, 32-43, and 139-48, respectively.

7.   The erasure of the traits of classical heroism from post-World War II fictional protagonists is illustrated by Ralph Ellison's *Invisible Man* and by Thomas Pynchon's creation in *Gravity's Rainbow* of Tyrone Slothrup, who literally fades into nothingness before the novel's conclusion. (I am indebted to Donald F. Larsson for this last observation.)

8.   In addition to the previously cited "Images of Women in Science Fiction," "Outta Space: Women Write Science Fiction," "*Amor Vincit Foeminam:* The Battle Between the Sexes in SF," and "SF and Technology as Mystification," Russ, a professor of literature as well as a creative writer, has witten "Towards an Aesthetics of Science Fiction," in *Science-Fiction Studies,* ed. R.D. Mullen and Darko Suvin (Boston: Gregg Press, 1976), pp. 8-15 and "What Can a Heroine Do? Or Why Women Can't Write," in *Images on Women in Fiction: Feminist Perspectives,* ed. Susan Koppelman Cornillon (Bowling Green, Ohio: Bowling Green University, 1973), pp. 3-20. Her most recent work is *How to Suppress Women's Writing* (Austin: Univ. of Texas Press, 1983). Russ has also contributed reviews to feminist journals and presented papers at professional conferences.

Gearhart is co-author of *Loving Women/Loving Men: Gay Liberation and the Church* (San Francisco: Glide, 1974) and author of *A Feminist Tarot: A Guide to Interpersonal Communication* (Watertown, Mass.: Persephone Press, 1977). With Jane Gurko, she is coauthor of "The Sword-and-the-Vessel versus The Lake-on-the-Lake," *Bread and Roses,* 2 (Spring 1980), 26-34, an excerpt from a longer study of contemporary lesbian and gay literature. She has also contributed "Woman Power: Energy Re-Sourcement" to *The Politics of Spirituality,* pp. 194-206.

Piercy is a feminist poet as well as novelist.

9.   Teresa De Lauretis, "Signs of Wander," and Samuel R. Delany, "Generic Protocols: Science Fiction and Mundane," in *The Technological Imagination: Theories and Fictions,* ed. Teresa De Lauretis, Andreas Huyssen, Kathleen Woodward (Madison, Wisc.: Coda Press, 1980), pp. 159-74 and 175-93, respectively, both define science fiction in this way. It is interesting, in light of this study's examination of typographical innovation by feminist authors, to note De Lauretis's typographical conflation to mark her own critical "wanderings" through this literature of "wonder." De Lauretis's and Delany's generic distinctions are akin to those of Suvin and Scholes; however, De Lauretis and Delany explicitly link their categorization to feminism in ways that Suvin and Scholes do not.

10. Delany, "Generic Protocols: Science Fiction and Mundane," p. 176.

11. Such mis/reading is the focus of Nancy K. Miller's "Emphasis Added: Plots and Plausibilities in Women's Fiction," *PMLA,* 96 (1981), 36-48. It is also discussed by Peter J. Rabinowitz, "Assertion and Assumption: Fictional Patterns and the External World," *PMLA,* 96 (1981), 408-19.

12. De Lauretis, p. 164.

13. Gayatri Chakravorty Spivak, "Three Feminist Readings: McCullers, Drabble, Habermas," *USQR,* 35 (Fall and Winter 1979-80), 29.

14. Working with ideas and terms formulated by Julia Kristeva and Roland Barthes, Jonathan Cullers notes that "subjectivity is not so much a personal core as an intersubjectivity, the track or furrow left by the experience of texts of all kinds." (*Structuralist Poetics: Structuralism, Linguistics, and the Study of Literature* [Ithaca, N.Y.: Cornell University, 1975], p. 140.) It is this awareness which Miller expands upon in her article, and it is Kristeva's redefinition of intersubjectity as "intertextuality" (in *Semioteke,* as cited by Cullers, p. 13) that both Spivak and I use here.

   (Rachel Blau Du Plessis also notes the "embedded elements of assertive discourse" in *The Female Man* and *Woman on the Edge of Time* in "The Feminist Apologues of Lessing, Piercy, and Russ," pp. 1-2. She does not, however, analyze these elements in terms of controversy among feminists or of the overall field of feminist speculative fictions.)

15. Lee Killough's hybrid detective-science fiction novel *Deadly Silents* (New York: Ballantine, 1981) renders this need to maintain a healthy skepticism toward political dogma or conventionally de-politicized legend literally: Killough's alien legends are all relayed in the subjunctive tense—for example, "The world *might* have begun when...." Killough's deliberately wary treatment of naturalized truths in an otherwise unremarkable "space opera" indicates the extent to which feminist theory has permeated the conventions of science fiction.

16. Ellen Morgan, "The One-Eyed Doe," *Radical Teacher,* No. 10 (1978), p. 10. *The Female Man* is an expanded version of Russ's award-winning short story "When It Changed," in *Again, Dangerous Visions,* Vol. I, ed. Harlan Ellison (New York: New American Library, 1972), pp. 271-81.

17. My analysis of *The Female Man* in this chapter is an expanded version of a paper I originally presented at the May 1980 National Women's Studies Association national conference in Bloomington, Indiana. This paper appears in *Extrapolation,* 23 (Spring 1982), 31-36 as "A Female Man? The 'Medusan' Humor of Joanna Russ."

18. Pamela Annas discusses *The Female Man* as an example of feminist androgyny in the previously cited "New Worlds, New Words: Androgyny in Feminist Science Fiction."

19. These interpretations are raised by, respectively, Bruce Kawin in his 1978 MLA presentation on Russ and Doris Lessing; Rachel Blau Du Plessis in "The Feminist Apologues of Lessing, Piercy, and Russ," p. 6; and Carol Pearson and Katherine Pope in *The Female Hero in American and British Literature,* p. 68. In *Archetypal Patterns in Women's Fiction,* Annis Pratt similarly sees *The Female Man* as a *bildungsroman,* p. 36.

20. Russ's parodic treatment of phallocentric criticism echoes the similar but serious critiques written by such feminist scholars as Mary Ellmann in *Thinking About Women* and Carol Ohmann, "Emily Bronte in the Hands of Male Critics," in *A Case for Equity,* ed. Susan McAllester (Urbana, Ill.: National Council of Teachers of English, 1971), pp. 60-67.

21. Russ's and her protagonists' perceptions are documented by such theorists as Carol Korsmeyer, "The Hidden Joke: Generic Uses of Masculine Terminology," in *Feminism and Philosophy,* ed. Mary Vetterling-Braggin et al. (Totowa, N.J.: Littlefield, Adams, and Co., 1977), p. 141.

22. This interpretation of *The Female Man* is akin to Rachel Blau Du Plessis's conception of it as a feminist apologue, but Du Plessis, despite recognizing Russ's devastating wit, considers the "plot ... clearly and amusingly nugatory" ("The Feminist Apologues of Lessing, Piercy, and Russ," p. 5). I argue that humor is an inherent structural element in the novel.

23. B. Ruby Rich, "The Crisis in Naming in Feminist Film Criticism," *Jump Cut,* No. 19 (1978), p. 11.

24. Hélène Cixous, "The Laugh of the Medusa," p. 888.

25. Russ's background as a dramatist (she received in M.F.A. in playwriting from Yale's Drama School) may account for the dramatic form of these interjections.

26. Although Pamela Annas also recognizes *The Female Man* as "a novel about coming into consciousness and, as a result, advancing out of stasis to the possibility of action" ("New Worlds, New Words: Androgyny in Feminist Science Fiction," p. 149), she does not comment on Russ's humor. Instead, she designates the "party game" litanies as a stylistic device, and she explicates the novel's title and this particular passage in full seriousness.

27. For example, the woman who totally rejects Whileaway's established conventions, who denies their existence and hence the existence of other Whileawayans, must be executed by the reluctant Janet in the performance of her Safety and Peace duties.

28. "The Great Goddess" issue of *Heresies,* No. 5 (Spring 1978) contains analyses and examples of the significance of ritual to some feminists. See, for example, Toni Head's "Changing the Hymns to Hers," pp. 16-18, and Kay Turner's "Contemporary Feminist Rituals" and "Song of Black Feather, Song of White Feather," pp. 20-27.

29. As Nelly Furman notes in relation to the constructive role of the reader in "authoring" a literary work, "Text [from the Latin *textus,* fabric, structure, text; past participle of *texture,* to weave] is not merely a synonym for literary work or some portion of a work. It is more precisely a literary *passage,* that is to say, a place of transition, an area which either leads to something different or a space where change is occurring." "Textual Feminism," in *Women and Language in Literature and Society,* ed. Sally McConnell-Ginet, Ruth Borker, and Nelly Furman (New York: Praeger, 1980), p. 49. Such passage or transition may also, then, occur when the message that prompts it is verbal rather than written—for example, a fairy tale or cultural myth. Roland Barthes notes that "the text is that *social* space which leaves no language safe . . ." (as cited by Furman, p. 52).

30. Pearson and Pope see this assassination as a symbol of the completion of a stage in the female hero's quest for selfhood. According to them, the female hero must "slay the inner dragon" of internalized self-hatred before becoming psychically whole. *The Female Hero,* pp. 66-67.

31. See Barbara Hillyer Davis, "Teaching the Feminist Minority," *Women's Studies Quarterly,* 9 (Winter 1981), 7-9.

32. Furman, p. 48.

33. In addition to works cited in notes 11 and 14 of this chapter, see, for example, Robert De Maria, Jr., "The Ideal Reader: A Critical Fiction," *PMLA,* 93 (1978), 463-74 and *The Reader in the Text: Essays on Audience and Interpretation,* ed. Susan Suleiman and Inge Crosman (Princeton: Princeton University Press, 1980). This anthology contains a bibliography by Crosman which indicates the expansion of interest in reception theory.

34. Stanley and Wolfe, p. 67.

35. "The Feminist Apologues of Lessing, Piercy, and Russ," p. 7.

36. Conversely, Jael's polarized, warring universe is an extrapolation of what the future might be like if our present social norms and ills go unchecked.

37. Rachel Blau Du Plessis, p. 3, interestingly notes that Janet Evason's initials—JE—like those of Charlotte Bronte's Jane Eyre are an acronym for the French "I."

38. See Joan L. Griscom's "On Healing the Nature/History Split in Feminist Thought" and Ynestra King's "Feminism and the Revolt of Nature" for discussions of radical cultural feminism. These articles are in *Heresies,* No. 13 (1981), pp. 4-9 and 12-16, respectively.

39. Ann Rush Kent, *Moon, Moon* (New York: Random House, 1976) and Z Budapest, *The Feminist Book of Lights and Shadows* (Venice, Calif.: Luna Publications, 1975).

40. Barbara Bowman, "Sally Gearhart's *The Wanderground:* The Aesthetics of Matriarchy," unpublished 1981 MMLA paper, p. 6. This generally insightful article is, aside from reviews, the only critical work focusing exclusively on *The Wandergound* I have been able to locate.

41. In *We Who Are About To* (New York: Dell, 1975), Russ rebuts the premise of women's individual and cultural survival in a non-high-technology future by depicting a space-wrecked female protagonist who would rather die than live a subsistence, solely baby-producing existence.

42. Whileaway has an extensive computerized support system and has sent Janet into another continuum through technological means. Yet individuals tend cows, and communities are small and dispersed in Whileaway.

43. De Lauretis, p. 165.

44. See Ann Rush Kent and Z Budapest. The historical persecution of women as witches is detailed in Mary Daly's *Gyn/Ecology* and Susan Griffin's *Woman and Nature,* both previously cited.

45. Ynestra King, pp. 13-14.

46. Naomi Mitchison's *Memoirs of a Spacewoman* (1962; London: New English Library, 1976) similarly depicts women's ability to communicate through the medium of a "naturally" receptive female body.

47. "The Sword-and-the-Vessel versus The Lake-on-the-Lake," p. 26. Not all feminists would agree with Gearhart's view of non-aggressive female sexuality; for an overview of this controversy, see *Powers of Desire: The Politics of Sexuality,* eds. Ann Snitow, Christine Stensall, and Sharon Thompson (New York: Monthly Review Press, 1983).

48. See Esther Harding's previously-cited *Women's Mysteries* for a discussion of matriarchal virginity.

49. See Merlin Stone's *When God Was A Woman* for general background on this usurpation and Adrienne Rich, *Of Woman Born,* pp. 238-40, for specific discussion of Demeter and Kore. Rich cites C. Kerenyi, *Eleusis: Archetypal Image of Mother and Daughter* (New York: Pantheon, 1967) extensively.

50. Susan Griffin's *Woman and Nature* details the destructive impact of such categorizations on women's lives.

51. Bowman, pp. 1-2.

52. According to *The Wanderground*'s copyright page, some of its stories first appeared in *Ms.; Quest: A Feminist Quarterly; The Witch and the Chameleon;* and *Woman Spirit.*

53. Barbara Bowman, p. 3, also notes this absence of traditional narrative closure in Gearhart's fiction.

54. Whileawayans believe that their men died as the result of a plague; Jael, however, tells Janet that it was Jael's own warring Womanland which secretly and deliberately rid Whileaway of men. Jael is scornful and angered at Janet's easy indifference to the threat patriarchy poses to women.

55. In addition to disagreement between radical separatists and other, more mainstream feminists who believe in a sexually-integrated future, there are some disputes arising out of

the male liberation movement. A few of this movement's spokesmen anger feminists (of both genders) with their assertions that androcentric norms, sexual stereotypes, and gender roles harm men *as much* as they harm women. An example of such polemic is Herb Goldberg, *The Hazards of Being Male* (New York: Nash Publications, 1976).

56. Phyllis Chesler, *Women and Madness* (Garden City, N.Y.: Doubleday, 1972) discusses the psychiatric establishment's labelling of inappropriate female behavior as "insane."

57. In addition to R.D. Laing's *The Divided Self* (1960; Middlesex, England: Penguin Books, 1971), a number of specifically feminist critiques and revisions of conventional psychiatric theory have been written in the last fifteen years. These included *Women and Analysis: Dialogues on Psychoanalytic Views of Femininity,* previously cited. Interestingly, Doris Lessing also terms her mentally-receptive yet clinically "insane" characters "catchers." (See, for instance, *Shikasta.*)

58. Again, this concept of the reader as author parallels that of Annis Pratt in *Archetypal Patterns in Women's Fiction,* p. 177.

59. See Mary Ellmann, p. 60, for a discussion of these conflicts.

60. These parallels are not necessarily linear ones. Rachel Blau Du Plessis, for example, sees a correlation between Jackrabbit and Connie's first husband Martin, who also dies a tragically early death ("The Feminist Apologues of Lessing, Piercy, and Russ," p. 3).

61. Realizing that Manland has no real-life models to contradict them, Womanland each year sends their enemies "wilder and wilder" specifications for the sex-change operations the weakest men are forced to undergo (FM, p. 169).

62. Piercy, among other comparisons, points out the differing attention paid to food in the three societies. Gildina's diet of artificial concentrates is unpleasantly similar to Connie's prison diet; the care given to cuisine in Mattapoisett parallels Connie's own enthusiasm for cooking, which is thwarted both by her limited budget before she is confined and by her brother Luis's prejudices about "appropriate" Anglo food and his "mad" sister's culinary skills when he finally does invite Connie as an out-patient to his home.

63. Blau Du Plessis, p. 4.

64. Blau Du Plessis, p. 3.

65. I am indebted to Rachel Blau Du Plessis for this term, p. 2.

66. This observation is made by both Susan Kress, "Politics of Time and Space: The Utopian Vision in *Woman on the Edge of Time,*" unpublished article, and Nadia Khouri, "The Dialectics of Power: Utopia in the SF of Le Guin, Jeury, and Piercy," *Science-Fiction Studies,* 7 (1980), 58-59. A revised version of Kress' article appears as "In and Out of Time: The Form of Marge Piercy's Novels," *Future Females: A Critical Anthology,* pp. 109-22.

67. Khouri, p. 58, interestingly notes that Piercy's positive future vision retains the "flavor" of what are now minority cultures.

68. Ellmann, pp. 78-82 and 119-36.

69. Stanley and Wolfe, p. 67.

70. See, for example, Shulamith Firestone, *The Dialectic of Sex* (New York: Bantam Books, 1970).

71. An historical example of this circumscribed prescriptive criticism is Christopher Caudwell, *Illusion and Reality* (1937; New York: Russell and Russell, 1955).

Chapter 4

1. Muriel Rukeyser, "The Speed of Darkness," in *About Women: An Anthology of Contemporary Fiction, Poetry, and Essays,* ed. Stephen Berg and S.J. Marks (Greenwich, Conn.: Fawcett, 1973), pp. 41-42.

2. Although I have concentrated on major themes in a wide range of contemporary women's speculative fiction, there are some aspects of feminism in this genre that I have not explicitly addressed. For example, much of James Tiptree, Jr.'s work (Tiptree is the pseudonym of Alice Sheldon) is primarily consciousness-raising in its depiction of the nexus between sexuality and violence in Western patriarchy. See "The Screwfly Solution," in *The Best SF of the Year #7,* ed. Terry Carr (New York: Ballantine, 1978), pp. 141-64, or "Your Faces, O My Sisters! Your Faces Filled of Light," written under the alternate pseudonym of Raccoona Sheldon, in *Aurora: Beyond Equality,* ed. Susan Janice Anderson and Vonda N. McIntyre (Greenwich, Conn.: Fawcett, 1976), pp. 16-35. Tiptree extends her consciousness-raising SF to include non-Western patriarchies' brutalization of women in *Up the Walls of the World* (New York: Berkeley, 1978); this novel's Black female protagonist has been subjected to cliterodectomy by her African stepfather.

    See footnote 18 in chapter one of this study for a bibliography of works which explore other aspects of feminist speculative fiction.

3. In addition to Scholes' and Suvin's analyses of SF's productive ability to "estrange" the reader, previously-cited, Daphne Patai explores this function of SF in "When Women Rule: Defamiliarization in the Sex-Role Reversal Utopia," *Extrapolation,* 23 (1982), 56-69. Patai draws upon the terminology of Russian Formalism in her use of "de-familiarization."

4. Even Sally Miller Gearhart questions the gynocentric "laws" of Mother Nature in *The Wanderground* through the depiction of the supposedly inferior, male "gentles" and their unexpected, slowly-developing psychic power.

5. Fritjof Capra, *The Tao of Physics: An Exploration of the Parallels Between Modern Physics and Eastern Mysticism* (Boulder, Colo.: Shambhala Press, 1975), pp. 154-60. I am indebted to Carol Pearson's articles and to Dr. Raymond Olderman for introducing me to Capra's work. See also Gary Zukav, *The Dancing Wu Li Masters: An Overview of the New Physics* (New York: Bantam, 1979), particularly pp. 91-114 and p. 260, for discussions of personal subjectivity in relation to this physics of probability, rather than of certainty.

6. W. Heisenberg, *Physics and Philosophy* (New York: Harper and Row, 1958), p. 58, as cited by Zukav, p. 114.

7. Zukav, p. 255.

8. Zukav, pp. 256 and 281-82.

9. Zukav, pp. 256-63.

10. See Zukav, pp. 281-317, especially pp. 316-17, on the "end of science" as we have traditionally conceived of it—the epitome of definable, obtainable knowledge.

11. See Kaplan, previously cited.

12. Robin Morgan's fascinating *The Anatomy of Freedom: Feminism, Physics and Global Politics* (Garden City, NY: Doubleday, 1982), published after this study was completed, extensively examines connections between the new physics and politicized feminisms.

    Other gestalts currently challenging dominant Western thought include non-Western patterns of business organization—specifically, the Japanese model of "familial" cooperation and dedication in industry. I am indebted to Professor Carolyn Shrewsbury of the Mankato State University Women's Studies Department for making this connection apparent to me.

13. I am indebted to Carolyn Burke's exposition of "phallogocentrism," a neologism coined by theoretician Jacques Derrida, in her "Irigaray Through the Looking-Glass," *Feminist Studies,* 7 (1981), p. 293.

14. Furman, p. 49.

15. Rejecting narratorial omniscience or purported objectivity, these authors also reject the concept of a uniformly "implied" or "ideal" reader who will necessarily bring to the text an "inter-textual" background or political bias comparable to their own. These works are not, therefore, congruent with reader-response theory which posits such ahistorically "ideal" or "implied" readers.

16. E.M. Broner, *A Weave of Women* (1978; New York: Bantam, 1981). In this novel set in contemporary Israel, an international group of women band together for mutual support and spiritual sustenance. They "weave" new, woman-centered religious rituals which subvert orthodox Judaism's traditionl biases against women.

   Another recent work of speculative fiction, Ardath Mayhar's *How the Gods Wove in Kyrannon* (New York: Ace, 1979) is more ambivalent in its use of weaving metaphors. It metaphorically refers to "gods" and "fate," but—instead of depicting supernatural invention—delineates characters self-sufficiently struggling for themselves.

17. Zukav, p. 315.

18. Jacques Derrida, as cited by Gayatri Chakravorty Spivak in the preface to her translation of Derrida's *Of Grammatology* (Baltimore: Johns Hopkins University Press, 1976), pp. lxxv-lxxvii, as quoted by Burke, p. 294.

19. Capra, pp. 67-68.

20. See, for example, Carolyn Burke's illuminating study of Luce Irigaray, especially pp. 288-305, or *New French Feminisms,* both previously-cited, and Ann Rosalind Jones, "Writing the Body: Toward an Understanding of *L'écriture Feminine,*" *Feminist Studies,* 7 (Summer 1981), 247-63.

21. "The Laugh of the Medusa," pp. 886 and 887, respectively.

22. Jones, pp. 250-52.

23. Burke, p. 289.

24. Luce Irigaray, "Woman's Exile," *Ideology and Consciousness,* 1 (1977), p. 64, as cited by Burke, p. 289.

25. Burke, especially pp. 302-03.

26. Hélène Vivienne Wenzel, "The Text as Body/Politics: An Appreciation of Monique Wittig's Writings in Context," *Feminist Studies,* 7 (1981), 275.

27. Neal Wilgus, "Interview with Suzy McKee Charnas," *Algol,* 33 (Winter 1978-79), 22.

28. Indeed, *From the Legend of Biel* had only one printing. Ace Books has not responded to my written inquiries about the possibility of reprinting this work or the current whereabouts and writing plans of Mary Staton.

29. Bryant, "My Publisher/Myself," previously-cited.

30. Dworkin writes:

this text has been altered in one very serious way. I wanted it to be printed the way it was written—lower cases letters, no apostrophes, contractions. . . .

my publisher, in his corporate wisdom, filled the pages with garbage: standard punctuation. he knew his purposes; he knew what was necessary. our purposes differed; mine, to achieve clarity; his, to sell books. . . .

there is a great deal at stake here. many writers fight this battle and most lose it. what is at stake for the writer? freedom of invention. freedom to tell the truth, in all its particulars. freedom to imagine new structures. (Pp. 197-201, as cited by Stanley and Wolfe, pp. 59-60)

31. Delany comments on this graphic "transmogrification" of *Babel-17* in his unpaginated, forwarding "note" to the 1982 reissue.

32. Linda Fleming employs the term "American SF subculture" for the social structures that have sprung from professional and amateur interest in SF in her "The American SF Subculture," *Science-Fiction Studies,* 4 (1977), 263-71. Beverly Friend's "The Science-Fiction Fan Cult" (Ph.D. dissertation, Northwestern University, 1975) is another significant study of this phenomenon.

33. Burke, p. 301. Within this quotation, Burke herself cites Stephen Heath's description of Lacanian psychoanalysis in Heath's "Difference," *Screen,* 19 (Autumn 1978), 52.

34. This summary of the American SF subculture draws upon my own personal experience as well as Linda Fleming's article.

35. Fleming, p. 265.

36. See, for example, Suzy McKee Charnas, *Janus,* vol. 3, no. 2 (1977), p. 40.

37. *The Shattered Chain* (New York: Daw, 1976). These short story collaborations are Marion Zimmer Bradley and the Friends of Darkover, *The Keeper's Price* (New York: Daw, 1980) and Marion Zimmer Bradley and the Friends of Darkover, *Sword of Chaos* (New York: Daw, 1982). Bradley has acknowledged the impact of feminist fandom on her writing at fan conferences.

38. See Janice Bogstad and Barbara Emrys, "Science Fiction and Women's Networking," *New Moon: A Quarterly Journal of Science Fiction and Criticial Feminism,* vol. 1 (Winter 1981-82), pp. 2-3 and 17, for a discussion of feminist networking, both actual and potential, through SF fandom.

39. Mary Daly employs this term for a non-sexist environment in which human potential may flourish in *Beyond God the Father,* pp. 40-43.

40. Jane Tompkins, "The Reader in History: The Changing Shape of Literary Response," in her *Reader-Response Criticism: From Formalism to Post Structuralism* (Baltimore: Johns Hopkins University Press, 1980), p. 204, as cited by Elizabeth A. Flynn, "Women as Reader-Response Critics," unpublished 1981 MMLA Conference paper, p. 2. Tompkins' original statement applies to the position of literature and literary criticism in classical Greece.

Bibliography

Ahearn, Marie L. "Why Doris Lessing's Move into Science Fiction." Doris Lessing Session, MLA Convention, Houston. 1980.

Annas, Pamela. "New Worlds, New Words: Androgyny in Feminist SF." *Science-Fiction Studies,* 5 (1978), 143-56.

Arnold, June. *Applesauce.* 1966; New York: Daughters, Inc., 1977.

_____. *The Cook and the Carpenter: A Novel by the Carpenter.* Plainsfield, Vt.: Daughters, Inc., 1973.

Atwood, Margaret. *Lady Oracle.* New York: Simon and Schuster, 1976.

Badami, Mary Kenny. "A Feminist Critique of Science Fiction." *Extrapolation,* 18 (1974), 6-19.

Barr, Marlene, ed. *Future Females: A Critical Anthology.* Bowling Green, Ohio: Popular Press, 1982.

Barry, Judith, and Sandy Flitterman. "Textual Strategies—The Politics of Art Making." *Screen,* 21 (Summer 1980), pp. 35-48.

Barthes, Roland. *S/Z: An Essay.* Trans. Richard Miller. New York: Hill and Wang, 1974.

Baruch, Elaine. "'A Natural and Necessary Monster': Women in Utopia." *Alternative Futures: The Journal of Utopian Studies,* 2 (Winter 1978-79), pp. 28-48.

Berger, Thomas. *Regiment of Women.* New York: Simon and Schuster, 1973.

Bittner, James. "Approaches to the Fiction of Ursula K. Le Guin." Diss. University of Wisconsin-Madison 1979.

Bogstad, Janice M., and Barbara Emrys. "Science Fiction and Women's Networking." *New Moon: A Quarterly Journal of Science Fiction and Critical Feminism,* 1 (Winter 1981-82), pp. 2-3, 17.

Bowman, Barbara. "Sally Gearhart's *The Wanderground:* The Aesthetics of Matriarchy." Science Fiction Section, MMLA Convention, Oconomowoc, Wisc. November 1981.

Bradley, Marion Zimmer. *The Ruins of Isis.* Virginia Beach, Va.: Donning, 1978.

_____. *The Shattered Chain.* New York: Daw, 1976.

_____, and the Friends of Darkover. *The Keeper's Price.* New York: Daw, 1980.

_____. *Sword of Chaos.* New York: Daw, 1982.

Branham, Robert J. "Fantasy and Ineffability: Fiction at the Limits of Language." *Extrapolation,* 24 (Spring 1983), 66-79.

Broner, E.M. "The Dirty Ladies: Earthy Writings of Contemporary American Women—Paley, Jong, Schor, and Lerman." *Regionalism and the Female Imagination,* 4 (1979), 34-43.

_____. *A Weave of Women.* 1978; New York: Bantam, 1981.

Broumas, Olga. *Beginning with O.* New Haven: Yale Univ. Press, 1977.

Bryant, Dorothy. *A Day in San Francisco.* Berkeley, Calif.: Ata Books, 1982.

_____. *Ella Price's Journal.* New York: New American Library, 1972.

_____. *The Garden of Eros.* Berkeley, Calif.: Ata Books, 1978.

_____. *The Kin of Ata Are Waiting For You.* 1971; San Francisco: Moon Books. 1976.

_____. *Miss Giardino*. Berkeley, Calif.: Ata Books, 1978.

_____. "My Publisher/Myself." *Frontiers,* 4 (Spring 1979), pp. 35-39.

_____. *Prisoners*. Berkeley, Calif.: Ata Books. 1980.

Budapest, Z. *The Feminist Book of Lights and Shadows*. Venice, Calif.: Luna Publications, 1975.

Building Feminist Theory: Essays from Quest, a feminist quarterly. New York: Longman, 1981.

Burke, Carolyn. "Irigaray Through the Looking-Glass." *Feminist Studies,* 7 (1981), 288-306.

Campbell, Joseph. *The Hero with a Thousand Faces*. New York: World Publishing, 1970.

Capra, Fritjof. *The Tao of Physics: An Exploration of the Parallels Between Modern Physics and Eastern Mysticism*. Boulder, Colo.: Shambhala Press, 1975.

Carr, Jaygee. *Leviathan's Deep*. New York: Playboy, 1979.

Carter, Angela. *The Passion of New Eve*. London: Arrow Books, 1978.

_____. *The Sadeian Woman and the Ideology of Pornography*. New York: Pantheon Books, 1978.

Caudwell, Christopher. *Illusion and Reality*. 1937; New York: Russell and Russell, 1955.

Charnas, Suzy McKee. Interview. *Janus,* 3 (Winter 1977), p. 40.

_____. *Motherlines*. New York: Berkeley, 1978.

Chesler, Phyllis. *Women and Madness*. New York: Doubleday, 1972.

Chodorow, Nancy. *The Reproduction of Mothering: Psychoanalysis and the Sociology of Gender*. Berkeley: Univ. of California, 1978.

Christ, Carol. *Diving Deep and Surfacing: Women Writers on the Spiritual Quest*. Boston: Beacon Press, 1980.

Cixous, Hélène. "The Laughter of the Medusa." Trans. Keith Cohen and Paula Cohen. *Signs,* 1 (1976), 875-93.

Culler, Jonathan. *Structuralist Poetics: Structuralism, Linguistics, and the Study of Literature*. Ithaca, N.Y.: Cornell Univ. Press, 1975.

Daly, Mary. *Beyond God the Father: Towards a Philosophy of Women's Liberation*. Boston: Beacon Press, 1973.

_____. *Gyn/Ecology: The Metaethics of Radical Feminism*. Boston: Beacon Press, 1978.

Davis, Barbara Hillyer. "Teaching the Feminist Minority." *Women's Studies Quarterly,* 9 (Winter 1981), pp. 7-9.

Davis, Elizabeth Gould. *The First Sex*. New York: Harcourt Brace, 1976.

De Beauvoir, Simone. *The Second Sex*. Paris, 1949; New York: Bantam, 1970.

Delany, Samuel R. *Babel-17*. 1966; New York: Bantam, 1982.

_____. "Generic Protocols: Science Fiction and Mundane." *The Technological Imagination: Theories and Fictions*. Ed. Teresa de Lauretis, Andreas Huyssen, and Kathleen Woodward. Madison, Wisc.: Coda Press, 1980, pp. 175-93.

_____. *The Jewel-Hinged Jaw: Essays on Science Fiction*. New York: Berkeley, 1977.

_____. *Triton*. New York: Bantam, 1976.

De Lauretis, Teresea. "Signs of Wonder." *The Technological Imagination: Theories and Fictions*. Ed. Teresa de Lauretis, Andreas Huyssen, and Kathleen Woodward. Madison, Wisc.: Coda Press, 1980, pp. 159-74.

De Maria, Jr., Robert. "The Ideal Reader: A Critical Fiction." *PMLA,* 93 (1978), 463-74.

Dodderidge, Esme. *The New Gulliver*. New York: Taplinger, 1978.

Draine, Betsy. "Competing Codes in *Shikasta*." Doris Lessing Session, MLA Convention, Houston. 1980.

Du Plessis, Rachel Blau. "The Feminist Apologues of Lessing, Piercy, and Russ." *Frontiers,* 4 (Spring 1979), pp. 1-8.

Dworkin, Andrea. *Woman-Hating*. New York: E.P. Dutton, 1974.

Earnest, Ernest. *The American Eve in Fact and Fiction*. Bloomington: Univ. of Indiana Press, 1975.

Edwardsen, Mary. "Introduction." *Union Seminary Quarterly Review*, 35 (Fall and Winter 1979-80), pp. 3-4.

Eliot, T.S. "Four Quartets." *The Complete Poems and Plays 1909-50*. New York: Harcourt Brace, 1971, pp. 117-45.

Ellmann, Mary. *Thinking About Women*. New York: Harcourt Brace, 1968.

Emrys, Barbara: "SF and Women's Studies." "Feminist SF: Shaping the Future" panel, Great Lakes Women's Studies Association Conference, Mankato, Minn. April 1981.

Emschwiller, Carol. "Maybe Another Long March Across China 80,000 Strong." *Joy in Our Cause*. New York: Harper and Row, 1974, pp. 161-70.

Extrapolation, 21 (Fall 1980). Ursula K. Le Guin issue.

Extrapolation, 23 (Spring 1982). Women and SF issue.

Firestone, Shulamith. *The Dialectic of Sex: The Case for Women's Liberation*. New York: Bantam Books. 1970.

Fleming, Linda. "The American SF Subculture." *Science-Fiction Studies*, 4 (1977), 263-71.

Flynn, Elizabeth A. "Women as Reader-Response Critics." Women and Literature Session, MMLA Convention, Oconomowoc, Wisc. November 1981.

Friend, Beverly. "The Science Fiction Fan Cult." Diss. Northwestern University 1975.

Frost, Robert. "Fire and Ice." *The American Tradition in Literature*. 3rd ed. Ed. Sculley, Bradley, et al. New York: W.W. Norton, 1967. Vol. II, p. 1083.

Fryer, Judith. *The Faces of Eve: Woman in the Nineteenth Century American Novel*. New York: Oxford Univ. Press, 1976.

Furman, Nelly. "Textual Feminism." *Women and Language in Literature and Society*. Ed. Sally McConnell-Ginet, Ruth Borker, and Nelly Furman. New York: Praeger, 1980, pp. 45-54.

Gardiner, Judith Kegan. "Evil, Apocalypse, and Feminist SF." Science Fiction Section, MMLA Convention, Oconomowoc, Wisc. 1981.

Gearhart, Sally Miller. *A Feminist Tarot: A Guide to Interpersonal Communication*. Watertown, Mass.: Persephone Press, 1977.

————. *Loving Women/Loving Men: Gay Liberation and the Church*. San Francisco: Glide, 1974.

————. *The Wanderground: Stories of the Hill Women*. Watertown, Mass.: Persephone Press, 1978.

————, and Janet Gurko. "The Sword-and-the-Vessel versus The Lake-on-the-Lake." *Bread and Roses*, 2 (Spring 1980), pp. 26-34.

Gilbert, Sandra M., and Susan Gubar. *The Madwoman in the Attic: The Woman Writer and the Nineteenth Century Literary Imagination*. New Haven: Yale Univ. Press, 1979.

Gilman, Charlotte Perkins. *The Charlotte Perkins Gilman Reader*. Ed. Ann J. Lane. New York: Pantheon, 1980.

Goldberg, Herb. *The Hazards of Being Male*. New York: Nash Publications, 1976.

Goldenberg, Naomi R. *Changing of the Gods: Feminism and the End of Traditional Religions*. Boston: Beacon Press, 1979.

Gomoll, Jeanne. "Out of Context: Post-Holocaust Themes in Feminist Science Fiction." *Janus*, 6 (Winter 1980), pp. 14-17.

Gornick, Vivian, and Barbara K. Moran, eds. *Woman in a Sexist Society: Studies in Power and Powerlessness*. New York: Basic Books, 1971.

Gould, Lois. *A Sea Change*. New York: Avon Books. 1976.

Griffin, Susan. "Rape: The All-American Crime." *Female Psychology: The Emerging Self*. Ed. Sue Cox. Chicago: Science Research Associates, 1976, pp. 290-303.

————. *Woman and Nature: The Roaring Inside Her*. New York: Harper and Row, 1978.

Griscom, Joan L. "On Healing the Nature/History Split in Feminist Thought." *Heresies*, No. 13 (1981), pp. 4-9.

Hall, Nor. *The Moon and the Virgin: Reflections on the Archetypal Feminine.* New York: Harper and Row, 1980.

Harding, Esther. *Women's Mysteries: Ancient and Modern.* New York: G.P. Putnam's Sons, 1971.

Harris, Daniel. "Androgyny: The Sexist Myth in Disguise." *Women's Studies,* 2 (1974), 171-84.

Haskell, Molly. *From Reverence to Rape: The Treatment of Women in the Movies.* New York: Holt, Rinehart and Winston, 1974.

Hedges, Elaine, and Ingrid Wendt. *In Her Own Image: Women Working in the Arts.* Old Westbury, N.Y.: The Feminist Press, 1980.

Heilbrun, Carolyn. *Toward a Recognition of Androgyny.* New York: Harper and Row, 1973.

Heresies, No. 5 (Spring 1978). "The Great Goddess" issue.

Holly, Marcia. "Consciousness and Authenticity: Toward a Feminist Aesthetic." *Feminist Literary Criticism: Explorations in Theory.* Ed. Josephine Donovan. Lexington: Univ. of Kentucky Press, 1975, pp. 38-47.

Johnston, Jill. *Gullible's Travels.* New York: Link, 1974.

Jones, Ann Rosalind. "Writing the Body: Toward an Understanding of *L'ecriture Feminine.*" *Feminist Studies,* 7 (1981), 247-63.

Jung, C.G. *The Basic Writings of C.G. Jung.* New York: Modern Library, 1959.

———. *The Development of Personality.* New York: Bollingen, 1954.

———. *Psychological Reflections.* New York: Bollingen, 1953.

———. *Psychology and Symbol.* Garden City, N.Y.: Anchor/Doubleday, 1958.

Kaplan, Alexandra G., and Joan P. Bear, eds. *Beyond Sex-Role Stereotypes: Readings Toward a Psychology of Androgyny.* Boston: Little, Brown, 1976.

Kaplan, Sydney Janet. *Feminine Consciousness in the Modern British Novel.* Urbana: Univ. of Illinois Press, 1975.

Kawin, Bruce. "Joanna Russ and Doris Lessing." MLA Convention, New York. 1978.

Kay, Karen, and Gerald Peary, eds. *Women and Film.* New York: E.P. Dutton, 1977.

Kent, Anne Rush. *Moon, Moon.* New York: Random House, 1976.

Kerenyi, C. *Eleusis: Archetypal Image of Mother and Daughter.* New York: Pantheon, 1967.

Kerouac, Jack. *On the Road.* New York: Signet, 1955.

Khouri, Nadia. "The Dialectics of Power: Utopia in the SF of Le Guin, Jeury, and Piercy." *Science-Fiction Studies,* 7 (1980), 49-60.

Killough, Lee. *Deadly Silents.* New York: Ballantine, 1981.

King, Ynestra. "Feminism and the Revolt of Nature." *Heresies,* No. 13 (1981), pp. 12-16.

Kolodny, Annette. *The Lay of the Land.* Chapel Hill: Univ. of North Carolina Press, 1975.

Korsmeyer, Carol. "The Hidden Joke: Generic Uses of Masculine Terminology." *Feminism and Philosophy.* Ed. Mary Vetterling-Braggin et al. Totowa, N.J.: Littlefield, Adams, and Company, 1977, pp. 138-53.

Kress, Susan. "Politics of Time and Space: The Utopian Vision in *Woman on the Edge of Time.*" Unpublished paper.

Kristeva, Julia. *About Chinese Women.* Trans. Anita Barrows. New York: Urizen Books, 1977.

Le Guin, Ursula K. *The Dispossessed: An Ambiguous Utopia.* New York: Harper and Row, 1974.

———. *The Language of the Night: Essays on Fantasy and Science Fiction.* Ed. Susan Wood. New York: G.P. Putnam's Sons, 1979.

———. *The Left Hand of Darkness.* 1974; New York: Ace Books, 1979.

Lerman, Rhoda. *Call Me Ishtar.* Garden City, N.Y.: Doubleday, 1973.

Lessing, Doris. *Documents Relating to the Sentimental Agents in the Volyen Empire.* New York: Alfred A. Knopf, 1983.

———. *The Making of the Representative for Planet Eight.* New York: Alfred A. Knopf, 1982.

———. *The Marriages Between Zones Three, Four, and Five.* New York: Alfred A. Knopf, 1980.

———. *Shikasta.* New York: Alfred A. Knopf, 1979.

_____. *The Sirian Experiments.* New York: Alfred A. Knopf, 1980.

Lewis, R.W.B. *The American Adam: Innocence, Tragedy, and Tradition in the Nineteenth Century.* Chicago: Univ. of Chicago Press, 1955.

Lippard, Lucy. *From the Center: Feminist Essays on Women's Art.* New York: E.P. Dutton, 1976.

Marks, Elaine, and Isabelle de Courtivron, eds. *New French Feminisms: An Anthology.* Amherst: University of Massachusetts, 1980.

Mayhar, Ardath. *How the Gods Wove in Kyrannon.* New York: Ace, 1979.

Mellon, Joan. *Women and Their Sexuality in the New Film.* New York: Horizon Press, 1973.

Merril, Judith. "Wish Upon a Star." *The Best of Judith Merril.* Ed. Virginia Kidd. New York: Warner Books, 1976.

Miller, Margaret. "The Ideal Woman in Two Feminist Science-Fiction Utopias." *Science-Fiction Studies,* 10 (1983), 191-98.

Miller, Nancy K. "Emphasis Added: Plots and Plausibilities in Women's Fiction." *PMLA,* 96 (1981), 36-48.

Mitchison, Naomi. *Memoirs of a Spacewoman.* 1962; London: New English Library, 1976.

Monk, Patricia. "Frankenstein's Daughters: The Problem of the Feminine Image in Science Fiction." *Mosaic,* 13 (Spring/Summer 1980), pp. 15-27.

Morgan, Elaine. *The Descent of Women.* New York: G. P. Putnam's Sons, 1971.

Morgan, Ellen. "The Feminist Novel of Androgynous Fantasy." *Frontiers,* 2 (Fall 1977), pp. 40-49.

_____. "The One-Eyed Doe." *Radical Teacher,* No. 10 (1978), pp. 2-6.

Morgan, Robin. *The Anatomy of Freedom: Feminism, Physics, and Global Politics.* Garden City, New York: Doubleday, 1982.

_____. *Going Too Far: The Personal Chronicle of a Feminist.* New York: Random House, 1977.

Norman, Dorothy. *The Hero: Myth/Image/Symbol.* New York: New American Library, 1969.

O'Faolain, Julia, and Laura Martines. *Not in God's Image.* London: Maurice Temple White, 1973.

Ohmann, Carol. "Emily Bronte in the Hands of Male Critics." *A Case for Equity.* Ed. Susan McAllester. Urbana, Ill.: National Council of Teachers of English, 1971, pp. 60-67.

Olander, Joseph, and Martin Harry Greenberg, eds. *Ursula K. Le Guin.* New York: Taplinger, 1979.

Orbach, Suzy. *Fat Is a Feminist Issue.* New York: Berkeley Books, 1978.

Ortner, Sherry. "Is Female to Male as Nature Is to Culture?" *Woman, Culture and Society.* Ed. Michelle Zimbalist Rosaldo and Louise Lamphere. Stanford: Stanford Univ. Press, 1974, pp. 67-87.

Patai, Daphne. "When Women Rule: Defamiliarization in the Sex-Role Reversal Utopia." *Extrapolation,* 23 (1982), 56-69.

Pearson, Carol. "Towards a New Language, Consciousness and Political Theory." *Heresies,* No. 13 (1981), pp. 84-87.

_____. "Women's Fantasies and Feminist Utopias." *Frontiers: A Journal of Women's Studies,* 2 (Fall 1977), pp. 50-61.

_____, and Katherine Pope. *The Female Hero in American and British Literature.* New York: R.R. Bowker, 1981.

Piercy, Marge. *Woman on the Edge of Time.* Greenwich, Conn.: Fawcett, 1976.

Pratt, Annis V. "Archetypal Approaches to the New Feminist Criticism." *Bucknell Review,* 21 (Spring 1973), pp. 3-14.

_____. *Archetypal Patterns in Women's Fiction.* Bloomington: Indiana Univ. Press, 1981.

_____. "'Aunt Jennifer's Tigers': Notes Towards a Preliterary History of Women's Archetypes." *Feminist Studies,* 4 (1978), 163-94.

Rabinowitz, Peter J. "Assertion and Assumption: Fictional Patterns and the External World." *PMLA,* 96 (1981), 408-19.

Raglan, Lord. *The Hero: A Study in Tradition, Myth, and Dream.* New York: Oxford Univ. Press, 1937.

Reed, Kit. "Songs of War." *The New Women of Wonder.* Ed. Pamela Sargent. New York: Vintage Books, 1977, pp. 121-75.

Rennie, Susan, and Kirsten Grimstad. "Spiritual Explorations Cross-Country." *Quest,* 1 (Spring 1975), pp. 49-51.

Renville, Maurine, et al. "Women's Survival Catalog: Women's Spirituality." *Chrysalis,* No. 6 (1978), pp. 77-99.

Rich, Adrienne. *Of Woman Born: Motherhood as Experience and Institution.* New York: W.W. Norton, 1976.

_____. "When We Dead Awaken: Writing as Revision." *Adrienne Rich's Poetry.* Ed. Barbara Charlesworth Gelpi and Albert Gelpi. New York: W.W. Norton, 1975, pp. 90-98.

Rich, B. Ruby. "The Crisis in Naming in Feminist Film Criticism." *Jump Cut,* No. 19 (1978), pp. 9-12.

Robinson, Lillian S. "Dwelling in Decencies: Radical Criticism and the Feminist Perspective." *A Case for Equity: Women in English Departments.* Ed. Susan McAllester. Urbana, Ill.: National Council of Teachers of English, 1971, pp. 33-43.

Romano, Deborah Larned. "Eating Our Hearts Out." *Mother Jones,* June 1980, pp. 20-30, 60-63.

Rosen, Marjorie. *Popcorn Venus.* New York: Avon Books, 1973.

Rosinsky, Natalie M. "A Female Man? The 'Medusan' Humor of Joanna Russ." *Extrapolation,* 23 (1982), 31-36.

_____. "Feminist Theory in Women's Speculative Fiction, 1966-81." Diss. University of Wisconsin-Madison, 1982.

_____. "Feminist SF: Shaping the Future." Feminist SF panel, Great Lakes Women's Studies Association Conference, Mankato, Minn. 1981.

Rukeyser, Muriel. "The Speed of Darkness." *About Women: An Anthology of Contemporary Fiction, Poetry, and Essays.* ed. Stephen Berg and S.J. Marks. Greenwich, Conn.: Fawcett, 1973, pp. 39-42.

Russ, Joanna. *"Amor Vincit Foeminam:* The Battle of the Sexes." *Science-Fiction Studies,* 7 (1980), 2-15.

_____. *The Female Man.* New York: Bantam, 1975.

_____. *How to Suppress Women's Writing.* Austin: University of Texas Press, 1983.

_____. "Images of Women in Science Fiction." Rpt. in *Images of Women in Fiction: Feminist Perspectives.* Revised ed. Ed. Susan Koppelman Cornillon. Bowling Green: Popular Press, 1973, pp. 79-94.

_____. *Kittatiny: A Tale of Magic.* New York: Daughters, Inc., 1978.

_____. "Outta Space: Women Write Science Fiction." *Ms.,* January 1976, pp. 109-11.

_____. "SF and Technology as Mystification." *Science-Fiction Studies,* 5 (1978), 250-60.

_____. "Towards an Aesthetics of Science Fiction." *Science-Fiction Studies.* Ed. R.D. Mullen and Darko Suvin. Boston: Gregg Press, 1976, pp. 8-15.

_____. *We Who Are About To.* New York: Dell, 1975.

_____. "What Can a Heroine Do? Or Why Women Can't Write." *Images of Women in Fiction: Feminist Perspectives.* Ed. Susan Koppelman Cornillon. Bowling Green, Ohio: Bowling Green Univ. Press, 1973, pp. 3-20.

_____. "When It Changed." *Again, Dangerous Visions.* Ed. Harlan Ellison. New York: New American Library, 1972. Vol. II, pp. 271-81.

Sargent, Lyman Tower. *British and American Utopian Literature 1516-1975: An Annotated Bibliography.* Boston: G.K. Hall, 1979.

Sargent, Pamela. "Women and Science Fiction." *Women of Wonder.* Ed. Pamela Sargent. New York: Vintage, 1974, pp. xiii-lxiv.

Scholes, Robert. *Structural Fabulation: An Essay on the Fiction of the Future.* Notre Dame, Ind.: Univ. of Notre Dame Press, 1975.

Schwarz-Bart, Andre. *The Last of the Just.* Trans. Stephen Becker. New York: Atheneum, 1960.

Science-Fiction Studies, 2 (November 1975). Ursula K. Le Guin issue.

Secor, Cynthia. "Androgyny: An Early Reappraisal." *Women's Studies,* 2 (1974), 161-69.

Sexton, Anne. *Transformations.* Boston: Houghton Mifflin, 1971.

Sheldon, Raccoona [James Tiptree, Jr.]. "The Screwfly Solution," *The Best SF of the Year #7.* Ed. Terry Carr. New York: Ballantine, 1978, pp. 141-64.

———. "Your Faces, O My Sisters! Your Faces Filled of Light." *Aurora: Beyond Equality.* Ed. Vonda N. McIntyre and Susan Janice Anderson. Greenwich, Conn.: Fawcett, 1976, pp. 16-35.

Sherfey, Mary Jane. *The Nature and Origin of Female Sexuality.* 1966; New York: Random House, 1972.

Showalter, Elaine. *A Literature of Their Own: British Women Novelists from Bronte to Lessing.* Princeton: Princeton Univ. Press, 1977.

Singer, June. *Androgyny: Toward a New Theory of Sexuality.* Garden City, N.Y.: Anchor/Doubleday, 1976.

Singer, Rochelle. *The Demeter Flower.* New York: St. Martin's Press, 1980.

Snitow, Ann, Christine Stensall and Sharon Thomson, eds. *Powers of Desire: The Politics of Sexuality.* New York: Monthly Review Press, 1983.

Spender, Dale. *Man-Made Language.* Boston: Routledge and Kegan Paul, 1980.

Spivak, Gayatri Chakravorty. "Three Feminist Readings: McCullers, Drabble, Habermas." *USQR,* 35 (Fall and Winter 1979-80), pp. 15-34.

Spretnak, Charlene. *Lost Goddesses of Early Greece.* Berkeley: Moon Books, 1978.

———, ed. *The Politics of Women's Spirituality.* Garden City, N.Y.: Anchor, 1982.

Staicar, Tom, ed. *The Feminine Eye: Science Fiction and the Women Who Write It.* New York: Frederick Ungar, 1982.

Stanley, Julia Penelope, and Susan J. Wolfe. "Toward a Feminist Aesthetic." *Chrysalis,* No. 6 (1978), pp. 57-71.

Staton, Mary. *From the Legend of Biel.* New York: Ace Books, 1975.

Stone, Merlin. *When God Was a Woman.* New York: Harcourt Brace, 1976.

Strouse, Jean, ed. *Women and Psychoanalysis: Dialogues on Psychoanalytic Views of Femininity.* New York: Dell, 1974.

Sturgeon, Theodore. *Venus Plus X.* New York: Pyramid, 1960.

Suleiman, Susan, and Inge Crosman, eds. *The Reader in the Text: Essays on Audience and Interpretation.* Princeton: Princeton Univ. Press, 1980.

Suvin, Darko. *Metamorphoses of Science Fiction: On the Poetics and History of a Literary Genre.* New Haven: Yale Univ. Press, 1979.

Tiptree, Jr., James. "Houston, Houston, Do You Read?" *Star Songs of an Old Primate.* New York: Ballantine, 1978, pp. 164-226.

———. "Mama Come Home." *Ten Thousand Light Years from Home.* New York: Ace, 1973.

———. *Up the Walls of the World.* New York: Berkeley Books, 1978.

Todorov, Tzvetan. *The Fantastic: A Structural Approach to a Literary Genre.* Trans. Richard Howard. Cleveland: The Press of Case Western Reserve Univ., 1973.

Trible, Phyllis. "Eve and Adam: Genesis 2-3 Reread." *Womanspirit Rising: A Feminist Reader in Religion.* Ed. Carol P. Christ and Judith Plaskow. New York: Harper and Row, 1979, pp. 74-83.

Wenzel, Helene Vivienne. "The Text as Body/Politics: An Appreciation of Monique Wittig's Writings in Context." *Feminist Studies,* 7 (1981), 264-87.

Weston, Jessie. *From Ritual to Romance.* Garden City, N.Y.: Doubleday, 1957.

Wilgus, Neal. "Interview with Suzy McKee Charnas." *Algol,* Winter 1978-79, pp. 21-25.

Wittig, Monique. *Les Guérillères.* Trans. David Le Vay. 1969; New York: Avon Books, 1971.

Wood, Susan. "Women and Science Fiction." *Algol/Starship,* Winter 1978-79, pp. 9-18.

Woolf, Virginia. *Orlando.* 1928; New York: Harcourt Brace, 1956.

Young, Donna J. *Retreat: As It Was!* Weatherbuty Lake, Mo.: Naiad Press, 1979.

Zukav, Gary. *The Dancing Wu Li Masters: An Overview of the New Physics.* New York: Bantam, 1979.

Index